Gabriele B. Clemens

# The Risorgimento

## Italy's Path to Modernity, 1770–1870

Translated by Kate Tranter

BÖHLAU

Bibliographic information published by the Deutsche Nationalbibliothek:
The Deutsche Nationalbibliothek lists this publication in the Deutsche Nationalbibliografie; detailed bibliographic data available online: https://dnb.de.



Cover image: The meeting at the Teano between Giuseppe Garibaldi and Vittorio Emanuele. Lithograph after the painting by Carlo Ademollo. © akg-images / Fototeca Gilardi.

Cover design: Guido Klütsch, Köln
Proof reading: Claudia Riefert, Berlin
Typesetting: le-tex publishing services, Leipzig
Printed and bound: Hubert & Co., Ergolding
Printed in the EU

**Vandenhoeck & Ruprecht Verlage | www.vandenhoeck-ruprecht-verlage.com**
E-Mail: info@boehlau-verlag.com

ISBN 978-3-412-53315-1 (print)
ISBN 978-3-412-53316-8 (digital)

## Contents

# Preface

This book offers an up-to-date overview of the history of the Risorgimento in Italy, (1770–1870). It not only considers standard topics of Italian political history but also socio-economic aspects and the results of recent research into Italian cultural history in the last twenty-five years. Risorgimento is the term given by historians to the period leading up to the foundation of the nation state of Italy in 1861. The name was taken from a liberal newspaper in Turin published by leading politicians associated with the 1848 revolution. Risorgimento can be translated as 'resurgence' or 'revival'. However, this title is somewhat misleading as it is not possible for a nation state to resurge or be revived if it has never previously existed. Italy's path towards becoming a modern nation state was extremely complex and was ultimately determined by shifts in power structures within Europe and processes of reform within Italy. Many books on the Risorgimento begin its history with the invasion of French troops in 1796. Here I have chosen a different time frame. Since any portrayal that begins with the Napoleonic period necessarily neglects the defining era of reform in Italy in the last decades of the eighteenth century, the first chapter here is dedicated to the final years of the *Ancien Régime*. The fall of the Papal States in 1870, when Rome was conquered and, with the exception of Trentino and Trieste, Italy's current borders were established, marks the conclusion of this Risorgimento period.

Compared to the relative lack of interest shown by German historians in what Reinhart Koselleck called the 'saddle period' (*Sattelzeit*) (1750–1850) and the subsequent decades up until the foundation of the nation state, Italian research on the history of the Risorgimento is considerably advanced. Over the last twenty-five years, it was shaped particularly by studies on cultural and discourse history which engaged with theories put forward by Benedict Anderson, Ernest Gellner and Eric J. Hobsbawm. These theories describe the founding of the nation state as an invention of intellectual elites. A major impetus in this context was undoubtedly provided by the Italian historian, Alberto M. Banti. No other book in recent years has triggered such heated discussions on the topics of nation and national feeling in the nineteenth century amongst historians in Italy and of Italy worldwide as his book *La nazione del Risorgimento*, published in 2000. Subsequent studies have no choice but to examine and discuss its arguments. It is received with extreme scepticism on the part of those whose approach is from the angle of cultural history or more classical political history, but with enthusiasm by those who themselves experiment with 'turns', be they iconological, linguistic, spatial or any other.

Banti set himself the task of deciphering the meaning and significance of national and patriotic vocabulary used at the time and constructed a 'canon' based on the structures and topics he had elicited. This canon was developed from samples of well-known and well-received literature as well as from historical works, political texts by the most important Italian intellectuals, historical paintings, and romantic opera.

In spite of the brilliance of individual studies, neither the reception of the contents of Banti's canon nor the power of its influence have ever been disputed – they are simply accepted unchallenged. However, it is questionable whether songs, poems, romantic tales, pictures and opera were sufficient to motivate people to fight for a nation state. How many volunteered for the struggle and which side did they fight on? Did the elite really all want the kind of nation state that finally emerged? The majority of Italians were faced with more existential problems and would hardly have been motivated to leave their house and home to fight for an abstract idea. What role was played by economic and power political motives? Who were the winners and losers in this complicated process? There was by no means a clear consensus amongst the political actors as to how the new state should be organised or even how far its geographical boundaries should extend.

The overview provided here gives a prominent voice to a group that was neglected in earlier studies, namely to those thousands of Italians who spent decades of their lives in political exile, mostly against their will. There has been sound initial research on their circumstances in exile and the reception of their European discourses in their home countries, primarily focussing on processes of historical transfer in Europe and America. When they returned to Italy, however, these exiles, mostly from aristocratic or bourgeois elites, were to occupy key positions and become active as a powerful force in the shaping of the liberal Kingdom of Sardinia-Piedmont and the young Kingdom of Italy in the second half of the nineteenth century. The transnational political, military and cultural experience they had gained in neighbouring European countries, sometimes over decades, influenced their political activity after 1848–1849. In this study transnational and particularly European transfer processes will be considered with respect to the above phenomena, but also to other aspects of Italian political, economic and cultural history, since all the protagonists moved naturally within a wider European context.

A further problem is that current studies on the history of Italy in the long nineteenth century largely neglect economic issues. Yet Italy's path towards becoming a modern European nation state cannot be fully understood without considering economic and social aspects. On the one hand, the most important politicians were at the same time very successful aristocratic agrarian landowners. Conte Camillo Benso di Cavour, the first prime minister of the new nation state, is just one example. On the other hand, it was precisely the enormous success of agriculture that was the driving force for industrial development. In this context and in general, in spite of the significant role played by the aristocracy in Italy until well into the nineteenth century, not only in the economic sector, the extent of their involvement has been hitherto underestimated.

Industrialisation in the north of Europe also led to a transformation of trade flows and new developments in agriculture in the south of Italy, the Mezzogiorno. The widely differing agricultural structures inevitably had a major impact on the stratification of wealth and education. Oppressive poverty in large parts of the rural population was a major problem for the individual states as well as for the young nation state. It led to considerable national, international and global migration. The question quite naturally arises as to what effect this poverty and lack of education had on processes of political participation. The ordinary people, repeatedly invoked by Giuseppe Mazzini, in fact took precious little interest in his political ideas.

Another issue is that an enquiry into the social and institutional reasons for the underdevelopment of the south of Italy always causes controversy. Historical facts still play an important role in current debates. However, it is important to point out that the post-World War II economic miracle in Italy was based on long-term growth whose origins went back to the early nineteenth century. Finally, this analysis will also consider more recent studies that focus on transfer processes of European business in Italy.

This history of Italy on the road to modernity could hardly have been realised without the material and non-material support of the following institutions and individuals. The German Research Foundation generously supported my application for a leave of absence from teaching and thus contributed significantly to the production of this book. My heartfelt thanks go to Christof Dipper, Malte König and Jens Späth. As intelligent and astute proofreaders, they not only corrected careless errors but prevented biased interpretations on my part by their critical comments and insightful remarks. Amerigo Caruso, Silvia Cavicchioli and Marco Meriggi were always at hand with their immense knowledge of the history of the Risorgimento to give me help and advice, and I am extremely grateful to them. I would also like to thank my team at the University of Saarbrücken, first and foremost Maike Jung, Doris Kurz and Moritz Sommer. Thank you also to Kirsti Doepner from Böhlau publishers. In a fringe meeting at the German Historians' Congress in Münster she positively encouraged me to write this book, something I had been wanting to do for a long time. This book is a revised version of the original German edition entitled *Geschichte des Risorgimento* published in October 2021. Finally, I would like to thank Kate Tranter for her careful and insightful translation of my original German academic text.

Gabriele B. Clemens
Saarbrücken, July 2025

# 1. The *Ancien Régime*

The Risorgimento, the process whereby Italy was united as a nation state, has always had a special place in the study and writing of Italian history. But when did it begin and end as a historical period? Periodisation can help history to be understood and interpreted, but at the same time period divisions are always controversial. For the Risorgimento period there is good reason to consider the French Revolution in 1789 as its beginning, since it shook the pre-existing Italian states to the core and meant that, as a result of the hostilities, they were either wiped off the map or radically reformed. However, there is also much to be said for beginning with the *Ancien Régime* since it is not possible to understand the changes brought about by the French Revolution without some knowledge of the Italian states before 1789. For this reason, this book begins about twenty years before the revolution, around 1770.

In the early modern period, there was no Italian territorial state. After the fall of the Roman Empire, the territory had been divided up into numerous dominions. In the Middle Ages a sea of around a hundred prospering city republics had formed in the north, but in the early modern period they were no match for the powerful neighbouring states that had emerged north of the Alps and were successively conquered by French and Spanish troops. The Austrian Habsburgs eventually prevailed in northern Italy. Although the formerly powerful maritime republics of Genoa and Venice were able to hold their ground and maintain power over their cities and surroundings, by the time of the outgoing *Ancien Régime*, they had long lost their role as global players. All that was left to the Venetian Republic was Corfu, the Ionian Islands and Dalmatia. Genoa still ruled over the Ligurian coast but, since it was unable to effectively counteract the Corsican autonomy movement, it was forced to sell the island of Corsica to France in 1768. In central Italy, the popes ruled for more than a thousand years; in the south, it was first the Arabs, then in succession the Normans, the Staufers, the French, the Spanish Habsburgs and the Bourbons. The only area in which an Italian dynasty, the House of Savoy, was able to retain its independence and gradually expand its territory was in the north-west.

During the wars of Spanish Succession (1701–1714) and Austrian Succession (1742–1748), that is until the middle of the eighteenth century, Italy was once again the object of military campaigns and European diplomacy. These frequent changes of rule only came to an end with the Treaty of Aachen in 1748. The territorial order that it created ensured stability and offered scope for reform and was more or less endorsed at the end of the Napoleonic era by the Congress of Vienna in 1815. Austria's dominant influence during the 'saddle period' (1750–1850) was reflected not least in its ownership of the Duchy of Lombardy, which was, like Mantua, ruled directly from Vienna. Although the Duchy of Tuscany was formally independent, it was also under Austrian control and the influence of Vienna was unmistakable. In central Italy the Papal States stretched over a wide area from Bologna to Gaeta, but after the Renaissance and the grandeur of the Baroque era, papal power had passed its peak. To the south of the Papal States was the Kingdom of Naples which ruled Sicily, the largest island in Italy, as a satellite state with its own viceroy. A branch of the Spanish Bourbons with family connections to Madrid and Vienna had been on the throne of this kingdom, known as the Kingdom of the Two Sicilies, since 1734. Maria Carolina (1752–1814), a daughter of Maria Theresia (1717–1780), was married to Ferdinand I (1751–1825) from the line of the Spanish Bourbons. She was a resolute queen who maintained very close relations to Vienna. Following the example of her brother, Emperor Joseph II (1741–1790), she attempted to modernise the south. In the north, the Duchy of Parma and Piacenza was also ceded to the Spanish Bourbons by the Treaty of Aachen. There, too, a daughter of the Austrian empress Maria Theresia, Maria Amalia (1756–1804), was married to the Duke of Parma. He was another Ferdinand (1751–1802), the grandson of the Spanish Queen Elizabeth (1692–1766), who for her part came from the House of Farnese, which had ruled the small dukedom before the male line became extinct. Directly adjacent was the Duchy of Modena under the Este dynasty, which worked as a kind of buffer zone between the Papal States, the Duchies of Tuscany and Lombardy, and the Republic of Venice.

The second largest island, Sardinia, previously the property of Spain and Austria, had belonged to the Kingdom of Sardinia-Piedmont since 1720. Although Sardinia-Piedmont is often compared to Prussia because of its military tradition, its progressive administration and its gradual rise from being a small duchy in Savoy to an important influential power in northern Italy, this comparison is flawed. In contrast to Prussia, Sardinia-Piedmont was constantly threatened by France and Austria. The Savoy dynasty, ruling the Kingdom of Sardinia from its capital Turin, was the only ruling family in Italy that was in fact Italian. From the Savoyards in the extreme north to the inhabitants of Lampedusa in the south, all Italians lived under absolutist regimes, even though the Catholic Church and the aristocracy remained extremely powerful. In the last decades before the clashes with revolutionary France, however, deep-seated reforms were introduced in the majority of Italian states, and the intellectual climate derived significant inspiration from Italian Enlightenment thinkers.

After the Treaty of Aachen in 1748, attempts at reform had intensified. These years are referred to by the poet Giosuè Carducci (1835–1907) as the symbolical beginning of the spiritual Risorgimento, a century before the revolution of 1848. This nationalist interpretation, however, goes back too far. Although demands of individual patriots and intellectuals for a nation state can be found in the run-up to the French Revolution, both the political and intellectual elites were generally still acting in isolation and only on a regional level. This is why this book looks at the different states individually when examining the various developments up until unification, thus making it possible to outline contemporaneous developments and identify the obstacles on Italy's path to modernity.

Researchers generally agree that a central feature of late eighteenth century Italian history was that Italian Enlightenment thinkers, famous throughout Europe, were actively involved in state reforms. This is in contrast to the French Enlightenment philosophers, who were publishing at the same time but typically kept their distance from the state. At this time all the Italian regions introduced a series of anti-feudal policies, judicial, administrative and financial reforms, steps towards secularisation (except in the Papal States), humanitarian reforms and moves towards greater tolerance. Both torture and the death penalty were abolished in some areas. The theoretical basis for these measures was an interest in natural law, with its idea of a contract with the rulers that granted rights to all subjects. The great British and French Enlightenment scholars Locke, Montesquieu, Voltaire and Rousseau were read and analysed and the *Encyclopédie* by Diderot and d'Alembert was printed in Livorno with a dedication to the Grand Duke of Tuscany. Yet there was a characteristic divide between those states which systematically included the best Enlightenment thinkers in their reform ideas (Lombardy, Tuscany, Naples-Sicily, Parma-Piacenza and Modena), and those which were content to rely merely on administrative reforms (Piedmont, the Papal States and the maritime republics of Venice and Genoa).

It is an undisputed fact that as a result of the reforms of Maria Theresia and her son Joseph, Habsburg-controlled Lombardy was the most progressive state in Italy. The most important administrative fiscal reforms and the establishment of the famous cadastre (real-estate register) were carried out under Maria Theresia, while basic steps towards secularisation as well as the abolition of both religious censorship and the Inquisition were introduced under the joint rule of mother and son. After 1780, Joseph, now as sole ruler, consistently pursued a reformist course by dissolving the guilds and introducing anti-feudal measures, even though this turned the rich patricians of Lombardy against him. Considerable impetus for reform came from the economist Pietro Verri (1728–1797) in Milan, where he held numerous administrative posts. The focus of his writings was on progress in trade and commerce. Although he was influenced by the Physiocrats, he attempted to reconcile free trade with progress in agriculture in his own way. He and his brother, the poet Alessandro Verri, published the short-lived, but highly respected magazine *Il Caffè* (1764–1766). Voltaire referred to the group as the *École de Milan* (the Milan school). It included the lawyer Cesare Beccaria (1738–1794), who was recognised as a radical criminal law reformer far beyond Italy. His 1764 magnum opus *Dei delitti e delle pene (On Crimes and Punishments)* was based on the philosophy of natural law and translated into twenty-two different languages. He argued that punishment imposed by the state should be proportionate in order to maintain order and that laws should be enforced consistently. Beccaria denounced the death penalty and also torture, which was abolished in the following year. A further forceful civil servant worthy of mention is Pompeo Neri, who established the cadastre system in Lombardy. He had previously introduced land surveys in the Duchy of Tuscany. Overall, it is striking that in both Habsburg duchies, qualified civil servants operated on the basis of their expertise. Beccaria in Milan was also responsible for the reform of criminal law.

As part of the Habsburg family corporation, the emperor's brother Leopold I (1747–1792) and his nephew Ferdinand III (1769–1824) naturally applied the same principles to reforming the Duchy of Tuscany. Here also they centralised the administration and abolished the guilds, clerical jurisdiction and the Inquisition. In addition, they introduced land reform favouring small and medium-sized landowners, had the marshes in the Maremma region drained and abolished the salt tax and local road tolls. This was opposed by the large patrician landowners, as it was in Lombardy, because they saw their influence threatened by the creation of a modern civil service and the ensuing reforms. They were, however, unable to prevent the abolition of entailment and the introduction of free trade. Due to its privileged inheritance rights, entailment had hitherto prevented the fragmentation of property while free trade undermined secure profits on the agricultural market. Nevertheless, the aristocratic elites were able to dominate both the central ministries and the provincial and local administrations, to which Leopold I had granted far-reaching administrative rights. They also used their monopoly of posts in the administration, the military and the diplomatic service as well as a dense network of patronage at court to make money for themselves.

In the years before the French Revolution, the sister of the Habsburg emperor Joseph II and of Leopold I of Tuscany, Maria Carolina, used her influence on her husband, Ferdinand, who had little interest in the affairs of government, to modernise their kingdom of Naples and Sicily with the help of leading Neapolitan Enlightenment thinkers. The policy of abolishing feudal privileges and introducing reforms began after 1770, against the opposition of the powerful *Baroni*. In the Basilicata, land reforms led to the partitioning of large estates. The power of the church was also diminished by the confiscation of monastic estates and the expulsion of the Jesuits. A supreme fiscal council, established in 1782, was to pursue financial and fiscal rationalisation, and domestic tariffs were reduced. Lord John Francis Edward Acton (1736–1811) was enlisted from Tuscany to reorganise the army and reconstruct the navy. The most influential Enlightenment thinker at court was undoubtedly Gaetano Filangieri (1757–1788), a member of the Neapolitan aristocracy who favoured a paternalistic state based on the rule of law and had published a five-volume work, *Scienza della legislazione (Science of Legislation)*, while only in his early twenties. The first volume appeared in 1780 and the last was published posthumously in 1791. European contemporaries considered it a seminal work on constitutional philosophy. In it Filangieri also castigated feudal law and argued for a legal system based on reason. This work won international recognition and established Filangieri's fame. On his Italian journey in 1787, Johann Wolfgang Goethe sought contact with him as a leading thinker in Naples, as did Benjamin Franklin, who had read Filangieri's writings when he was the American ambassador in France and corresponded with him. He sent Filangieri as a philosopher of law his draft of the US Constitution, asking him for comment. In the eighteenth and nineteenth centuries, the more than seventy editions and translations of Filangieri's standard work made a significant contribution towards integrating the Italian debate on the end of the *Ancien Régime* into the context of European Enlightenment.

Another notable southern Italian reformer, Domenico Caracciolo dei Duchi di San Teodoro (1715–1789), shared a parallel career path with Benjamin Franklin. As diplomats, they both came into contact with Enlightenment ideas which were to influence them for the rest of their lives. The stations of Caracciolo's diplomatic career took him to Turin, London and Paris, where he met Jacques Necker (1725–1802) and Jean Baptiste d'Alembert (1717–1783). In 1781 Caracciolo was first appointed viceroy in Palermo (1780–1786), where he enthusiastically pursued Enlightenment reforms. His measures focussed on a fairer distribution of taxes and the establishment of a cadastre. Although this was prevented by the powerful feudal nobility, their privileges were nevertheless restricted. Queen Maria Carolina then summoned Caracciolo to Naples, where, under his direction, the reform process was to be accelerated.

Whereas in Naples the queen deliberately invited intellectuals from the academies and Masonic lodges to the court and entrusted them with high, administrative offices, Enlightenment thinkers in the Papal States and in the Kingdom of Sardinia-Piedmont had to expect persecution. Nevertheless, a process of reform and modernisation began in both these states too. In the Papal States, Clement XIV (1705–1774) had succumbed to international pressure and abolished the intransigent Jesuit order. His successor, Pius VI (1717–1799), opposed any new ideas in the field of religion and philosophy, but concentrated on economic measures which were altogether comparable to those in the neighbouring states. Agriculture was to be supported by mercantile policies and a cadastre was also introduced here.

The Kingdom of Sardinia-Piedmont was considered a model of efficient modern administration. Reforms had begun at the beginning of the eighteenth century under Charles Emmanuel III (1701–1773). The kings in Turin were able to achieve what Louis XV and Louis XVI had attempted in neighbouring France in vain: they succeeded in opposing feudalism to some effect. Although the fiscal privileges of the nobility and the church were efficiently curbed, the alliance between the crown and the church and the crown and the aristocracy was closer in Piedmont than in any other of the secular states in Italy. The nobility did forfeit some of its feudal rights in the eighteenth century but continued to enjoy privileges resulting from career opportunities in the military and the administration and so grew to be an aristocracy of civil servants supportive of the state. Aristocratic families who had generally not gained their titles until the early modern period focussed their loyalty on the House of Savoy. A symbolic image of the rise of the House of Savoy was the extension of their royal palace in Turin, modelled on the magnificence of French architecture.

More recent academic studies, however, are not content with only featuring the most prominent Enlightenment scholars and their works. They also analyse the wider fields of communication, the dissemination of ideas, academic sociability, public opinion, the history of book editions and their distribution, and the history of libraries and reading. It is important to see these exceptional intellectuals within the context of their historical environment in order to gain a better understanding of the political and social climate in the decades before the revolution. They were part of a public sphere which operated transnationally across Europe, flourishing in spite of censorship and bans on public meetings.

The academies and Masonic lodges in particular were used by the elites as a place to discuss topical issues. Networks of intellectuals emerged across Europe, closer communications were established and the production of books grew exponentially. The academy movement was crucial to this process everywhere but was particularly significant in Italy because of the disproportionately higher number of academies and their older traditions. In Naples alone, a total of 197 academies can be traced between the fifteenth and twentieth centuries. The figure for Rome in the same period is 185 and the situation was similar in other major Italian cities. Before 1800, nearly 2,000 academies or learned societies can be documented in approximately 350 larger towns and cities. Most of them were established in or near government seats or former capital cities: Bologna, Florence, Ferrara, Milan, Naples, Padova, Palermo, Rome, Siena, Venice and Verona. Many of these academies originated in a similar way, namely as private humanistic circles. They often began with a small group of friends who exchanged experiences, debated various issues, sought contact with like-minded people both at home and abroad and also enjoyed socialising. Some of these private initiatives were very short-lived, some developed into important academies such as those in Naples, Mantua and Padova. In this early phase, it was common to give them whimsical names, such as *Accademia degli Audaci, Accademia dei Cupi, dei Delicati, dei Depressi (Academy of the Daredevils, of the Sinister Ones, the Delicates and the Depressed)*. A few of the academies which were established in this period lasted longer, such as the famous Roman *Accademia dei Lincei (Academy of the Lynxes)*.

During the eighteenth century, the number of scientific academies to be founded increased and with the introduction of rules, committees and regular meetings they developed into institutions. The royal academies in Naples (1778) and Turin (1783) were founded during this period. They belong to the type of state foundations which were spreading throughout Europe and were modelled on the Royal Society in London (1660), the *Académie royale des sciences* in Paris (1665) and the academies in Berlin (1701), Saint Petersburg (1724) and Stockholm (1739). These were prestigious institutions supported by the local rulers and, in terms of their financial resources and the reputation of their academicians, differed considerably from the older, smaller academies largely based on private initiatives. Scientific rigour was paramount. The eighteenth century also saw a surge of new agricultural academies committed to the advancement of agriculture and the protection of a rapidly growing population from failed harvests and famine. They began in 1753 with the *Accademia dei Georgofili* in Florence and one in Palermo in the same year and were to be followed by forty more agricultural societies. Agricultural issues were not, however, the only specialist focus of academies. They were joined, for example, by academies specialising in archaeological research. The king of Naples established the *Reale Accademia Ercolanese* in 1775, whose purpose was to evaluate the findings of the excavations in Herculaneum and present them to an elite European public. The results of the excavations were published by academy members in magnificent books which the king gave to diplomats to be passed on to European rulers. The most important Italian academies were in close contact with the great academies in London, Saint Petersburg, Stockholm and Paris by means of networks of correspondence and honorary memberships. In Paris the majority of the foreign correspondents in the *Académie royale des sciences* were Italians. As a result, the publications of Italian scientists were distributed more quickly and efficiently.

The Italian academies may not have been directly aimed at the common good, but they did pursue scientific and cultural interests in the same way as the French learned societies, the *sociétés savantes.* In the eighteenth century they both shared a faith in enlightenment and progress, as did the numerous Masonic lodges. Large lodges in this internationally connected Freemason movement began to be founded in the first half of the eighteenth century in Britain, France, Italy and Germany. They can be counted as among the first societies to admit people of different social status. They were meeting places for members of both the aristocracy and the bourgeoisie, particularly diplomats, officers, merchants, intellectuals and the occasional high-ranking cleric. After attending the mystical meetings, whose rituals were derived from the mediaeval masons' guilds and the traditions of the Knights Templar, fellow Masons met for discussion. The focus of these largely egalitarian gatherings was the ideal of a humanitarian ethic which held that sincerity, altruism, tolerance and self-criticism would lead to the perfect cultivation of the individual. In the first half of the century a wave of early lodges was founded in Naples, Florence and Venice. The church responded with condemnations and excommunications, and Freemasons were arrested and tortured. In the milder political climate of the last third of the century, a second surge of new lodge foundations began, including in Livorno, Turin, Genoa, Milan, Naples, and even Rome. The founding of the lodges and their activities depended heavily on diplomats, merchants and military officers with experience in Europe, as well as the many European aristocrats who had travelled to Italy on their Grand Tour. To undertake such a tour, which led first to Paris and then to Italy, was considered part of good breeding and education in high society. One purpose was for the young nobles to get to know life at the European courts and another was for them to broaden their cultural knowledge. Particularly in Italy, there was ample visual material for the wealthy elite to further their aesthetic education and understanding of art. In the evenings they were admitted to the social circles of the urban elite in the lodges and salons.

The Masonic lodges were naturally under close police scrutiny. For the rulers, the meeting of a large number of elite groups to discuss tolerance, equality, the mind and humanity was cause for alarm. Another use of the lodges was to build up political networks. The lodge *Mystérieuse*, set up in Turin in 1768, was where officers met. The crown prince, Victor Amadeus III (1726–1796), who was a member, instrumentalised the lodge as a kind of parallel court to stir up opposition against his elderly father (Charles Emmanuel III, 1701–1773) and his powerful minister Giambattista Lorenzo Bogino. In the same way as other lodges, the *Mystérieuse* became the preferred meeting place of aristocratic society, where the assembled 'brothers' could win prestige and build up networks outside their strong family structures.

The fate of Freemasonry in Naples was discussed throughout Europe, since it was there that the young queen, Maria Carolina, exploited her involvement in the lodge to free herself from the overpowering influence of her father-in-law, Charles of Spain, and his right-hand man, prime minister Marquess Bernardo Tanucci. In Vienna her father, Francis Stephen, was a committed supporter of Freemasonry and was the first ruler to belong to a lodge and entrust his sons' education to a Master of the Lodge. In the southern Italian Kingdom of Naples, however, Freemasonry was outlawed. In spite of this, in 1773, the queen assisted the imperial ambassador Josef Wilczek and Neapolitan aristocrats to found a large national lodge with the indicative name of *lo Zero (Zeal)*. One of its many members was Gaetano Filangieri. When it became public two years after its foundation that young cadets from the royal regiment had joined the lodge, Charles and Tanucci exerted intense pressure on Ferdinand IV, Maria Carolina's husband, to enforce the ban on Freemasonry. Amid great publicity lodge members were arrested on Capodimonte outside the gates of Naples and put on trial, a move that reverberated throughout Europe. Members of the lodge were charged with treason, which, with a guilty verdict, could result in the death penalty. The trial developed into a tough power struggle, since the Freemasons were well-connected and used their international contacts to mount public protest. The trial was eventually dropped and the lodge members went free. Maria Carolina was celebrated as the heroine of the Freemasons and the raid on Capodimonte and its aftermath soon found its way into the historical memory of Enlightenment thinkers as a victory of reason over intolerance and arbitrary rule.

Supporters of the Enlightenment, however, were not restricted to the academies and lodges for the exchange of ideas. They also met in the many city salons and cafés, where they were spied on. Ideas were circulated by means of a flourishing culture of letter writing and above all by means of print media. The last third of the eighteenth century produced a huge increase in printed material. At the beginning of the century, 45,000 books were printed annually in the Italian states and by the end of the century this figure had risen to 60,000. In Naples twice as many books were available for purchase as a hundred years earlier. Whereas in other Italian cities production was frequently for the local and regional market, Venice was able to maintain its traditional reputation as the European capital of printing and between sixty and eighty per cent of its printed output was exported. As well as supplying all the Italian states, *La Serenissima* exported to Spain, southern Germany, Vienna, the Balkans and Greece. However, the era of companies owned by patricians in Venice had passed its peak and a wave of printing shops opened in the other Italian states. As in Venice, it was mostly patrician or aristocratic capital that flowed into this expanding market, which meant that the businesses were to a certain extent protected from state persecution. Apart from in Venice, the book trade was dominated by French dealers from the Dauphiné. They had representatives in the most important Italian cities and organised transnational trade in the western Mediterranean via family and kinship connections. The most popular import was French literature.

The numerous more risk-averse printers and publishers were often small businesses with one or two printing presses who were dependent on orders from the state, the aristocracy and the church. Towards the end of the eighteenth century, however, a new type of political printers and publishers emerged who gained more influence during the Napoleonic era. Censorship and surveillance were the order of the day and the Catholic Church regularly placed the works of French and Italian Enlightenment thinkers on the index. The greatest freedom in publishing was still enjoyed in Tuscany. However, it became clear that the circulation of books, whether permitted or not, could at best be hindered or delayed but not entirely prevented. This meant that by the end of the eighteenth century, Italian elites possessed excellently stocked libraries in which the major works of the European Enlightenment held a natural place.

# 2. Italy under French rule (1789–1814)

The effects of the revolution that shook France to its core could also be felt in large parts of Italy. Especially after the summer of 1792 when the revolution became increasingly radicalised, the unfolding of events in their neighbouring country was watched by Italy's dazed rulers with increasing horror. Their reaction was to abandon their enlightened reform policies and reintroduce strict political control. The Masonic lodges, although previously supported, had to close, censorship was tightened and political suspects were more closely monitored and imprisoned. While many supporters of the revolution fled to France, Maria Carolina in Naples and Maria Amalia in Parma were forced to look on helplessly as their sister Marie Antoinette died on the scaffold. This and many other murders of French aristocrats turned them, and not only them, into bitter enemies of the revolution, bent on revenge. Added to that, in the summer of 1789, after the Storming of the Bastille and the looting of French castles in neighbouring countries, the brothers of the French king and thousands of aristocrats, officers and priests fled the country to the Kingdom of Sardinia-Piedmont amongst other places. There in Turin, they agitated against the revolutionary government in Paris.

In contrast to the rulers, the peasant underclasses looked to France with high hopes. They wished to be able to rid themselves of the oppressive burdens of rents and taxes. Although there had been previous peasant uprisings, the abrupt abolition of feudal rights in August 1789 in Paris added fresh impetus to their demands. Revolutionary fervour spread across the border: there were mass anti-feudal protests in Piedmont in 1792 and in 1793 in distant southern Italy. The liberal achievements of the revolution were also welcomed by isolated intellectuals but the majority remained cautious. Since the enlightened elites supported the reform process, they were sceptical of the developments in France and publicly repudiated the great revolutionary events known as *Journées*, such as the Storming of the Bastille and the Women's March on Versailles, and mass protests of any kind. After the death of the king, they feared a further increase in political radicalisation, not without reason.

## 2.1 The politicisation of the Jacobins (1789–1796)

The number of Italian Jacobins who, as champions of a radical revolution, fought for their cause on Italian soil was relatively small. Their most famous figurehead was undoubtedly Filippo Buonarroti (1761–1837), a descendent of Michelangelo

Map 1 Italy 1789.

Buonarroti. He was the son of a family of Tuscan patricians with close ties to the Grand Duke of Tuscany. He was made a page at court in 1773, studied law in Pisa and became an ardent advocate of Jean-Jacques Rousseau and his concept of the social contract. Like other patricians, Filippo invested in the burgeoning book trade and also worked as a journalist. As a result of his dissemination of revolutionary ideas, he was under constant state surveillance, which he evaded by fleeing to Corsica in 1789. He continued to be involved in journalism there and published *L' amico della libertà italiana* and the *Journal patriotique de Corse*. It was probably his radical revolutionary views that recommended him for the post of commissioner in the district of Corte in 1792. The task of these commissioners was to monitor political sentiments during the radical phase of the revolution. Buonarroti acquired French citizenship and in 1793 fought against the Corsican counter-revolutionaries. As an eminent champion of Jacobin principles, he was sent back to his old homeland as a revolutionary agent. In April 1794, he was appointed commissioner of the republic of Oneglia, which he governed until 12 May 1795. This small town on the Ligurian coast had been conquered by France during the War of the First Coalition. Oneglia briefly became an experimental laboratory for Jacobin reforms and the headquarters of Italian revolutionaries. It was organised according to republican principles with collective ownership and was supported by the peasants in the surrounding countryside. After the end of the reign of terror, Buonarroti was harassed once again by the moderate directorate due to his vision of a social revolution. The principle of a combination of revolutionary patriotism, utopian communism and radical republicanism which he had propagated was no longer desirable. This small patriotic Jacobite movement was able to achieve very little during its time and in other Italian cities such as Turin, Bologna, Naples, Palermo and Rome any revolutionary stirrings were immediately supressed. However, in the long term, it had a major impact on the political discourse and political movements in the nineteenth century. These patriots, as the Italian Jacobins called themselves, were the first to articulate the demand for the peninsula to be transformed into a nation state.

The republican experiment in Oneglia was only feasible during the short phase when the French Jacobins were in power. The Italian radicals hoped to be freed from the 'yoke of tyranny' by further French military offensives. After the collapse of the Republic of Oneglia, Buonarroti used every means at his disposal to persuade the directorate in Paris to intervene in Italy. The continuation of hostilities that followed did in fact gradually bring the whole of Italy under French rule, with the exception of Sicily and Sardinia, which were British protectorates. In the process, soldiers and officers imported revolutionary ideas and publications. However, their promises of 'liberty, equality, fraternity' as well as 'war on the palaces, peace to the huts' remained unfulfilled since, in principle, these were wars of conquest based on power strategies. They may have been followed by fundamental reforms and modernisation, but in the spirit of the liberal elites, not of the Jacobins.

The Italian rulers participated in several European coalitions against revolutionary and Napoleonic France in an attempt to protect themselves from any further expansion by their powerful neighbour. This, however, proved futile and they were unable to prevent their loss of power. The first to be affected was Piedmont, which had allied itself with Austria, Prussia and Britain in the War of the First Coalition. In 1792–1793 revolutionary troops invaded and annexed Savoy and Nice, invoking the principle of natural borders. Prussia withdrew from this First Coalition in 1795, but Britain and Austria were determined to continue the war. The Habsburgs hoped for a further expansion of their power in Italy. France responded with the grand war plan conceived by Lazare Carnot, who, as one of the five members of the directorate, was responsible for military affairs. The French armies were to inflict a defeat on Austria by marching on it both from the Rhine through Franconia and Bavaria and through northern Italy.

In March 1796 the command of the army in Italy was handed to Napoleon Bonaparte, at that time only twenty-seven years old. He used the opportunity to demonstrate his extraordinary tactical talent and to establish his reputation as a general. As a result of his success, he became one of the leading figures in France. The prestige he earned in these campaigns created the basis for his subsequent independent tactics – Napoleon frequently ignored directives from the government, conducted unauthorised diplomatic negotiations or prolonged hostilities without appropriate orders. As early as April 1796, King Victor Amadeus III had to accept a ceasefire which left Piedmont to Napoleon as a staging area and confirmed the surrender of Nice and Savoy. On 10 May 1796 the French defeated the Austrians completely unexpectedly in the legendary battle of Lodi. When Napoleon entered Milan, its residents hailed him as their liberator. Tuscany declared its neutrality and was initially unaffected by the war. In June 1796, the French troops advanced further south into the Papal States, also taking Emilia Romagna which belonged to the Papal States and the duchies of Parma-Piacenza and Modena. At the end of 1796, Napoleon, at the head of an exhausted army, managed to turn an impending defeat into a victory by overcoming the rearguard of the Austrian army on the bridge at Arcola. This episode was immortalised in a famous painting by Antoine Gros, whose iconic depiction contributed towards Napoleon's reputation as a brilliant strategist. By February 1797, he had defeated the Austrians at Mantua and Trento. After occupying large parts of Venice's *terra firma* in the same month, he forced the collapse of the aristocratic republic of Venice. The last doge, Ludovico Manin, had no choice but to abdicate. The Italian campaign had achieved its military aim: Austria had been driven out of Lombardy and was in a weak diplomatic position.

## 2.2 The era of the 'sister' republics – the *Triennio* (1797–1799)

The term *Triennio* is used by Italian historiographers to describe the years between 1797 and 1799. They were distinguished by pathbreaking liberal reforms within the judicial system and the administration and also by the costs of occupation and rises in taxes and food prices. Military conquests were consolidated by means of diplomatic treaties. In February 1797, the Pope was forced to surrender Emilia Romagna in the Treaty of Tolentino and the size of the levies it demanded, fifteen million francs, exacerbated the economic problems already existing in the Papal States. Even before this, in December 1796, local liberal patricians had founded the

Cispadane Republic, made up of Reggio Emilia, Modena, Bologna and Ferrara. By agreeing to the Treaty of Campo Formio in October 1797, Austria sanctioned further French conquests in northern Italy, giving up Lombardy in exchange for Venice, Dalmatia and Istria. This disappointed the Jacobins, who had hoped that these areas would also become part of the new Cispadane Republic. Emperor Francis II further agreed to the mandatory transformation of the oligarchic, aristocratic Republic of Genoa into the Ligurian Republic. The Cisalpine Republic had previously come into existence in Lombardy, and after the treaty of Campo Formio, the Cispadane Republic was merged with it. A sovereign and formally independent state, this enlarged Cisalpine, with Milan as its capital, became a refuge for democrats and moderate liberals from southern and central Italy. Its 3.5 million inhabitants had previously lived in six different states, so the creation of this new state in northern Italy represented a significant step forward for the supporters of a nation state. Napoleon returned to Paris and, just ten days after the signing of the Treaty of Campo Formio, was given command of the *Armée d'Angleterre* with the task of overcoming France's strongest enemy. Since he deemed a direct attack on Britain unlikely to succeed due to the poor state of the French fleet, he concentrated on confrontations with the British over power in the Mediterranean. His aim was to fight the British in Egypt.

In Italy, meanwhile, the extent of French power continued to increase. Only two months after the Treaty of Campo Formio, there was renewed unrest in Rome. On 28 December 1797, Jacobin patriots protested outside the French embassy, the Palazzo Corsini on the Via Lungara. Papist soldiers intervened and the French embassy counsellor, General Duphot, was killed in the turmoil. This and other attempts at rebellion instigated by the patriots provided a pretext for action. Louis-Alexander Berthier (1753–1815), who had taken over supreme command of the troops from Napoleon, marched to Rome and took the city on 10 February. On 28 February 1798, the end of papal secular rule and the beginning of the Roman Republic were proclaimed on the forum, staged as a sovereign act of people. The number of people who participated in this revolutionary act is estimated at no more than between five and seven hundred. Berthier himself wrote in his private correspondence that he had seen no sign of patriotic feeling in the city, only bewilderment.[1] The pope, Pius VI (Giovanni Angelo Braschi), refused to relinquish his secular power whereupon he was arrested and deported to France, where he died on 20 August 1799 at the age of nearly eighty-two. This was the temporary end of a thousand years of papal power in Rome and the Papal States. The election of the new pope, Pius VII, had to take place in Habsburg Venice.

In Naples, the government used the apparent power vacuum after Bonaparte's departure to begin new hostilities. Spurred on by Queen Maria Carolina and Lord Acton, Ferdinand IV ordered his troops to march northwards. When they reached Rome, they were vigorously repulsed by General Championnet who, to add insult to injury, launched a counterattack conquering southern Italy and forcing the royal couple to flee to Sicily. Back in Naples the Jacobin patriots proclaimed a republic in January 1799. Two months later the French succeeded in invading Tuscany. The King of Piedmont had already been forced to abdicate in December 1798, and he also fled to his island, Sardinia. Thus, by spring 1799, the French were in control of the whole of the Italian mainland with the exception of Venice. Resigned and disappointed, the Jacobins were forced to look on as the French simply annexed Piedmont and divided it up into French departments.

The politics of the *Triennio* years from 1797 to 1799 had many different facets. The French generals, as representatives of the *Grande Nation*, conducted negotiations with the local Jacobins and liberals in accordance with the orders of the directorate, which for its part concluded treaties with those monarchs who were still in office. At the same time, Napoleon acted as the representative of the revolution, permitting the creation of 'sister' republics, and took it upon himself to lead his generals on new campaigns to spread the French revolutionary model. In spite of the term 'sister' republics, these entities were all ruled with massive interference from Paris. On the other hand, the liberal Italian elites willingly seized the opportunity for political participation which had not existed before the invasion of the French troops and which was lost again after the Congress of Vienna. The local members of the aristocracy and bourgeoisie who had leading political, social and economic positions by virtue of their property, education, career and family, commonly known as 'notables', were in favour of republics that were formally independent.

It is no coincidence that Italian researchers attach considerable significance to this three-year period of the *Triennio*. For many historians it marks the beginning of modern Italian history. The *Triennio* is seen as a momentous phase of independent political projects and relative autonomy. After around three hundred years of 'foreign rule' this was the first time the Italian elites were in a position to govern themselves, albeit not independently of France. During these three ephemeral and transitory years, fundamental political and legal innovations were introduced and, regardless of the political regimes that succeeded them in the following decades, their effects were long-lasting.

Bonaparte cooperated with the Italian liberals and filled important posts from their ranks. He used the Jacobins, in contrast, only in the transition phase after the military conquest and only to systematically exclude them from all offices after power had been consolidated. In spite of all the regional differences, during the three years of their existence these republics shared common features. They were all aligned to the French constitution of 1795: they introduced equality before the law, reformed taxes and modernised the administration. The only exception was the southern republic in Naples, which was established autonomously by a group of democratic patriots led by the philosopher and lawyer Mario Pagano (1748–1799). He drew up a constitution modelled on the French republic of 1793.

It is worth noting that, apart from this singular case, politics on the Italian peninsula, whether ruled directly or indirectly by France, always followed Parisian directives. The Italian constitutions of 1797 guaranteed consistent separation of powers and civil liberties. As in Paris, the executive was in the hands of a five-member directorate. The legislature was determined by two chambers, a council of elders and a general council, which appointed the directorate. The deputies were elected on the basis of census suffrage, i. e. determined by wealth, a system which favoured the bourgeois elite and therefore naturally disappointed the Jacobins. The newly-established bodies used their first laws to abolish all privileges based on social position. From then on, every citizen was equal before the law. This modern citizenship was associated with the idea of freedoms – freedom of thought, of religion, of the press and of association. Of further fundamental significance was the reorganisation of the judicial system and the administration. It included the adoption of the French court system, public and oral hearings, and the equality of every individual before the law. The aristocracy lost not only their titles and heraldry, but also their patrimonial jurisdiction and with it much of their power in the countryside.

The administration was also modernised and centralised. Following the French model, the new republic was divided into departments and districts of approximately equal size, each named after natural features such as rivers, mountains and the sea. The aim of this system was to break with traditional territorial names and the memories associated with them. Each department was governed by a council of five members. Justices of the peace and administrative officials were elected. Although the constitution also provided for the election of an administrator at the head of each department, they were in fact simply instated by Bonaparte. In any case, the final decision-making power in the republics rested with the highest military officers present. The adoption of the French model of state policy towards the church proved problematic. The introduction of civil registers, civil marriage and options for divorce were readily accepted and in themselves caused a massive loss of influence for the church. But how far should the separation of church and state and the freedom of religion go? This was endlessly debated. So, for example, the Ligurian and Cisalpine republics decided to retain Catholicism as their state religion.

There was initial euphoria amongst the political actors. In official speeches, they praised the generosity of the mother republic and celebrated the genius of Napoleon Bonaparte. The *Tricolore* was taken as a model and introduced in the Cisalpine Republic in green, white and red, later becoming the flag of the national movement and the Italian nation state. Official titles and symbols were also adopted from France. Since these new terms were derived from the ancient Roman Republic, which was glorified by revolutionaries, they were readily accepted in Italy. The Cisalpine Republic is often referred to as a Jacobin republic, but a glance at the main actors in Milan shows that, in reality, it was dominated by liberal politicians. As in Paris, the directorate was plagued by governmental crises, staff fluctuation and its own temporary nature. Between June 1797 and April 1799, three successive directorates were in power and these five posts were occupied by a total of sixteen men. They came without exception from the aristocratic and bourgeois elite of northern Italy, a third of them from rich patrician families in Milan, Bergamo or Bologna, and the other two thirds were socialised in merchant or legal circles. They were by no means hot-headed young politicians, but mature men between the ages of 35 and 60, many of whom had studied law. There were no radical Jacobins to be found in their ranks. The mark of the so-called Jacobin constitutions in Italy was that, as a result of the shocking experience of Robespierre's terror and in the same way as the French model of 1795, they reversed their stance in favour of the notables and turned their back on the common people.

Not only in the Cisalpine Republic, but also earlier in the Cispadane Republic and Naples, it was particularly young aristocrats in the south who seemed prepared to give up their privileged career opportunities and feudal rights. In return, they took significant advantage of the power offered to them by the constitutions and the new political bodies, whose deputies were elected from the exclusive group of high property owners. This was the basis on which the transformation of an aristocratic republic into one on more democratic lines could be accepted by the aristocracy in Lucca and Genoa. French innovations were not seen as revolutionary because all that happened was that the previously dominant groups were reshuffled. The patrician order did not collapse – ultra-conservative politicians were simply replaced by younger liberals from the same families. The political subjects of the republican constitutions were the propertied classes.

However, 'sister' republics did not enjoy widespread popularity in Italy. One problem was that, although state sovereignty existed formally on paper, high taxes and levies still had to be paid to Paris. There was also the issue of the constant demands of the local army. The 'sister' republics were expected to make their contribution to the wars and the endless military campaigns were extremely onerous for the Italians; officers, troops and their horses had to be provided for and the high level of levies paid. It is difficult to estimate exactly how much money flowed from the occupied territories to France, as the full extent is not known. During the Italian campaign, money and palaces were requisitioned throughout the country.

The French army also immediately carried out targeted thefts of artworks in all the areas it conquered. Looting art may not have been new, but it was new that the stolen objects were chosen according to the aesthetic theories and guidelines of the modern art world. The invading troops were swiftly followed by a group of commissioners who were instructed by the directorate to secure artefacts, books, archaeological finds and so on for the *Grande Nation*. Not everything that was valuable was indiscriminately removed; instead, particular pieces were selected in order to present as complete a collection of valuable masterpieces in Paris as possible. The ideological justification for this extensive relocation of cultural assets was the claim that the revolution was universal, and this was part of official museum policy. Artworks were requisitioned in the neighbouring European countries, initially in what is now Belgium, then in Luxembourg and the Rhineland states and from 1796 in Italy, where the haul was particularly rich as a consequence of the exceptional cultural heritage of the Renaissance and Baroque periods. Its legitimacy was based on the bold pretext that works of art and science were a product of liberty and had therefore to be taken from the tyrants and given an adequate home in the land of *liberté*, i. e. in France. In Paris, they were to promote national education by equipping newly founded institutions such as the *Bibliothèque nationale* and the art museum in the Louvre with particularly valuable exhibits and making them available to the general public. Paris was thus stylised as the European capital of culture. Spoils from Italy were taken to Paris in lavishly staged triumphant processions. From then on it was possible to visit the Louvre in Paris and admire Raphael's *School of Athens* from the Ambrosiana art collection in Milan, the *Massacre of the Innocents* by Guido Reni from Bologna, Andrea Mantegna's quadriptych from the high altar of San Zeno in Verona and the statue of *Laocoon and his Sons* from the Vatican museums, to name just a few of the most outstanding works. The *Triumphal Quadriga,* the four bronze horses that had decorated the facade of the St Mark's Cathedral in Venice since the thirteenth century, was also removed and carried off to Paris.

In the summer of 1799, the fledgling republics collapsed under attacks from two sides. On the one hand there was a massive expansion of conservative resistance incited by the church, and on the other, European powers took advantage of Bonaparte's absence in Egypt to renew their coalition. The uprisings and the anti-French sentiment against the occupying forces had a strong religious component and were often blended with elements of popular antagonism towards the advocates of 'atheism'. This was combined with urban discontent and resentment on the part of the disaffected peasants towards those who had profited from the new regime by buying large estates which had previously belonged to the church but been secularised and auctioned off in the republics. The overall situation led to a 'white terror', which denounced Jacobins, patriots and French soldiers with equal vigour and celebrated the deposed rulers and the imprisoned pope, whose martyrdom had already become a symbol of all the excesses of the new era.

Acts of violence were carried out with particular ferocity in Campania, Calabria and the interior of Tuscany where they assumed the form of outright guerilla warfare. In May 1799, an army of priests and fanatical peasants from the area of Arezzo, the so-called *Armata Aretina*, with their battle cry of *Viva Maria,* terrorised eastern Tuscany and Umbria. After taking Arezzo and Siena, they invaded Florence in July and relentlessly pursued anyone who had the semblance of a Francophile patriot. In Piedmont a group of officers loyal to the king led the *Massa cristiana* movement, a group of partisans influenced by the clergy. The most violent clashes, however, took place in southern Italy.

The political instrumentalization of the popular movement was most evident in Naples. Here the leader of the irregulars was Fabrizio Ruffo di Baranello (1744–1827), who came from a respected ruling family in Calabria. He had made a career in the Papal States. In contrast to most men at the courts in Rome and Naples, Cardinal Ruffo was not a reactionary but an advocate of enlightened reforms. He offered to reconquer the mainland for the exiled king and set out in February 1799 with a handful of companions. This was a conservative undertaking, but similar in daring to the more popular campaign that Garibaldi would lead from Palermo to Naples sixty years later. Supported by a legendary bandit called Fra Diavolo, Cardinal Ruffo mobilised the peasants in Campania and Calabria for his Christian, royalist army, rapidly swelling their numbers by promising the peasant underclasses charity and social relief. On 13 June 1799, these so-called *Sanfedisti* (*Army of the Holy Faith*) marched into Naples, supported by Admiral Nelson's recently landed British troops. It was Ruffo's aim to strengthen the Bourbon monarchy and after the French had left, he offered to make peace with the Republicans. But the cardinal had underestimated the desire for revenge driving Maria Carolina and Ferdinand: encouraged by Nelson, they sought to eradicate the patriots. Ferdinand waited until Ruffo was victorious, then returned to Naples with his court and had the Jacobins and the Italian patriots condemned by special tribunals. The republican leaders, who had campaigned for a modern bourgeois state, were murdered. Looking back on this, Pietro Colletta (1775–1831), a Neapolitan officer, contemporary witness and liberal historian, who himself had been imprisoned, wrote in his *History of the Kingdom of Naples*:

> The best-known of the kingdom died, approximately three hundred of them without even counting the deaths in the battles or the riots. Among these unfortunates were some from the Caraffa, Riario, Colonna and Caracciolo families, five Pignatelli and members of twenty other illustrious families. At their side can be seen the most famous men of letters and science. […] Never has a city or kingdom so rich in talent become so impoverished as a result of so many deaths.[2]

Nowhere else had so many young nobles been so enthusiastically committed to a republic. 534 patriots were captured and convicted and 119 of them were executed, among them intellectual aristocrats such as Eleonora Pimentel, Luisa Sanfelice and Ettore Caraffa. This had a lasting effect on contemporary remembrance of *Novantanove* (99), which stood for the hopes and failures of the revolutionary circles in Naples. The patriots who had been killed thus became early martyrs of the democratic and liberal nation state movement.

The monarchs, on the other hand, interpreted the Naples Republic as a reprehensible attempt on the part of the aristocracy to incite popular sentiment against absolutism and were convinced that they deserved no less than to have their power crushed. The property of the families involved was confiscated and the Restoration that followed led to a complete return to the old system of government. For a time, Maria Carolina even pursued plans to seize feudal estates in order to ruin the aristocracy. However, she overlooked the fact that this would have had a considerable effect on the church. A substantial portion of the feudal property in the south was owned by the church and the king was absolutely dependent on its support.

The French had been unable to help their political allies. Whereas Naples had fallen before the troops of the Second Coalition had reached the city, it was military victories in northern and central Italy that led to the collapse of the republics. The Second Coalition was sealed by Britain, Austria, Russia, the Ottoman Empire, Portugal, Naples and the Papal States by the beginning of 1799 and soon proved successful in Italy. Austrian and Russian troops under general Alexander Suvorov reconquered lost territory in Italy. In April 1799, the French had to withdraw from Lombardy and the government of the Cisalpine Republic fled to France. In May, the Austro-Russian troops had reached Turin and in September 1799 the Roman Republic came to an end. Only André Masséna held his ground in Genoa. The French retreat was accompanied by massive repression against patriots in all the territories, although the rulers in the north were more merciful and astute than those in Naples. All the republics were abolished and the institutions of the *Ancien Régime* restored.

At the turn of the century the papacy was also restored. The papal conclave convened in Austrian-controlled Venice from December 1799 to March 1800. It was divided into two irreconcilable factions which would continue to dominate discussions on ecclesiastical policies. On the one hand were the moderate, liberal *Politicanti* (*the Politicals*), who were more open to political changes in Europe, and on the other the *Zelanti* (*the Zealots*), who hoped for a complete restoration of the *Ancien Régime.* Cardinal Luigi Barnaba Conte Chiaramonti (1742–1823), who was elected Pope Pius VII, was sympathetic towards the moderate wing. Both Austrian and Neapolitan troops accompanied the new pope to Rome. He proved to be tolerant of revolutionary achievements as long as they did not violate Catholic doctrine. In line with this moderate stance, he chose as his cardinal secretary of state Ercole Consalvi (1757–1824), who attempted to govern by enlightenment principles. This naturally antagonised the *Zelanti*, who were dominant in the Papal States. This conflict was to play a crucial role throughout the nineteenth century. The majority of the high dignitaries of the Papal States were not prepared to compromise in any way and were resolutely opposed to any liberal or even moderate reforms.

The restoration of the monarchy, however, lasted only a short time (1799–1800). Austria and Russia had completely different aims in the war and the Second Coalition collapsed. In Vienna the focus was on consolidating power in Italy while the Russian troops lost battles in Switzerland and laid the blame on the lack of support from their coalition partners. The tsar withdrew his troops. Meanwhile, Napoleon Bonaparte had hurried back to Paris from Egypt, and as a result of the badly organised coup d'état on 18 Brumaire VIII (9 November 1799) had assumed power. He replaced the incompetent directorate with a three-member committee of consuls, which he himself led as First Consul. Napoleon's offer of peace was rejected by Britain and Austria. London attempted to establish a balance of power in Europe and secure its own supremacy in the Mediterranean whereas Vienna wanted to renegotiate the terms of the Treaty of Campo Formio and so redraw the map of Italy.

As First Consul, Napoleon decided to renew hostilities against the European powers. Following periods of peace, new European coalitions repeatedly attempted to reverse or at least revise French gains, but to no avail. Although Napoleon had to surrender the Mediterranean to the British after the catastrophic defeat at Trafalgar, he was unbeaten on the continent until 1808. At the height of his power his empire stretched from Hamburg to Rome and he also controlled the 'model states' reaching from Warsaw to Madrid and Reggio Calabria. The military victories meant that the territories on the Apennine peninsula were being constantly re-organised. A change of ruler had become an everyday occurrence for their subjects.

Napoleon first rushed to conquer Lombardy. This second Italian campaign entailed crossing the Great Saint Bernard Pass in winter on donkeys. The picture of this Alpine crossing painted by Jacques Louis David as powerful propaganda shows Napoleon storming the pass mounted on an Arab steed. The names of Hannibal and Charlemagne are symbolically inscribed on the rocks at the bottom of the picture. Bonaparte did indeed succeed in repeating the victories of 1796, defeating the Austrians surprisingly quickly near Marengo in the province of Alessandria. General Moreau was in command of the army invading Germany and also won a crushing victory over the Austrians. Vienna found itself forced to agree to a ceasefire. The peace treaty agreed on 9 February 1801 in Lunéville in Lorraine saw Austria renouncing its territorial claims on the left bank of the Rhine and Lombardy restored as the Cisalpine Republic. In principle, the treaty of Lunéville endorsed the treaty of Campo Formio, but Bonaparte went further and forced Austria to renounce Tuscany as a secundogeniture, although it was permitted to retain Venice. Two further peace treaties completed the process of incorporating Italy into the Empire: first the Treaty of Pressburg (26 December 1805) after Napoleon's victory over the Third Coalition and then the Treaty of Vienna (Schönbrunn) (14 October 1809), following the renewed defeat of Austria.

After the Treaty of Pressburg in 1805, Napoleon again occupied Naples and again Maria Carolina and Ferdinand fled into exile in Sicily, this time for ten years. While the islands were still under the protection of Britain, as a result of the provisions of the Treaty of Vienna, after 1809 the whole of the Italian mainland belonged directly or indirectly to the Grand Empire. Napoleon had appointed himself emperor in December 1804, and during this period he founded the Bonaparte dynasty. He installed his brothers and brothers-in-law as kings in the newly conquered territories. Louis became King of Holland, Jérôme, King of Westphalia and Joseph, King of Naples, who, after his accession to the Spanish throne, was succeeded by his brother-in-law Joachim Murat. Power relations in the duchies of Tuscany and Parma were extremely complicated. In 1801 Napoleon had negotiated an agreement with Spain and the Bourbon(-Parma) dynasty that, after the death of Duke Ferdinand, the Duchy of Parma should go to France. In return the House of Bourbon would be compensated with the Duchy of Tuscany which the Habsburgs lost in the Treaty of Lunéville in 1801. From then on it was called the Kingdom of Etruria and the crown went, as agreed, to the Spanish prince Louis Francis. The Habsburg previously in power, Ferdinand III, was compensated with the secularised Archbishopric of Salzburg. On the death of Louis Francis, his wife Maria Luisa, sister of the Spanish Queen, became regent but in 1807 she also lost her kingdom. As in the case of the Papal States, Napoleon was provided with an excuse to invade and then annex Tuscany/Etruria by its failure to strictly observe the anti-British Continental System. This was a blockade on continental ports imposed by Napoleon in an effort to bring Britain to its knees by exploiting its dependence on exports, because the French navy could not hope for a victory at sea. Tuscany was then divided into departments and incorporated into the Grand Empire. Since the Pope also refused to adhere strictly to the Continental System, in 1808 the remaining regions of the Papal States were also occupied, annexed and divided into departments. Once again, the secular power of the popes was ended. Pius VII responded by excommunicating Napoleon but suffered the same fate as his predecessor: he was taken first to Savona and then to France, where he was imprisoned.

Napoleon came from the minor aristocracy, and as such suffered from the stigma of being an upstart. His remedy was to systematically set up connections between his dynasty and the major European aristocratic families by means of intermarriage. He also expected this family consortium to display maximum solidarity and loyalty. He married his brother Jérôme to Katharina von Württemberg, his stepson Eugène Beauharnais to Auguste of Bavaria and his brother Louis to Hortense, Beauharnais' sister. Only Joseph remained married to a bourgeois – his first wife was a merchant's daughter. Napoleon's brother Lucien Bonaparte refused to enter into a marriage for the dynasty and fled into exile in Rome. After the collapse of the Papal States, he fell into the hands of the British while fleeing to America and was taken prisoner. The emperor's sisters in their turn married officers or generals. Caroline was married to Murat and Pauline to Camillo Borghese, who came from one of the oldest noble families in Italy and was instated in Piedmont as governor general. After the collapse of the Republic of Lucca Elisa Bonaparte and Félix Baciocchi were promoted to become the rulers of Lucca. Napoleon's marriage policy is likely to have been modelled on that of Maria Theresia and of the aristocracy in general.

Regardless of who was in power, between 1792 and 1814 the Italian territories were fundamentally modernised and reformed according to the principles of the liberal revolution. The reforms differed only slightly, depending on whether they were introduced in areas annexed by France, where the Italians became French citizens with the same rights and duties, or whether they were in one of the two kingdoms in the south and north. It was Napoleon's confirmed conviction that his subjects in the empire and the 'model states' would be won over to him and his system by an egalitarian judicial system, free enterprise, civic equality, freedom of religion, a modern and functioning administration and the abolition of privileges. He succeeded in many cases, particularly with the notables involved. The Napoleonic era had its most lasting impact in the areas of northern Italy that were annexed early on, and it achieved least in those areas such as the territories of the former Papal States, Tuscany and the Kingdom of Naples that belonged to the empire only for a short time. The reforms were particularly enduring in those areas of northern Italy that belonged first to the Cisalpine Republic, then to the Italian Republic and from 1805 to the Kingdom of Italy.

## 2.3 Italy under Napoleon

After the return of the French and the victory at Marengo, the Cisalpine Republic was re-established and initially placed under the authority of an envoy from the French government. However, complaints were soon heard about chaos, corruption and inefficiency in the new administration and it proved necessary to reorganise the government and draw up a constitution. It was passed by members of the aristocracy, the clergy, the bourgeoisie and representatives of the liberal professions, acting on the maxim of Emmanuel Joseph Sièyes that power should come from above and trust from below. In the first Italian campaign Bonaparte had styled himself as the liberator but after the success of the second campaign and the Treaty of Lunéville, he appeared as the deliverer of peace and a figure who would restore order – in cooperation with the northern Italian notables.

After the autumn of 1801 Napoleon invited 500 of these notables from the Cisalpine Republic to an assembly to be convened between Paris and Milan. He settled on Lyon, a subversive city in which as First Consul he wanted to demonstrate his power. 452 of them accepted the invitation to the congress which took place in February 1802, with Napoleon present. The famous Italian poet Ugo Foscolo, who was one of the deputies, wrote a speech en route to Lyon in praise of the assembly, celebrating Bonaparte as the bearer of peace.

A constitution had been prepared beforehand in Paris. It was assumed that the deputies would do no more than discuss it at the congress. Substantial changes were unwelcome. After long debates the only option was to agree to the reintroduction of a system based on the model of a constitution with a directorate. This time it was the constitution of the year VIII (1799). Bonaparte adopted a similar approach with the Swiss. Since a civil war had been raging between conservative federalists and liberal unionists for years in Switzerland, he invited select notables from all the Swiss cantons to Malmaison near Paris for consultations. After some deliberation they voted to accept a constitution drafted by Napoleon and his advisors. This Act of Mediation passed in Malmaison was to determine the federal structures of Switzerland even after 1815.

A consequential outcome of the meeting of deputies in Lyon was the proclamation of the Italian Republic, replacing the Cisalpine Republic. Its name was of great significance, since this was the first time a state on the peninsula had been called Italian – a noteworthy signal. A few years later, when Napoleon created a state on Polish soil, he refused to call it Polish. To the great disappointment of the supporters of a nation state, what was formed there was no more than the Grand Duchy of Warsaw. The Republic of Italy was still a model state dependent on Paris with Napoleon as its president. However, its vice presidency was conferred on one of the leading liberal notables, Francesco Melzi d'Eril. Previously one of the most influential politicians in the Cisalpine Republic, he contributed significantly to the creation of the new state.

Melzi d'Eril (1753–1816) came from one of the numerous aristocratic families in Milan. He attended the prestigious Brera college and as a young man kept company in the salons with important Enlightenment thinkers such as Pietro Verri and Cesare Beccaria. On his travels through Europe, Melzi came to appreciate British parliamentarianism and wrote enthusiastically in his journals about the progressive economic system in Britain. He welcomed the liberal phase of the French Revolution, received Bonaparte on his arrival in Milan and was frequently consulted by him. Melzi was also involved in attempts to re-organise the strained finances of the Cisalpine Republic. After the battle of Marengo, he was one of the few Italian notables with whom Napoleon conferred in Paris during the preparations for the assembly in Lyon. His greatest moment came when he was appointed vice president of the Italian Republic. In the three years of its existence, he was able to use the considerable authority granted him by the constitution to make significant contributions to the establishment of state structures.

Map 2 Italy 1810.

In contrast to the Cisalpine Republic, any vestiges of a sovereignty of the people were erased in the Italian Republic and its legislative power degenerated into a mere appendage of the omnipotent executive. There were no longer elections in the new republic: the deputies in the committees were appointed for life from above by the president from the ranks of landowners, merchants and the well-educated. Apart from a *Consulta* consisting of eight members, there was a legislative assembly with sixty-five members, of which one third were exchanged every two years. It was, however, only empowered to debate laws submitted to it. Power was clearly in the hands of the president, his vice president, his deputy, the new ministers and the administration. It amounted to an administrative monarchy with a strong executive and a centralised administration. Since Bonaparte was seldom present, the responsibility for governing the state lay with Francesco Melzi d'Eril.

In the subsequent three years, Melzi as vice president succeeded in introducing key reforms. The initial focus was on rectifying the disastrous state of public finances, which he achieved by selling secularised church property. A further Herculean task was creating a national army that was for the first time based on conscription. The modernisation of the education system and fundamental reforms to the judicial system according to liberal principles was a further challenge. In 1803 Melzi also successfully negotiated a Concordat with Pope Pius VII. Modelled on the Concordat concluded between France and the Pope in 1801, it regulated the relationship between the church and the state. In order to be able to implement his reforms locally Melzi resorted to a novel type of civil servant introduced in France after 1800 as a new instrument of power, the prefect. Each department was headed by a prefect chosen by Melzi. They received their orders from the ministers, to whom they had to report regularly about their administrative activities. On the level of the *arrondissements,* the prefects for their part had sub-prefects under them who again had local mayors as subordinates in the municipalities. For the people, this system was most conspicuous in the person of the prefect, not least because of his magnificent blue uniform with its gold embroidery. It was the task of the prefect to implement the laws, to guarantee public order with the help of the police, to control the lower administrative divisions, enforce conscription and monitor the public mood. There was very little room for local autonomy in the system, although that naturally depended on those in office.

Bonaparte allowed Melzi remarkable scope for his civil service policy. The structure of the civil service was completely novel. All the functionaries were appointed by the state and were representatives of the new state administration and jurisdiction. Previously jurisdiction had been based on noble privileges, and the coexistence of the state and the nobility had been the order of the day. The new reforms literally robbed the nobility of its judiciary function. Would they be prepared to serve the new system? After all, the success or failure of the reforms depended crucially on the functionaries and their quality. Melzi filled the higher positions almost exclusively with young northern Italian representatives from liberal-conservative and enlightened, noble and bourgeois circles. When appointing prefects and vice prefects, he strove to recruit mainly members of the aristocracy with experience of office. He was able to fill thirteen out of nineteen prefectures with patricians and *nobili,* members of the aristocracy. The new and old elites came together in the civil service. One of the motives for the nobility to become involved in the republic in leading positions stemmed from their perception of themselves as aristocrats:

Fig. 1 Andrea Appiani, Napoleon I Bonaparte (1769-1821) as King of Italy, c. 1806–1808.

they believed that their position in society and their experience of it traditionally qualified them to govern.

Overall Melzi strove to achieve the greatest possible autonomy for the Italian Republic. After Napoleon had crowned himself emperor, however, there was no more room in his empire for republics. In 1805, he converted the Italian Republic into a monarchy and, symbolically using the iron crown of Lombardy, crowned himself King of Italy in Milan and appointed his stepson Eugène Beauharnais as his deputy. In spite of his great merits, there was no place for an independent figure like Melzi in the new kingdom. He was relegated to the honourable post of the Royal Keeper of the Seal at court, an office with a high income and considerable prestige but no political influence. His reform measures, however, were kept unchanged. Nevertheless, after 1805 the nobility began to withdraw remarkably often from leading positions. In 1806, 76 per cent of the prefects and sub-prefects came from the nobility but by 1814, this figure had fallen to 42 per cent.

In those areas of Italy that had been annexed by France and divided into fifteen departments, only laws that had been passed in Paris were applied. What is noticeable here is the very high percentage of officials from other regions. While in northern Italy Melzi had deployed prefects in their home region, in the Italian departments and in France itself they were often relocated and not employed in their home towns. The purpose of this policy of appointing prefects from elsewhere was to avoid conflicts of interest, nepotism and corruption. In the Italian departments, French notables or notables from other regions of Italy were selected. However, the appointment of civil servants from other regions or of French origin reinforced the perception of the otherness of the new regime and the extent of the changes.

Furthermore, many nobles in these departments were opposed to Napoleon's new system, so the question remains as to who did in fact identify with it. It was most likely to have been the younger nobles who had been educated in Paris. One of them was Conte Cesare Balbo di Vinadio (1789–1853), who undoubtedly pursued one of the most remarkable careers. He came from an aristocratic family of civil servants in Piedmont and studied law in Paris. As early as 1807 he was appointed auditor in the Council of State in Paris. In 1808 he was secretary general of the administration that implemented liberal reforms in the annexed departments of Tuscany and was appointed to the same position in 1809 in the Roman *Consulta* in the annexed Papal States. Further stages of Balbo's career took him to Ljubljana as French government commissioner and finally to Holland as police commissioner. During the Restoration, he was initially sidelined for a few years by the Piedmontese king, but later became one of the staunchest protagonists of a liberal nation state. Balbo was one of those Italians who enjoyed a remarkable career in the service of Napoleon and was crucially influenced by this experience.

After 1806, the restructuring of the state also brought gains and losses to the Kingdom of Naples. By the standards of the emperor, his brother Joseph's government was only in the early stages of the reform process. Joseph selected experienced French and Neapolitan figures for his ministerial posts. The constitution and the structure of the state was similar to that in Milan, except that here the prefects were called intendants. A gradual process of transformation can be observed for the south of Italy. Where previously the capital Naples with its approximately 400,000 inhabitants had dominated everything, thanks to the many seats of the newly created provincial governments, genuine urban life emerged. An immense urban periphery gradually transformed into a modern structure, based on a variety of centres, which in their turn administrated the rural peripheries. This was particularly the case in Bari, Avellino and Catanzaro. In the case of one of the most pressing problems, however, that of rampant gangsterism, particularly in Calabria, very little was achieved. Although the Napoleonic police force model was applied in the new Kingdom of Naples, there was no existing law enforcement group to rely on and the period of rule was too short to establish an efficient police force.

It proved to be extremely difficult to end feudalism in the south. 30 per cent of the land belonged to the aristocracy and another 20 per cent to the church, while the remaining 50 per cent was shared between state institutions or the crown. Tied to them were the lower courts, feudal servitude, monopolies on mills and presses and income from tithes and rents. There were no independent farmers, only small tenant farmers and peasant workers who bore the costs of the feudal system more or less alone. Joseph's reform plans were able to make no progress in this sensitive area, and it was not until 1808 that his successor Joachim Murat was able to prevail. He succeeded Joseph on the throne when he was given power over Spain. The new king, who came from Quercy, was sensitive to the problems of the peasants and in February 1809 he abolished the feudal regime with all its rights and privileges for the nobility. In contrast to his predecessor, he consistently appointed southern Italians as ministers, counsellors of state and intendants, thus helping the government to gain acceptance. However, that did little to change the continued existence of large landowners, and also failed to solve the problems of impoverishment which affected large sections of the population.

The effect of the Napoleonic period in Italy was felt essentially as a result of tighter administration, tax burdens and liberal reforms. The reform measures, which were not always successful, did not focus on social problems or the widespread oppressive poverty. The consumption tax introduced in 1809 even exacerbated the hardship of the lower classes. Ordinary people became acquainted with the Napoleonic empire primarily as conscripts, which led to considerable antagonism. The representatives of the regime also strove to consolidate their power by prestige politics and creating a new society. This period saw a huge transfer of landed property, the beginnings of a society of bourgeois notables and an extensive redistribution of artworks from which the aristocratic and bourgeois elites profited almost exclusively.

## 2.4 Secularisation and property speculation

Secularisation led to a redistribution of wealth on a scale previously unimaginable in many areas of western Europe at the end of the eighteenth and beginning of the nineteenth centuries. In 1783 Joseph II of Austria secularised seven hundred monasteries in his hereditary lands. The revolutionaries in Paris hoped that seizing church properties would enable them to pay off the enormous national debt accumulated by Louis XV and Louis XVI. Within two decades, a huge number of church properties were sequestered, expropriated and sold, not only in France but also in the areas occupied and annexed by the French. A close look at the question of who profited from this huge transformation process reveals one clear winner from the outset – the French state. It collected huge sums of money to cover its national debt and finance its many wars. However, those who purchased secularised church property were also considerably enriched.

In the early sales at the beginning of the 1790s, the revolutionary governments pursued their aim of social reform by dividing up the monastic estates into reasonably priced units and selling them off locally, allowing instalments to be paid over a long period of time. In the Italian territories, however, the sales were based on a completely different principle. Here the aim was to make as much profit as possible. As with all the measures introduced by the Paris government, they were implemented at different times: in Piedmont, Lombardy and Emilia Romagna before 1800, a good deal later in the Kingdom of Naples and Toscana and not until after 1809 in the Papal States. In Piedmont King Charles Emmanuel IV had obtained permission from the Pope to begin sales in 1794 in order to rescue his completely insolvent state budget. The sales continued during the Napoleonic period. Lombardy, however, was something of an anomaly, since only those who were in possession of promissory notes were allowed to bid for national goods. This led to valuable monastic lands being obtained by those who were already the richest. In the Cisalpine Republic, lists of the highest taxpayers were drawn up. The first four categories which included *decurions* (members of the administration), patricians, nobles and rich merchants who, until 1799, had to pay the largest part of the 36 million lira levies received promissory notes which were then compensated with monastic lands at the national estate sales. This meant, for example, that in the Cisalpine Republic a total of 62 million lira was collected, of which 30 per cent was accounted for alone by the Department of Olona and its capital Milan.

In Venetia, which was incorporated into the Kingdom of Italy in 1806, national property to the value of 16 million French francs was auctioned off. On the southern Italian mainland, which had also only been occupied by France since 1806, the domain directorate proceeded in the same way as in the north. Properties were not auctioned off for cash as had originally been planned, but for promissory notes.

Here again the land was sold in order to pay off public debts. In the Kingdom of Naples, however, only 20 per cent of the confiscated church property was put to auction while the main part was used to endow state administration and public bodies, including schools. In Tuscany, annexed in 1808, an impressive 29 million francs was realised from monastic properties in the three years between 1810 and 1813.

Bourgeois army suppliers and merchants in Italy acquired land from church institutions based on mandatory loans, but above all it was the wealthiest families who profited, most of whom came from the nobility. A novelty was that Jews were permitted to buy land for the first time because they were equal before the law. Whereas in France and the adjoining Belgian and German territories to the east more commoners than nobles purchased these highly coveted plots of land, on the Apennine peninsula it was the nobility who were able to considerably expand their already existing dominance in land ownership. In Piedmont, every second noble listed in the tax registers participated in the state auctions, whereby of the nearly 400 purchasers from the nobility, 60 per cent belonged to the older landed gentry and 35 per cent to nobles at court or in the military. In Tuscany the participation of the nobility in the sales of state lands was on a similarly high scale to Piedmont. In the department of Arno alone, 137 nobles bought around a third of all the goods offered, investing 7.6 million francs. In the Kingdom of Naples, sales of confiscated church property also led to a notable concentration in the hands of the noble families. There only 7 per cent of the total buyers purchased 65 per cent of the land for sale. Overall, existing ownership patterns in Italy were reinforced and the nobility was able to maintain its position as by far the largest property owner until well into the nineteenth century. The aristocracy also joined the bourgeoisie in skilfully participating in army supply networks and financial transactions, which offered a huge potential for speculation. Any of the bourgeoisie who managed to acquire wealth through this kind of business and become large landowners strove to become part of the nobility. It was Napoleon's hope that this policy of strongly favouring the rich would ensure the loyalty of a noble-bourgeois elite. He had no interest in how these measures were viewed by the peasants, who had little chance of acquiring land. He was primarily concerned with the approval and support of the notables.

This concentration of property ownership and wealth also had long-term consequences for political participation. In addition to the social prestige, risk-free financial liability, guaranteed mortgage security and more or less inflation-resistant capital investment which land ownership brought with it, it had a further distinctive element: it determined participation in political power and decision-making processes. In the annexed territories Napoleon recruited his political elite to committees such as the general council and district and department councils exclusively from the six hundred highest taxpayers in each department, with the greatest proportion of tax income coming from land tax. In the Italian kingdoms, Napoleon and Murat also selected deputies for their committees from the ranks of the wealthiest. The city councillors were again chosen from the hundred most highly taxed individuals in their municipalities. When drawing up regulations for their governments, both Piedmont and later Italy retained the principle that the ownership of land should determine political participation. A very high level of income was required in order to be eligible and this again was calculated on the basis of the amount of property tax paid. In summary, it can be said that in the Napoleonic empire and the nascent Italian nation state, property ownership was the foundation of the social, economic and political order.

## 2.5 The Old Masters as objects of prestige

It would be misleading to portray the nobility solely as the great profiteers of the French epoch. In the case of their art collections, often built up over centuries, they suffered bitter losses. The art market, which historians frequently ignore, was thrown into turmoil by the revolutionary upheavals. Owning precious works of art was more than a mere hobby or a source of tasteful interior decoration. Investing into art in the dimensions seen here was always also connected to power, politics and prestige. After the French conquest and the immediate abolition of the feudal system, the Italian aristocratic families were forced to pay taxes and levies. They were given promissory notes for the latter, but they first had to find the sums demanded. The greater the ownership of land the higher the taxes to be paid. Many noble families sold artworks on a large scale during these crisis years in order to overcome their lack of liquidity. It was by no means a novelty to sell artworks; the Italian art market flourished in the eighteenth century long before the invasion of the revolutionary troops. But in the Napoleonic era Italian art collections began to suffer substantial losses, a situation that continued throughout the century. It did not only apply to works that were simply requisitioned for the Louvre. They were mostly returned after the Congress of Vienna in 1815. It was also the case for private sales which remained valid during the Restoration. This process can be illustrated by the example of the nobility in Rome. After the treaty of Tolentino in 1798 the Pope financed the huge war debt in part by means of the obligatory debenture bonds from the Roman aristocracy. They in turn were forced to sell artworks, which mainly found their way to the London auction market by means of British art dealers, artists and ambassadors. After 1800 over three hundred so-called Old Masters were auctioned in London, all of which had formerly belonged to Roman families. They included pictures by Carracci, Garofalo, Giorgione, Guercino, Raphael and Reni which nowadays hang in the most famous national museums worldwide. Mantegna's *The Birth of Christ*, Titian's

*Venus and Adonis* and Raphael's *Saint Catherine*, all of which can be admired in the National Gallery in London, originally came from Roman collections.

At the same time, new collections were being rapidly assembled by the new rulers: the Bonaparte family on the one hand and the high dignitaries of the new political system in Italy on the other. One example is the considerable collection built up within only a few years by the emperor's stepson Eugène Beauharnais. As viceroy of Italy, he acquired the majority of the paintings in his collection in the royal capital Milan. His mother Josephine also had her residence in Malmaison furnished with exquisite Old Masters. By far the most valuable collection of the Bonaparte family, however, was created by Napoleon's uncle Cardinal Joseph Fesch. In 1796, he resigned from the priesthood and during the Italian campaigns became a supplier to the army, a type of business that could create enormous profits. Fesch sometimes accepted artworks in payment for his services and bought Old Masters from secularised monasteries. After his appointment as Bishop of Lyon in 1802, he set up art galleries both there and in Paris. The total number of paintings in his possession was estimated at 16,000.

Apart from the imperial family, politicians and diplomats who had risen swiftly under Napoleon, especially the liberal Francophiles in the Italian Republic and the later Kingdom of Italy, took advantage of the opportunities presented on the art market. Due to the unsatisfactory state of research, only the collectors and patrons Giovanni Battista Costabili Containi, Ferdinando Marescalchi, Francesco Melzi d'Eril and Giovanni Battista Sommariva can be mentioned here, all of whom built up considerable art collections within a short space of time. Around 1800 Costabili Containi was one of the staunchest supporters of the French revolution and the Napoleonic system, which enabled him to enjoy an illustrious career. He was the general administrator of the crown possessions in the Kingdom of Italy, was showered with honorary titles and, in 1809, elevated to Count of the Empires. During his time at the Napoleonic Court in Milan he was friendly with Viceroy Beauharnais. By the end of his life, Costabili Containi's collection of paintings had risen to over six hundred.

Giovanni Sommariva also succeeded in pursuing a remarkable career during the French period, first as city councillor in Milan, then as secretary of the Cisalpine Republic, and finally as one of its five directors. Although after 1800, during its second phase, he was one of Napoleon's closest confidants, when the Italian Republic was founded, he lost influence to his rival Melzi d'Eril and withdrew to Paris, where he had already bought a palace in 1800. He continued to act on a grand scale there as a patron of contemporary artists and collectors. Back home Giovanni Sommariva lavishly furnished not only his palace in Milan, but also his country estate Montmorency and the Villa Tramezzo (now Villa Carlotta) on Lake Como, always competing with his political rival Melzi d'Eril, whose villa was close by on the lake. For d'Eril it was perfectly natural to enhance his political status by means

Fig. 2 Titian (Tiziano Vecellio), Venus and Adonis, c. 1554.

of exceptional patronage. As befitted this status, he purchased the palace of the Calvachino family in Milan where he exhibited part of his collection. The villa on Lake Como was a further prestige object. He employed the most famous artists of the period to decorate it, amongst them the sculptor Antonio Canova who also worked for the viceroy.

A final example is the patrician Ferdinando Marescalchi from Bologna, who also enjoyed a stellar career during the Napoleonic era. After 1802, he lived in Paris as foreign minister, initially of the Republic of Italy and then of the Kingdom of Italy. He used his time in Paris to acquire a collection of over four hundred Italian Old Masters. Marescalchi's ultimate aim was to exhibit his pictures in a permanent collection in Bologna. However, his valuable collection met the same fate as those of Sommariva and Costabili. Soon after his death, his heirs cashed them in. Although collector's fever may well have been at play in some of these cases, art collections of such dimensions were perfectly suited to display ostentatious luxury and enhance prestige. Art collecting and patronage also created new arenas for old and new elites to meet as equals.

## 2.6 Napoleon's amalgamation policies: elite sociability and the Italian courts

Political, cultural and social clubs and societies also received an important boost during the Napoleonic era. During the short republican phase, Jacobin clubs were permitted where free political debate was possible for the first time. After the transfer of power, Napoleon abolished this type of society – free debate was henceforth undesirable. What was permitted and encouraged were elite societies, which he hoped would create a new elite loyal to the state. The Freemason societies, which had been prohibited at the end of the *Ancien Régime*, also gained new impetus. In 1805 the Grand Orient lodge was founded in Paris with Joseph Bonaparte as its Grand Master. Other family members assumed high offices. Eugène Beauharnais followed their example in Milan where he set up a 'mother lodge' with twenty-eight branches in the countryside. It was mostly officers and civil servants who met there together with the intellectual and landowning elites. Murat used his lodges in Naples to distance himself from Napoleon, who was constantly dictating government policy, not only to him as his brother-in-law. Murat separated his own Grand Orient lodge from that in Paris and went on to found a total of a hundred-and-twelve lodges in the Kingdom of Naples as meeting places for his elites. In the annexed departments, lodges were established at least in every city with a prefecture; in Tuscany alone, there were four. Freemasonry was also no longer prohibited in Rome and there a Calabrian merchant, Giuseppe Tartaro, founded the *Vertu Triomphante,* a secular lodge loyal to the government, which was granted its patent by the Grand Orient of France in 1808. Although it was state functionaries who met here, the activities of the Freemasons were kept under close police surveillance. Aristocrats were permitted to meet not only in the Freemasons lodges but also in exclusive clubs, such as the *Casino Nobile* in Milan. During the Restoration Freemasonry was prohibited once again, one of the reasons for increasing disaffection with Vienna.

Cultural commitment was also welcomed and controlled by the state. In every major centre in the departments of the empire a *Société des recherches utiles* was to be set up, under the control of the Ministry of the Interior in Paris. The aim of these 'learned' societies was to improve general education as well as to provide practical support for trade and agriculture, such as by introducing new production methods or improving yields in the spirit of the French economic theory, Physiocracy. In order to promote 'the common good' and 'usefulness' by means of voluntary activities for the benefit of fellow citizens, there was a need not only for 'cameralism', i. e. strict management of the economy and public finances, but also for statistics to enable descriptions of the land and for historical research concerned with local history in its narrow sense. The members of these societies were carefully selected and made up of functionaries and local intellectuals presided over by the prefect. Relations with the state were very close even in societies whose aim was to promote culture. The literary academy of Milan and the *Société scientifique et littéraire*, founded in 1812, connected the new men in power with the nobility of the *Ancien Régime*, although the city council was dominated by the aristocracy. Under Napoleon Milan experienced an inspiring theatre and opera scene with celebrated composers. This gave rise to close local networks of notables who met regularly in political meetings, chambers of commerce, cultural societies and in the evenings at the opera.

The absolute pinnacle of elite sociability was to have access to court. The newly created Italian courts played a central role in the demonstration of power. While in the annexed departments, former capitals such as Florence, Rome and Parma were downgraded to prefectures, Beauharnais in Milan and both Joseph and Murat in Naples, together with their wives, cultivated elaborate courts. In Turin, Pauline Bonaparte and her husband Camillo Borghese, the governor general, were also expected to take on this role of 'substitute monarchs', but Pauline, the emperor's capricious sister, rarely resided in the capital. The courts of Milan and Naples, like those in Kassel and Amsterdam, were structured according to Napoleon's Parisian model, for which he in turn had employed Louis XVI's master of ceremonies. Ceremonial pomp with its considerable symbolic significance seemed indispensable. Its cultural codes were deliberately followed for the orchestration of courtly ceremonies. The aim was to maintain a court no different from the courts of other European sovereigns, but also to demonstrate the principles of monarchy to its civil servants and subjects. Court etiquette, travel rituals and birthday and christening celebrations for the royal family were all designed to make the Italians loyal supporters of their dynasties.

In Milan a court was created worthy of a capital. Eugène Beauharnais surrounded himself with members of the old aristocracy and the newly created nobility of merit. Patricians from Milan and the provinces were selected for the highest offices as dignitaries and chamberlains. The ladies of the palace came from various high-ranking families, including the Confalonieri, the Belgiojoso, the Porro Lambertenghi and the Trivulzio. Military and clerical hierarchies were also integrated into court society as support for the crown. It was important for the court to display luxury combined with artistic taste. Vincenzo Monti, who was celebrated by the Italians as *Dante redivivo* (*Dante reincarnated*), was promoted as poet to the court. The royal residence in Milan and the summer residence in Monza were redesigned and redecorated by the most renowned artists and architects, including the royal architect Luigi Canonica, and Antonio Canova, one of the best sculptors of his time. At court the ruling couple received distinguished representatives from the fields of politics, science and the arts. Following the example of the Louvre, the neoclassicist painter Andrea Appiani created a public museum in the Brera academy, for which the king had eight hundred paintings purchased from all over Italy. After the demise of the kingdom, they remained in the Brera. Both Joseph Bonaparte and Murat used Neapolitan court society to unite the old aristocracy and the new functionaries as a new elite loyal to the state, according to Napoleon's wishes. After some hesitation, the aristocracy returned to the court, drawn by the lucrative posts and glamorous parties which had not been offered to them by the miserly Ferdinand IV.

## 2.7 Infrastructure and education

During the Napoleonic era important new initiatives were launched in the fields of infrastructure and education. A telegraph link was set up between Paris and Milan. For economic and strategic purposes, large road and canal building projects were promoted. Napoleon had the Simplon pass fortified to make it suitable for stage coaches so that the Rhone valley was connected to Lake Maggiore via the Swiss Valais. From there both passengers and goods could travel to Milan using the considerably modernised mediaeval canal (*Naviglio Grande)*. At the same time the Po River was made navigable as an east-west route and the Pavia canal was built connecting the Po with Milan. In Naples Joseph Bonaparte and Murat had the *Valle della Sanità* built, a link road to Capodimonte with complicated bridges, and had the *Via Foria* widened. In the centre of Turin, a monumental bridge was erected over the Po. The engineers responsible for these ambitious projects were trained at schools specially established for the purpose. In addition, large-scale archaeological campaigns were carried out such as the excavations in Portici near Naples or in the Roman Forum and the Colosseum.

Improvements such as the botanical gardens in Milan were carried out to make the cities more pleasant. Murat's plan to transform what is today the *Piazza del Plebiscito* into a *Forum Murat* with a rotunda with semi-circular colonnades comparable to the Roman Pantheon was eventually realised by Ferdinand I. The same happened with the *Arc du Triomphe de Simplon* in Milan, designed by Luigi Cagnola. This was to be a neoclassical monument lending the capital more radiance and supporting the cult of the rulers. Building began at the same time as the *Arc du Triomphe* in Paris but was not completed until Milan was under Austrian rule. The architect of the *Arc du Triomphe* in Paris, Charles Perciers, was for his part inspired by the *Arco di Tito* (*Arch of Titus*) in Rome. In Rome itself a large number of architectural and urban development projects were set up, including Valadier's aesthetic improvements of the *Piazza del Popolo*. Further, rationality and principles of hygiene prevailed over religious traditions and, whereas previously in Italy the dead were buried close to one of the numerous churches in a city, the cemeteries were now moved outside the city walls. Another significant improvement was the installation of public street lighting. The introduction of consistent house numbering also made orientation in the cities easier. However, many of the ambitious projects conceived in the Napoleonic era never developed beyond the planning phase or were never completed.

The outcome of reforms to the school system in this period also remained inconclusive. The task of improving the situation in primary schools was shifted to the local authorities. In the Kingdom of Italy, it was their task to provide the elementary schools: instruction was free but not compulsory. Their number increased from around 2,000 in 1807 to around 4,000 four years later. The quality of teaching was poor by today's standards; nevertheless, 70 per cent of bridegrooms and 48 per cent of future wives in Milan were able to sign their marriage certificates. In contrast, the literacy rate in southern Italy at the beginning of the nineteenth century is estimated at 20 per cent.

On the level of further education there were grammar schools and lycées for boys which were much better equipped. In the annexed departments, the public education law was implemented and there was at least one institution for further education in every larger city, although girls still had to rely on private tutors or convent schools. It proved generally difficult to extricate the state schools from the influence of the church since teaching had previously been in the hands of the clergy. An additional problem was that the nobility preferred the exclusive old-style institutions in Milan or the boarding schools in Monza and Nerviano which were allowed to remain in existence.

The existing universities were reformed in order to educate the elite state functionaries. Alongside Turin, Parma, Pavia, Pisa, Siena and Perugia, Rome occupied a leading position in the university landscape. Since Rome was considered the 'second' city of the empire, its university was particularly well endowed with forty-two professorships. This approach stemmed from the idea of general cultural influence and the hope that education would eventually triumph over the resistance and diametrically opposing doctrines of the Church. The international church colleges were quite simply declared political and abolished. The only theological faculties to be established were in Turin, Pisa and Rome. A *Scuola normale superiore,* modelled on the Parisian *École normale supérieure,* was established in Pisa and still exists today. Its express mission was to forge the best civil servants of the future. It was not difficult to appoint staff since there were many applications from scholars moulded during the Enlightenment period. Overall, it has to be said, however, that in the strategically important areas of education and poor relief, the institutions created on the French model were slow to produce positive results. This was particularly true for public welfare, which had previously been organised and run by the numerous religious orders. After they were abolished, the measures taken by the state to alleviate the misery of the poorest were inadequate.

## 2.8 The military

Compulsory military service had more far-reaching consequences than any other of the aspects mentioned above. It was completely new to the Italians and affected large sections of the population. In the eighteenth century the absolutist rulers were still waging so-called 'cabinet' wars. Armies were made up of mercenary troops and there was absolutely no desire for the participation, let alone mobilisation of the general public. Only in the kingdom of Piedmont-Savoy was a well-functioning military built up and the officers closely attached to the House of Savoy. It could look back proudly on its military traditions and the victories that had led to a steady expansion of its territories. The Savoyards owed their rise from being a minor princedom to becoming a middle-sized power and finally a kingdom to the military. In the other Italian states, however, no significant role was played by an independent army.

All the territories in Italy that were successively annexed by France after 1796 were subject to Parisian military law. In the Republic and Kingdom of Italy as well as in the Kingdom of Naples the army was modelled on its French counterpart with very little variance. Conscription had been introduced for the first time in France in 1793 under the pressure of military defeats. As there was no end to the military conflicts, it remained in place, only changing in certain aspects such as the age of conscription and the length of service. In principle every man between the age of 20 and 25 was liable to military service as long as he was unmarried and in good health. Members of the clergy were exempt. It was also possible to find a substitute, but this option was only open to the wealthy as it cost between 1,800 and 2,000 francs, the equivalent of the annual salary of a judge. As the wars continued, a substitute became more and more expensive, so that ten years later the price was 4,000 francs. The length of service was initially five years but was generally much longer during wartime. The scale of conscription depended on the state of the war, meaning that the majority of recruits were drafted during the last years of the Empire.

The Cisalpine Republic attempted to create a volunteer army, but with very little success. Voluntary Polish legions were deployed in Lombardy after 1796 under General Jan Henryk Dąbrowski and with the approval of Napoleon. They were spectacular but ultimately unsuccessful. These legions had a total strength of 30,000 men, who fought in various campaigns and suffered severe losses in return for vague promises from Napoleon. Poland had been divided up between Russia, Austria and Prussia and the Poles hoped Napoleon would help it to become a single united kingdom again. It was in this context that what was later to become the Polish national anthem originated. In contrast, the Italian soldiers in this first volunteer army enlisted more for financial reasons than out of an idealistic desire to fight for the Cisalpine Republic.

In the Republic and Kingdom of Italy the Minister of War organised the military strictly according to the French system. 18,000 men were to be conscripted, taken from the departments, relative to the size of their population. The local mayor and a selection committee drew up lists of young unmarried men eligible for conscription according to their age and then drew names by lot. Widowers with children, families with only one son or where one son was already in service were to be exempted. Here again it was possible to provide a substitute and again this was only feasible for the wealthy due to the high costs. From the start there were major problems with 'draft dodgers', young men who tried to evade conscription, for example by fleeing to Switzerland or to the mountains, or who were hidden by their families. The state initially had great difficulty in asserting its authority since the administration and gendarmerie were not yet fully developed. This meant that they were unable to prevent draft dodging and that the state lacked the means to fulfil its quota of conscripts. With the duration and consolidation of the regime, conscription became more efficient but the conscripts began to realise that it was easier to first allow themselves to be conscripted and then to desert. Desertion reached epidemic proportions and posed a serious problem for the king and his ministers and officials. A tougher scale of penalties introduced in 1808 did little to help – most sentences were passed in *contumacia* (absence of the delinquent). The state proved incompetent and its subjects lacking in patriotism. In addition, many deserters joined robber bands and so became a palpable threat to public order. Police records report significant cases of desertion and related banditry. In 1809, a year with both a particularly high number of conscriptions and rising food prices due to a new consumption tax, the violent clashes between the state and the gangs in the Marche and Romagna became extreme. Around 2,000 men died in the armed fighting or on the gallows.

Napoleon's increasing need for more soldiers meant that in the last crisis-ridden years of his regime, men who were supposed to be exempt, i. e. only sons, young men whose brothers were already in the army and married men, were called up. Families lived in fear and insecurity and among the population the impression was that the poorest in town and country were in any case particularly hard hit by conscription. In order to build more trust, the results of the chance draw from the year lists were published, but with little effect. Many of those who were caught preferred prison or community labour to military service. The death toll in the Italian army was high. From 1797 onwards a total of 165,000 conscripts and 44,000 volunteers were mobilised, including 8,000 men from Istria and Dalmatia as well as Italians and Poles. The loss is estimated at approximately 125,000 dead and wounded. Despite all the suffering, the positive element of the emotions and experiences these young men were subjected to should not be underestimated. Although the Italian troops were incorporated into the French army while they were fighting, they fought under their own green, white and red flag. Whether and to what extent the lower ranks developed a sense of patriotic national identity is unclear, but it can be assumed that this was certainly the case for the Italian officers.

Similar findings apply to the Kingdom of Naples. Here, however, there was even less time available to build up a powerful army. After 1806–1807, Joseph and his successor Murat also largely imposed French structures on their kingdom. The problems with draft dodgers and deserters were the same in the south but took on even greater proportions. In the former territories of the Papal States conscripts also evaded military service in large numbers. In Viterbo and Velletri a third of conscripts went into hiding. As in the north, rebellious deserters retreated to the mountains and joined the existing gangs of brigands. Very young draft dodgers and deserters were imprisoned, convicted and hung publicly in Rome on the *Piazza del Popolo,* at the *Bocca della Verità* and outside Santa Maria in Trastevere, the city's notorious deprived quarter. These hangings are likely to have played a decisive role in fanning the flames of hatred against Napoleonic rule. Camille de Tournon, the prefect, was not the only person to have misgivings about these measures.

Bonaparte's power was based to a large extent on his sensational military successes, which he owed not only to his troops but also to his officers. The French army offered them excellent opportunities for promotion. In 1805 in the Kingdom of Italy he established elite troops, the Guard of Honour and the Veliti. While the Guard of Honour was made up of sons of the highest taxpayers, the Veliti were recruited from wealthy middle-class families. They were both fitted out with splendid uniforms which gave them high prestige. Many young Italians fought in their ranks, fascinated by the myth of Napoleon, and motivated by the career prospects and a thirst for adventure. But beyond these elite troops there were also excellent opportunities for advancement, and the military leaders, trained at their own military schools in Modena and Pavia, became progressively more nationalistic. Towards the end of the Kingdom of Italy, 12 out of 17 major generals, 18 out of 40 brigadiers and 41 out of 73 colonels were Italian. After the fall of Napoleon, the Italian army was unceremoniously disbanded by the Austrians. This was an affront and an unparalleled humiliation for Napoleon' s highly decorated generals. It is no coincidence that so many aristocratic officers were involved in the revolts and revolutions of 1820–1821.

## 2.9 Religious policy and popular religion

Napoleon's policy towards the church led to one of his most agonising defeats. In vain he had hoped to reach a compromise with the papacy by means of the concordats concluded for France (1801) and the Kingdom of Italy (1803). However, from 1806–1807, relations between the Papal States and the emperor deteriorated once again. The Napoleonic Code introduced in the annexed departments and in the Kingdom of Italy permitted divorce, which was an absolute affront to devout Catholics and the church hierarchy. Furthermore, more monasteries were dissolved in Veneto after 1806 without previous consultation with the Curia as was stipulated by the concordat. Similarly, the Italian concordat was extended to the Duchy of Lucca without any consultation and the imperial catechism was also introduced into the Kingdom of Italy in the same way The Pope protested several times against these measures and finally resorted to a weapon offered to him by the concordat. He refused to consent to the appointment of nine bishops in the Kingdom of Italy. Ultimately, however, it was Napoleon's Continental System that led to the final escalation. When the Pope refused to close his ports to British goods, the emperor ordered the conquest of the remaining Papal States. The Marche was occupied and united with the Kingdom of Italy so that the Italian concordat also applied there. Napoleon rigorously turned the remaining areas of the Papal States into two departments, which were annexed directly by the empire. When the Pope was imprisoned, he retaliated by excommunicating the emperor. In 1810–1811, half of all bishoprics in the Kingdom of Italy were vacant. At the same time the number of parishes had been greatly reduced due to structural measures and almost all church organisations, with the exception of those dedicated to nursing the sick, had been abolished. Added to this was the problem of priests refusing to swear an oath to the state. They were removed from office, causing their angry parishioners to declare their solidarity with them.

The religious question was one of the main reasons for opposition to Napoleon from his deeply devout Catholic subjects, expressed particularly vehemently in the former Papal States but in essence throughout the regions of Italy. Although the Romans tended to be passive and apathetic during the Napoleonic period, they were still unsettled by the process of modernisation that broke with centuries-old ways of thinking and acting. The attacks on the established church also had tangible economic consequences. The banishment of Pope Pius VII and numerous cardinals and the flight of aristocrats and artists led to a considerable reduction of the traditional employment and welfare opportunities of those who worked for them and were dependent on them. Further conflicts arose as a result of religious practices. In reaction to the secular state attempting to limit forms of popular religious expression, they became ever more intensive. There was a remarkable flourishing of the cult of the Virgin Mary and the belief in miracles. Miraculous healings were attributed to the absent pope, whose picture was circulated in Rome in its thousands and fuelled anti-Napoleonic sentiment among the illiterate lower classes. A particularly popular image depicted the Virgin Mary ordering the Pope to excommunicate Napoleon. For four years Napoleon fought against an absent opponent, a phantom that was more difficult to overcome than his British military counterpart Wellington because it was intangible, immaterial and moral – a saint. Furthermore, traditional popular religious mindsets predicting the imminent end of the world, disasters or fundamental social transformation meant that natural disasters such as earthquakes and floods, which became more frequent in 1811 and 1812, were perceived as a sign from God and punishment for Napoleon.

## 2.10 The crisis of the years 1811–1814

As shown above, the majority of the people suffered as a result of indirect taxes, conscription and the years of economic crisis combined with price rises during the last years of the regime. In 1814 nearly 100,000 Italians were in the various armies. French rule remained alien to most people because it catapulted them into the modern age and confronted them with numerous revolutionary reforms and new challenges. The new state attempted to regulate the furthest corner of every village and it was precisely this that frequently led to it being rejected. Added to this were the negative effects of the Continental System and the consequences of Napoleon's economic policy, which strongly favoured his own empire at the expense of the kingdoms ruled by his relatives. In 1808 a trade agreement was set up between France and the Kingdom of Italy which cut customs duties by half for raw materials and agricultural products exported to France and also for manufactured French goods imported to Italy. This treaty was not exactly a programme of support for northern Italian proto-industry. The effect of the Continental System on the major Italian ports, however, was nothing less than disastrous. In Venice trading collapsed. In Genoa and Livorno, it caused the end of trade with the Levant and Spain. Whereas 1,048 ships used the harbour in Livorno in 1795, by 1800 the figure was a mere 713, in 1811 seven and in 1812 only one. These figures demonstrate not only the negative costs of the wars to the economy but also the disastrous effects of the Continental System. In Naples, whose port suffered severely from the blockade, Murat tolerated the smuggling of British goods, which was in any case ubiquitous, and introduced customs policies to protect local manufacturers from French products.

The collapse of Napoleonic Italy, however, was not caused by the repeated but isolated outbreaks of unrest, nor by the discontent of the people and their aversion to the demands of modernity, but by continuing hostilities in large parts of Europe. Napoleon's troops were, for example, unable to contain the guerilla warfare in Spain. His fatal error, however, was to take military action against Russia. The tsar, Alexander I, also violated the terms of the Continental System and continued to have large amounts of grain and timber imported to Britain across the Baltic. Napoleon then declared war on the tsar and in the summer of 1812 marched into Russia with his *Grande Armée,* made up of about 700,000 mainly young and poorly-equipped soldiers. The tsar simply retreated into the vast expanse of the interior, had all food supplies cut off and set fire to Moscow when it was taken by the French. Extreme weather conditions and shortages of supplies eventually forced Napoleon to retreat from Russia. An estimated 600,000 soldiers from all over Europe lost their lives in this campaign. A final successful coalition was formed between Russia, Prussia, Austria, Britain and eventually the smaller German states in order to regain lost territory and defeat Napoleon once and for all.

The collapse of French Italy began when the coalition troops invaded once again. In September 1813 the Austrians entered Venetia. Eugène Beauharnais and Murat had to decide whether they were in a position to save their kingdom, with whom they should form coalitions and when it would be wise to surrender. As Napoleon's defeat loomed in 1812–1813, Beauharnais hoped to be recognised as king by the allies. But Talleyrand only offered him the Grand Duchy of Genoa. Supported by Melzi and other high-ranking officials and military officers, he sided with the emperor against the Austrians but was forced to sign a ceasefire in April 1814.

In Milan this power vacuum led to riots and attempts by the aristocracy to form a government. On 20 April a hostile crowd, incited by patricians, rose up against the senate and high-ranking officials. These uprisings against Napoleonic rule in its final phase were part of a European phenomenon, triggered by crushing military service and heavy tax burdens. Lynchings were the absolute exception, but in Milan Francesco Prina, the detested minister of finance and an aristocrat from Modena, was murdered by an angry mob and his palace ransacked. The senate was driven out and members of the Milanese nobility formed a temporary government. They had already gained some administrative experience under the Austrians and in the Napoleonic system. A few days later the government co-opted representatives for each department in Lombardy and again the choice fell exclusively on aristocrats, many of whom had served under Napoleon. (Former) supporters of Napoleon and his dedicated opponents united in this crisis and fought together for an autonomous Lombardy.

The administrative system was immediately 'cleansed', a measure that mainly affected bourgeois and Jacobin ministers and prefects. There was no consensus on the future of Lombardy except for the desire for independence. Five different political factions were facing each other. One consisted of those who defended the Napoleonic system, among whom Melzi d'Eril stood out with his elaborate plans for the future. A second was committed to a united Kingdom of Italy under the leadership of Murat. This plan was mainly supported by the Freemasons and the Carbonari. A third comprised those who were in favour of an independent Kingdom of Italy but without a French monarch. The patricians debated two further political solutions, both of which would have given top priority to their own position. These were, on the one hand, the older patricians who expressed downright hatred of the Napoleonic system and supported the old estate system. On the other hand, the liberal-conservative patricians, who were mostly younger, were in favour of British liberalism and entertained vague ideas of a nation state. The influential figures in this faction were the young counts Frederico Confalonieri and Luigi Porro Lambertenghi, who were to become key figures in the liberal opposition movement over the next few years.

At the end of April 1814, the provisional government sent three envoys to Paris to negotiate with the foreign ministers of the victorious powers for the autonomy and legitimate rule of Lombardy. This vision of restitution to its former legal status was briefly fuelled by Lord Bentinck, the British special envoy in Milan, who indicated his country's possible support for the provisional government. However, his main aim was to maintain the peace in Milan and in any case his role was merely that of an observer. Wild rumours and plans for Lombardy's political future circulated, such as the creation of an autonomous kingdom of Lombardy including parts of Piedmont and Genoa. On 18 May Federico Confalonieri, one of the three envoys, wrote from Paris to Carlo Verri, the president of the regency, about a conversation with Castlereagh, the British foreign minister, in which he had vented independence, a constitution and national representation as their aims. When he was allowed an audience with Emperor Francis I a week later, Conte Confalonieri expressed rather more modest aims. Here he spoke of independent administration, a king of Lombardy and national representation. This Paris delegation failed on every count – no one supported its demands. The desire of patricians from Lombardy, Venice, Lucca and Genoa to negotiate for autonomous republics was thwarted once again at the Congress of Vienna.

Murat's attempt to keep the Kingdom of Naples or even to create a united Kingdom of Italy out of the ruins of bankruptcy was similarly unsuccessful. As a relatively independent king with an understanding manner, he enjoyed some popularity with the Italians. He initially turned his back on Napoleon and with his troops conquered central Italy, i. e. territories belonging to the empire. He was recognised as an ally by Austria in the Treaty of Naples of January 1814, in which Murat undertook to support the allies with 30,000 troops and not to conclude a separate peace treaty with France. This ran counter to the claims of the Spanish Bourbons, who insisted on their dynastic rights and were waiting in exile in Palermo to be reinstated as the monarchs of Naples. Emperor Francis, however, agreed to reject Ferdinand's claims. This seemed to be the way for Murat to secure the throne for himself, but Metternich was simply playing for time. When Napoleon returned to France from exile on Elba, and during the infamous 'Hundred Days', Murat made the wrong choice by siding with his brother-in-law in the hope of conquering the whole of Italy through a fresh military intervention. In March 1815 he rushed to join his troops who were still in central Italy. While negotiations continued in Vienna, thousands of volunteers joined him in this war which was short but psychologically important. Popular as he was, Murat called for all Italians from Sicily to the Alps to rise up and drive out the Austrians and found a nation state of Italy. He was supported by backers of the *Carboneria*, secret societies that were staunch proponents of an independent nation state. Murat managed to take Modena but failed outside Ferrara, had to retreat to Ancona and accept crucial defeat against the Austrians in the Marche near Tolentino. He did not have enough soldiers, ammunition or money. In the middle of May Austrian troops marched into Naples. Murat fled first to Marseille, then on to Corsica and in October 1815 made a last vain attempt to reconquer Naples with a small band of supporters. He was captured in Pizzo in Calabria and Ferdinand I had him summarily court-martialled and shot.

The future destiny of the Italians was negotiated at the Congress of Vienna in 1815. Decisions were reached by the major powers, with Austria and its influential chancellor Metternich leading the way. They forced through the traditional claims of the dynasties that had ruled the Apennine peninsula before 1798. In addition, Austria was to be the dominant power in the region. How would the new/old princes govern? Would they attempt to revert to the principles of the *Ancien Régime* or would they accept the Italian legacy? Did the majority of their subjects really have an interest in being thrust back into the same state of affairs as during the *Ancien Régime?*

## Notes

1 Albert Dufourcq, Le régime jacobin en Italie. Études sur la République romaine, Paris 1900, p. 100.

2 Pietro Colletta, Storia del Reame di Napoli dal 1734 sino al 1824, 2 vols., Capolago 1834, vol. 2, p. 123.

# 3. The Congress of Vienna, Restoration and Revolutions

After more than twenty years of war and several million dead, and with Napoleon defeated and deposed as emperor, the major powers restructured the European order. At the end of May 1814, after the initial signing of the Paris Peace Treaty, it was decided to convene an international conference in Vienna to negotiate the territorial and constitutional reorganisation of Europe. The events and outcomes of this conference were largely determined by the victorious allies, Russia, Prussia, Austria and Britain. Serving as the representative of the French Bourbons returning from exile, Talleyrand skilfully steered France back into the diplomatic arena after its defeat. His concept of the legitimacy of dynastic monarchs had a powerful influence on the conference. When negotiations began in Vienna in October 1814, different claims to territory and power soon clashed and it was not until after Napoleon's return during the Hundred Days that the major powers found themselves forced to reach a consensus. The negotiations were then hurried forward and the Final Act of the Congress was signed on 9 June 1815, nine days before the Battle of Waterloo. It succeeded in creating a European order and balance of power that guaranteed a long period of peace. No single power was to dominate Europe in the same way as the empire of Napoleon.

## 3.1 The new, old political state order

Although disputes over borders and territorial claims were bitter, there was overall agreement on domestic policies. All the European powers hoped to quell any future revolutionary tendencies immediately and permanently. There was no doubt that the constitutional or absolutist monarchies should remain in existence and return to power, and the legitimacy of the historically established dynasties as sovereigns was therefore extolled as the antithesis of the sovereignty of the people and revolution. The monarchies were to be based once again on the pre-revolutionary divine right of kings and in future also on their mutual solidarity. In order to maintain peace, it was agreed that in the event of revolutionary uprisings, neighbouring states could take military action to intervene. Austria was to exercise this right in Italy on a regular basis over the subsequent decades. As a result of the diverging geostrategic claims of Prussia, Russia and Austria, negotiations over the configuration of the territories of the German Confederation were complex and protracted, whereas in Italy the only competing demands were in relation to the smaller duchies in the north.

Map 3 Italy 1815.

Metternich's geopolitical plans proved crucial for the restructuring of Italy. In November 1814 he rejected a suggestion by the Spanish envoy Gómez de Labrador that a panel of experts should be convened to discuss a new order in Italy, as had been done for the German states. Yet Italian representatives of the various political interest groups had already arrived to put forward their case. One of these was Eugène Beauharnais, who received no territory but a large sum of money as compensation. In contrast, those who advocated the restoration of sovereign aristocratic republics left empty-handed. The city of Genoa, for example, had dispatched Antonio Brignole-Sale (1786–1863) with a corresponding proposition. He was a former Napoleonic prefect and a patrician from one of the most respected families. Although he had been provided with considerable financial resources by the city senate to win favour with the diplomats, his mission was a complete failure and Genoa was assigned to Piedmont. For a long time, the people of Genoa found this decision to annex it to one of the most conservative states on the peninsula difficult to accept. Ascanio Mansi, sent by the city of Lucca to retrieve its autonomy, was similarly unsuccessful.

Delegations from Lombardy and Venice suffered the same fate. In Lombardy the aristocracy still hoped that even if it was not possible to gain autonomy, they could at least have a politically active role in the negotiations at the Congress of Vienna. Two models continued to be discussed: keeping Napoleon's centralist institutions or returning to the old oligarchic regional and local institutions. Each of the larger municipalities in Lombardy sent their own representative of the old conservative nobility to Vienna. None of the cities wanted to be dominated by the metropolis Milan or be represented by it at the Congress. These ultraconservative delegates wanted a restoration of the rights and privileges of the noble estates from the time of Maria Theresa. As it was, they had very little influence within the chorus of the major powers.

In fact, the major powers at the Congress of Vienna had already decided the fate of Lombardy and Venetia. They were allocated to the Habsburg monarchy and the only unsolved problem was how they should be integrated into its existing system of hereditary provinces. In those provinces far removed from the negotiations of grand diplomacy, the people's hopes for more sovereignty were dashed. The patricians were accustomed to power and neither in Lombardy nor in Venetia did they welcome complete dependence. At the negotiating table in Vienna, they had expected to be able to express their wishes, albeit not without the support of one of the major powers. The provinces in Milan and Venice that were administered separately and directly from Vienna managed to secure some participation in decision-making bodies, successfully negotiated by Giacomo Mellerio from Lombardy and the Venetian Conte Alfonso Porcia. It was, however, very little in comparison to their original plans.

The restoration of the Papal States was entirely undisputed. Pius VII had returned to Rome in January 1814 and his interests in Vienna were represented by Marquess Ercole Consalvi. The Final Act of the Congress of Vienna returned the papal provinces Bologna, Romagna and Ferrara to the Papal States. In Ferrara the Austrians had to be granted garrison rights. The Kingdom of Sardinia-Piedmont was strengthened by territorial gains and restitutions so that it could fulfil its role as a strong buffer state between France and Austria. It acquired the Ligurian coast including Genoa, a strategically and economically valuable city, and regained Nice and Savoy. The negotiations over the Kingdom of Italy were more complicated until the Hundred Days when Murat changed sides to back Napoleon again. The Spanish Bourbons exerted huge pressure for Ferdinand IV, also a Bourbon and in exile in Palermo for ten years, to be reinstated on the southern Italian mainland. The Congress of Vienna stated that he should become Ferdinand the First of the Two Sicilies, not the Fourth, since his previous personal union of Naples and Sicily had now become a true union of the kingdom under a new name. In an additional agreement with Emperor Francis I, he undertook to model his domestic policy on that of Austria, thus ruling out the enactment of any later constitution. In principle this additional agreement was superfluous since, as King of Sicily, Ferdinand had only agreed to the constitution of 1812 in Palermo under great pressure from Britain and was now able to rescind it. However, the agreement makes very clear the extent to which Austria intended to exert its influence, even on the formally independent Italian states. Its political principles were in any case omnipresent in those countries ruled by members of the Habsburg family 'corporation'.

The Grand Duchy of Tuscany once again became a secundogeniture of the Habsburgs, which meant that Ferdinand III (1769–1824), the son of Emperor Leopold, was restored to his throne in Florence. This restitution was decided undebated by the five powers at the beginning of June 1815. However, horse trading then began over the smaller duchies, since both the Habsburgs and the Bourbons had to provide for their deposed female sovereigns. Particularly protracted negotiations were conducted over the former Bourbon Queen of Etruria and the former French empress from Vienna, both named Maria-Louise. Austria finally prevailed and their Maria-Louise became Duchess of Parma-Piacenza and Guastalla, although she was forced to renounce any hereditary titles for her four-year-old son, Napoleon, previously King of Rome. Britain and especially France were determined to prevent the further existence of any ruling dynasty stemming from Napoleon Bonaparte. The Bourbon Maria Luisa had to accept the Duchy of Lucca for herself and her son Charles. Both duchies fell to Tuscany and the Duchy of Modena respectively before 1848 as a result of laws of succession passed in Vienna. Modena then went to Austria-Este, resulting in the Habsburgs having two secundogenitures in Italy. A further decision of the Congress of Vienna was to endorse two small sovereign states, the Republic of San Marino and the Duchy of Massa and Carrara. Metternich was unable to push through his plan for a *Lega Italica* similar to the German Confederation. This *Lega* would have been of a purely defensive nature, guaranteeing a balance of power and creating a loose federal system for the purpose of law enforcement. The Papal States and Piedmont rejected the idea outright. Any restriction of their sovereignty was out of the question. However, Metternich had achieved his main aim, namely the restoration of the Italian state system as it was during the *Ancien Régime* with no constitutions. Austria thus became the pre-eminent power and in future ruthlessly suppressed any revolutionary stirrings or independence movements.

How did the new and old rulers govern after the Napoleonic period? How did they deal with the liberal heritage and was it in fact possible to return to the *Ancien Régime*? As in the period before 1789, a difference has to be made between the individual states, since in spite of all their conservatism, the range of political action was considerable. The state with by far the most liberal conditions was Tuscany. Ferdinand III and his ministers Vittorio Fossombroni and Neri Corsini re-introduced the enlightened legislation of his father, Leopold. They also brought back free-trade and opened up the ports, leading to a recovery and sharp rise in the volume of trade in Livorno. Many people were attracted to Florence from Italy and Europe by its relatively liberal atmosphere. A compromise of this kind between restoration and reform was unthinkable for the Papal States, the Kingdom of the Two Sicilies and Sardinia-Piedmont.

In the Papal States, the French administration and judiciary were abolished and canon law re-introduced. Leading civil servants were recruited from the ranks of the high clergy with an aristocratic background, barring aspiring talents from the bourgeoisie from any opportunity for advancement. Political participation was made impossible and the Masonic lodges were banned once again. Any attempts at reform by Pope Pius VII and his Secretary of State, Marquess Ercole Consalvi, a supporter of the Enlightenment, were doomed to failure because of the opposition of the arch-conservative nobility, the *Zelanti.* After the death of Pius VII, they elected Leo XII pope, a man from their own ranks who backed a severely repressive government.

In Naples, on the insistence of Metternich, the king originally attempted to take the middle road. Under his first minister, Luigi de' Medici, many of the Napoleonic reforms remained in force. An efficient, modern administration was to be established using Murat's civil servants and new capable individuals from the ranks of Bourbon supporters. The aim of this compromise policy was an administrative monarchy, but this went far too far for the ultra-conservative aristocracy. They demanded a return to the *Ancien Régime.* The reactionary minister of police, Canosa, immediately adopted a harsh policy of repression against all 'Jacobins' and liberals but, under pressure from Austria, was eventually removed from office. A further step towards the *Ancien Régime* was the concordat negotiated with the Pope in 1818, which created a new alliance between the monarchy and the church.

The greatest champion of the Restoration was the King of Sardinia-Piedmont, Victor Emmanuel I. On 20 May 1814, after sixteen years of exile in Sardinia, he returned with his entourage to the capital Turin. A liberal marquess, Massimo d'Azeglio, was on the Piazza Castello and an eyewitness of this triumphant procession. In consternation he wrote in his diary: 'They were all dressed in antiquated style, with powdered hair in pigtails and eighteenth-century tricorn hats in the fashion of Frederick II.'[1] And it was not only his clothing that revealed the spirit in which Victor Emmanuel was returning. The court calendar of 1795 was reinstated and with it the old court restored. The Royal Constitution of 1770 was re-introduced, legal equality of all citizens was abolished, rigid social distinctions were endorsed and feudal rights and entail commissions re-established. All important posts were reserved for the nobility. In 1817 the ranks of civil servants and officers were ruthlessly purged. Victor Emmanuel and his advisors also seriously considered the absurd idea of demolishing the bridge over the Po in Turin, built by Napoleon, as part of their restoration policy.[2] The arch-conservative minister Joseph de Maistre determined cultural policy and the schools were once again run by the clergy. Apart from in the Papal States and the Duchy of Modena, the attempt to return to the *Ancien Régime* was nowhere more pronounced in Europe than in the Kingdom of Sardinia-Piedmont. Liberal writers such as Ludovico de Breme and Silvio Pellico migrated to Milan, where they contributed to the journal *Conciliatore*. It was only in the annexed former Republic of Genoa that Napoleonic laws concerning the judiciary and the military were allowed to remain in force in order to contain the discontent of the traditionally anti-Piedmontese population.

In Lombardy, the aristocracy once again enjoyed privileges, but Austrian policy towards them led to a new attempt at rebellion. This was in spite of the fact that Vienna had granted them a voice in what were called the central and provincial congregations, that is the local state assemblies. The high property threshold for eligibility meant that seats which could have been filled by representatives of the bourgeoisie were taken by patricians. However, these assemblies won very little recognition due to their lack of decision-making powers. In the rural municipalities, on the other hand, the influence of the patricians increased once again. But those who had held important, lucrative positions in the senate or at the court in Napoleonic Italy and had received awards and noble titles from the emperor Napoleon for their loyalty were thwarted for a long time. After the return of the Habsburgs, they either did not or did not try to find a place in the administration or, perhaps more significantly, at the new court. The rational French administrative system was retained, which annoyed the patricians. They had no interest in posts in its rigid career system since it blocked their privileged access and forced them to adhere to its rules.

What seemed to the patricians to be even more drastic and emotionally powerful in the long term, was their exclusion from the court of the new kingdom. Even after 1815, social status in Italy was not determined solely by property ownership and, as in the Napoleonic period, affiliation with the court could have been an exclusive symbol of prestige. Rigid Austrian-Bohemian etiquette, however, completely denied a considerable number of time-honoured patrician families the right of admission to court. A commission tasked with reviewing aristocratic ranks in Lombardy simply lumped all of the traditional patrician families together with the lower-ranking *nobiltà,* since there was no equivalent noble rank in the hereditary lands of the Habsburgs. As a result, the rank of patrician was no longer recognised. When the viceroy, Archduke Rainer, arrived at his residence in 1819 and turned to the question of who exactly was to be admitted to court, the disputes over honour and rank rapidly escalated. A list of eligible families was drawn up following the rules of the Viennese court. The Master of the Household, Count de St Julien, then wrote a letter to all those who were considered aristocrats but were not on the list, asking them to provide proof of their rank. Since the patricians had assumed that they were naturally eligible for court, they had not thought to check their lineage. The ladies showed up to a public reception in Monza in magnificent gowns but were turned away.

This was a perfect scandal. Many of those who were excluded belonged to the oldest and most venerable families of patricians. Two fundamentally different concepts of nobility were irreconcilably opposed to each other here. In the Catholic countries of the Holy Roman Empire of the German Nation, four or more noble ancestors were required for even the lower nobility to gain coveted access to church benefices and charitable institutions and also to the court. This was why, in the ancestral homelands of the Habsburgs, a completely different marriage policy was pursued to that in Lombardy, where the principle of openness towards rising bourgeois families had guaranteed prosperity. According to the strict Austrian regulations, however, such marriages led to admission to the court being barred. In Monza, for example, the very women who would have lent the court its desired social glamour before 1815 were excluded. Their husbands also closed ranks and stayed away. These were members of the most illustrious and by far the richest families. For the Milanese aristocracy, this social degradation was anything but insignificant and contributed to the utter failure of Metternich's wish to establish a court as a means of reconciliation. In Italy, Austria earned itself the reputation of destroying the aristocracy. From then on, the nobility in Lombardy met in exclusive circles in their own *palazzi* and shunned the court. Network building and political discourse took place in other non-state institutions such as academies, societies and salons, each of which developed in its own method of becoming part of a quasi counter-court.

## 3.2 National and constitutional ideas after 1815

in 1815 supporters of a nation state both in Germany and Italy were neither influential nor large in number. Yet the conservative administrative monarchies were decisively rejected, at least in intellectual, democratic and liberal circles. Researchers often regard France as the source of revolution, overlooking the fact that there was a comparable revolutionary potential in Italy both before and after the Congress of Vienna. Political and constitutional crises and revolutions had occurred in Italy in 1799, 1820–1821, 1831 and 1848–1849. Nevertheless, however much they strove for change, there was no consensus amongst the opponents of the regime over the future political direction. On the contrary, they had different and conflicting visions. First were the advocates of a democratic nation state, second the supporters of autonomous aristocratic republics, third those favouring a federal Italy under the leadership of the Pope, (the so-called Neo-Guelphs), and fourth the proponents of an Italian nation state in the form of a moderate liberal monarchy, ruled by the House of Savoy. These four ideas, together with a fifth represented by the still dominant archconservatives, were to determine political discussion and activities from the Congress of Vienna until the founding of the nation state in January 1861 and beyond. A description of these five groupings is followed here by a discussion of the cultural historical research into nationalism which has both dominated and enriched Italian historiography in the last twenty-five years.

1). The Jacobins and representatives of the Carboneria with their political writer, Giuseppe Mazzini, a well-known figure throughout Europe, were active on the left-wing political fringe. As supporters of an Italian republic, they had already been persecuted in the Napoleonic period and had retreated into secret societies, particularly the so-called Carboneria. Nothing is known for certain about the beginnings of this movement or the reason for its name – *carboneria* can be translated as 'charcoal burning'. It is possible that their supporters used it to allude to the forest as the place where their secret meetings were held. Their political aims, on the other hand, were very clear: to fight for human rights and against despotism. At these private meetings bourgeois citizens and officers from the nobility came together, particularly those who had fought at the side of Murat during the Napoleonic wars. Members of Napoleon's family were also part of the movement, including the later Napoleon III. The Carboneria could be found all over Italy but especially in the Mezzogiorno and the duchies of central Italy. Its members were mainly responsible for the Italian revolutions of 1820 and 1821.

Their most eminent representative and mastermind was undoubtedly Giuseppe Mazzini (1805–1872). He was a professional revolutionary who gained crucial political experience with the Carboneria. Initially he was influenced by his bourgeois father, a doctor and professor of Pathology at the University of Genoa, who was a staunch supporter of the Ligurian Republic and politically involved in it through a Jacobin newspaper. Giuseppe Mazzini narrates that although he grew up in Genoa during the Napoleonic period, he was deeply impressed in his childhood by his father's memories of that short-lived republic. On the other side of the family was his extremely pious mother, who taught him religious values and a strict sense of morality and moral principles, including the duty to sacrifice oneself for a great cause. His dissatisfaction with restoration politics and his distrust of the church led him to take part in the first wave of protests against the Restoration regime in 1820 even as a grammar school pupil and to become even more involved in 1821. After studying law, he founded trade journals with his political friends in order to disseminate his political views in secret. However, strict censorship prevented both the *Indicatore Genovese* and the *Indicatore Livornese,* which was published in the neighbouring Grand Duchy of Tuscany, from lasting very long. When the July revolution broke out in France in 1830, Mazzini was disappointed by the inconsistency and lack of revolutionary drive of his comrades in the secret societies. He was arrested by the police for provocation, taken to the fortress of Savona and only released on condition that he went into exile.

Mazzini realised that political secret societies and publications alone would not be enough for him to reach his goal and, based on this insight and experience, he founded the group *Giovine Italia* (*Young Italy*) in Marseille, which fought openly for a republican nation state of Italy. He promoted the idea that this could only be achieved by means of education and resistance, and that this education would have to be carried out by means of constant preaching or missionary work by 'apostles'. The movement was to be a crusade that taught ordinary people that war was inevitable, a desperate and decisive war that knew no other peace than victory or death. In contrast to other contemporary revolutionary theories, Mazzini's ideas were always characterised by a strong religious component, an idea that can be summed up briefly as *Dio e Popolo (God and the people).* Faith alone, faith in God and faith in the people, were sufficient to give a movement and a nation the power to accomplish great deeds. All his principal ideas can be found in his writings of the early 1830s, right down to the phrases that were repeated unchanged even in his very last articles. The foundation for Mazzini's faith and for his plan for the renewal of the human race was the Italian people and the creation of an Italian nation. During his long exile in London, he became the prophet of a missionary vision of Italy.

2). The supporters of autonomous aristocratic republics, whose projects were rejected at the Congress of Vienna, tend to be overlooked by historians. For the majority of the Italian elites in northern and central Italy, the cities and their past were a key element of their identity and their political self-image. Numerous publications appeared in the nineteenth century on the mediaeval communes and their model character for contemporary constitutional issues. At the forefront was the pioneering six volume *Histoire des républiques italiennes au moyen-âge* by the Genevan economist and historian Jean Charles Simonde de Sismondi, published between 1807 and 1818 and translated into many languages. This work was to become the ideological handbook for supporters of aristocratic republics. For Sismondi a correlation existed between the emergence of Italian city republics and the political autonomy and unity of Italy. According to his *Histoire,* liberal political constitutions, which were the key achievement of mediaeval city republics, led to these city states being culturally and economically superior to every other form of society in mediaeval Europe. He considered the democratic way of life to be realised in its longest and purist form in the Constitution of Florence. His conception of

Fig. 3 Alfonso Chierici, The Clandestine Flag, Portrait of Giuseppe Mazzini, 1862.

life under this constitution focused on a group of politically experienced statesman who controlled city politics independently of the prescribed rotation of offices and so functioned as a kind of political class. This idea of history also shaped Sismondi's belief in the need for a political aristocracy in the nineteenth century. A series of newspaper articles written in 1858 by the Milanese Carlo Cattaneo, entitled *La città considerata come principio ideale delle istorie italiane (The city as an ideal principle of Italian history)*, was no less influential. According to Cattaneo, liberty, autonomy and political responsibility could only develop in the urban environment of the individual. Switzerland and the United States of America were his political ideals. He wrote the history of Italy as the history of a hundred cities that had evolved in constant conflict, leading to a maximum degree of liberality, vitality and material and cultural wealth and also to progress and efficiency. In Cattaneo's opinion, the municipalities formed the nation and offered a haven of freedom within that nation. For him it was the task of future national legislation to spread municipal rights throughout Italy.

Patricians were only too happy to take up this line of argument to insist on their particular capacity for politics in the nineteenth century. Prominent members, such as Marquess Gino Capponi in Florence, pointed to the centuries of experience and merits that the patricians had already acquired. Capponi and other representatives of moderate liberalism felt that, because of its traditions, virtues, ideas of honour and lifestyle, the aristocracy was predestined for a major role in the politics of Tuscany. It was not only in Genoa and Milan that ideas like this were discussed. For the patricians of Lombardy, the legacy of the *Lega Lombarda* was also of particular significance. This heroic northern Italian confederation of cities, which had fought for autonomy, was considered one of the few successful manifestations of Italian unity in its history. In the Treaty of Constance of 1183, it had wrested significant concessions from Frederick I (Barbarossa), who had been defeated at Legnano. The *Lega* was a major reference point for the identity of the Lombards, who had adopted a leading role in this historically memorable achievement. It has been politically appropriated and instrumentalised to this day. For the traditional and power-conscious patricians of northern and central Italy, integration into a unitary, levelling nation state under the leadership of Savoy was not an attractive political option.

3.) Mazzini's ideas initially inspired Vincenzo Gioberti (1801–1852), the main visionary behind the idea of founding a Neo-Guelphist nation state. He came from a bourgeois family in Turin, had a curious and encyclopaedic mind and was well-versed in Italian music, philosophy and literature. Gioberti believed that, given their extraordinary artistic legacy, Italians were living beneath their potential, and he developed a concept of nationhood based on the superiority of Italians in the field of culture. After studying theology, he taught at the University of Turin where he probably came into contact with supporters of the Carboneria and aroused suspicion as a sympathiser of *Giovine Italia.* He shared the fate of many opposition figures by being arrested and going into exile, first to France, and then to Belgium. He soon fell out with Mazzini and his revolutionary practices, which he considered to be totally unrealistic, given existing power relations. As a theologian, he developed the idea of a federal Italian nation state with the Pope as its honorary head. In his most popular programmatic text *Il primato morale e civile degli Italiani* (1843), he also based his arguments on mediaeval history. In the Investiture Controversy, he argued, it was the Pope and his allies the Guelphs who had protected Italy from the claims to power by the Hohenstaufen kings and their supporters, the Ghibellines (the Italian name for the Swabian town of Waiblingen where the Hohenstaufen family originated). For Gioberti, only the Catholic Church as a universal institution would guarantee order and harmony. At the same time, he called for its modernisation and for fundamental liberal church reforms. He assumed as a theologian that a nation state could only be founded as a federal state and in cooperation with the papacy, not in conflict with it. Gioberti may have reproached Mazzini for lacking a sense of reality in his revolutionary ambitions, but it was not clear in the case of his own ideas how his idealised image of liberal Catholic rule could be reconciled with the existing arch-conservative conditions in the Papal States. Pope Pius IX (1846–1878), who at the beginning of his pontificate seemed to be a more liberal pope, later put *Il primato morale e civile degli Italiani* on the index of forbidden books.

4.) The most influential group turned out to be those politically liberal-conservative elites whom Italian historiography calls the *Moderati*. These moderates worked together with a series of individuals who either lived in exile or in relatively liberal Florence. The most prominent figure in this group was Cesare Balbo Conte di Vinadio. He had gained significant political and administrative experience in the Napoleonic period. After the failure of the revolution in 1821, he also went into exile in Paris for several years and worked as a historian and writer. His analysis of Gioberti's works led to the publication of his *Delle speranze d'Italia (On the hopes of Italy)*. Balbo, like Gioberti, favoured a federal structure for Italy. However, he criticised Gioberti for ascribing far too great a role to the Pope, and for his excessive and dangerous enmity towards France. He also relativised Gioberti's claims to high culture with the reminder that other nations had also produced outstanding cultural achievements. Balbo's idea was to create a strong monarchist state, while he considered it unlikely that a nation would develop spontaneously as a result of cultural values. There had been no resistance to the invasion of the French in the 1790s, he pointed out. Only a dynastic state would succeed where cultural forces had failed. For Balbo, this state could only be the Kingdom of Sardinia-Piedmont. He also attached the greatest significance to Austria's hegemonic policy in Italy; for him, that was the central problem. The only way of solving it in his opinion would be for the European powers to agree to an expansion of the power of Vienna in the Balkans at the expense of the Ottoman Empire, in return for which Austria would have to give up Lombardy-Venetia. There was no provision for a centralist, united Italian state in this concept either. It was also questionable to what extent the Savoy dynasty was prepared to become the head of a liberal constitutional monarchy.

5.) Less attention has been paid in recent decades to the extent to which the arch-conservatives intervened in political discussions and debates after the Congress of Vienna, by no means leaving the field to opponents of the regime. They created an ideology to counteract desires for liberal reform and the nation state movements and participated energetically in the Europe-wide battle for political sovereignty over the interpretation of such concepts as nation, religion and patriotism. One of its most influential figureheads was Joseph de Maistre, extolled by his followers as *sommo filosofo del secolo (the greatest philosopher of the century).* A lawyer from a French-speaking, noble family in Savoy, in his youth he sided with the Enlightenment and Freemasonry but became increasingly radicalised due to his experience of the revolution. He was a royalist and diplomat who remained loyal to the king in exile. His writings – '*Considérations sur la France*' (1796), '*Du Pape*' (1819) and '*Les Soirées de Saint-Pétersbourg ou Entretiens sur la Gouvernement Temporel de la Providence*' (1821) – were published in fifty-nine editions and translated into seven European languages between 1800 and 1870. After 1814 his publications were for a long time amongst the most widely read books in the western world. Between 1816 and 1821, the arch-conservative Joseph de Maistre, chief ideologist and minister, determined Piedmont's cultural policy and comprehensive conservative reorganisation. In his texts this 'oracle' of the counter revolution also justified an unprecedented policy of oppression. With other arch-conservatives, he stressed both the significance of the connection between the throne and the pulpit and the eminent role of the monarch. This specific application of religious policy was a reaction to the challenges of the modern era. Christian pathos formulae, empathetic metaphors and visualisations were to contribute to an anti-revolutionary demobilisation of the wider public. The conservatives constantly reverted to paternalistic and ecclesiastical religious paradigms in order to idealise the ethos of service and pro-monarchist patriotism: 'With God, for King and Fatherland'.

In the same way as de Maistre, the Swiss lawyer Karl Ludwig von Haller went out of his way to demonise the revolution. Von Haller's six volume *Restauration der Staatswissenschaft (Restoration of Political Science),* in which he developed his programme for conservative stabilisation, soon spread throughout Europe and made a considerable contribution to political discourse in conservative networks. In it he quite simply equated revolutionary principles with liberal reforms and the desire for a nation state. Royalists were, he maintained, the only legitimate defenders of patriotic traditions. Edmund Burke's *Reflections on the French Revolution* was also held in high esteem in reactionary circles, as were the anti-revolutionary and anti-liberal writings of the French priest Félicité de Lamennais, particularly his *Paroles d'un croyant (Words of a Believer).*

Conservative circles also instrumentalised the cult of monarchy and emphasised the importance of the army as an institution capable of promoting national cohesion. They also called for honour, loyalty and fidelity as the most important elements of conservative patriotism. In order to underpin their conservative position in the public sphere they used various forms of communication including speeches, historiography, correspondence and local politics, as well as the cultivation of memorials and historical paintings. These royalist proponents of arch-conservative regimes were absorbed by religion, a paranoid fear of revolution, and the cult of the monarchy. They held countless ministerial posts and dominated courtly society.

Whereas research previously concentrated on political theorists or on the great men who made history, whether they were kings, ministers or generals, in the last twenty-five years broader areas of public discourse and forms of politics beyond cabinet tables have been analysed. However, no other book in Italy has led to such heated discussions on the topics of the nation and national feeling in the nineteenth century as Alberto M. Banti's work *La Nazione del Risorgimento* published in 2000. It was greeted with great scepticism by those with structural historical and classical political approaches, but with enthusiasm by those who themselves experiment with various different linguistic, spatial and other turns. It is by no means the first Italian study to develop Benedict Anderson's ideas on nationalism further and to pursue the question of how the creation of the nation state could be described as a process beyond the development of parliament and democracy. However, in the course of the cultural turn, Italian historiography has addressed the phenomenon of the construction of national identity with remarkable intensity, focusing on the 'invention' of the nation as the work of intellectual elites. After unity was complete, both in military and constitutional terms, particularistic and regional interests had to be integrated into the new state and centralist strategies were preferred in Italy.

Besides unification of the state, it was also necessary to instigate a process of 'inner' nation-building, since for centuries it had been regional and local traditions and identities that had determined how people lived together. This problem is symbolised in the famous saying attributed to Massimo d'Azeglio: *Fatta l'Italia bisogna fare gli Italiani* (*Once we have created Italy we will have to create the Italians*). The creation of a national identity is an extremely complex process which has to be conveyed and constantly re-affirmed by means of national models, objectives, ideals and myths. Attempts were made, for example, to instil national values in schools and in the military. Historical images and myths can be and were spread by means of songs, memorials, plaques, monuments, pictures and street names. Research has focused in particular on the diverse forms of state symbolism, mainly the cultivation of monuments, political festivals and political architecture, as well as iconography. A further effective method of creating national identities was to instrumentalise historiography. The depiction of Piedmont's illustrious leading role in the process of the unification of Italy therefore dominated both school textbooks and many standard academic works.

Banti provides a shift of focus. His starting point is not 1861, as was the case with earlier studies, but the French revolution period, which upset the whole of the

Italian peninsula by exporting its revolutionary ideas, waging wars and reorganising territories. He takes discourse analysis in its purest form to the extreme. His interest centres on the questions of what nation and the fatherland meant to the women and men of the Risorgimento and what these words meant to those who decided to take action in the first half of the nineteenth century – to act dangerously, to risk exile or imprisonment or even their lives. Banti set himself the task of deciphering the meaning and significance of the contemporary use of patriotic words related to 'nation'. He identified models and themes which he refers to as the 'canon', a word he uses only in quotation marks and admits to having constructed himself. This 'canon' is made up of well-known and well-received literature, historical works and political texts by the most important Italian intellectuals, including their private correspondence and memoirs. The material available for him to draw on is vast.

Banti analyses the fundamental semantic change in the word 'nation' since the French Revolution, and the political experiences associated with it. More revolutionary ideas reached Italy with the revolutionary troops, who also brought with them newspapers, books, manifestos and pamphlets, which became increasingly widespread after 1796. To a certain extent, both new and well-established meanings and connotations of nation were combined in political rhetoric. There were, for example, the concepts of 'sovereignty' and 'legitimacy', which had been discussed for decades, beside such catchwords as 'state', 'citizen', 'liberty', 'fatherland' and 'the people'. These were accompanied by two new aspects of the concept of 'nation' not known before. In the first, the actors understood nation as an elemental and deep-rooted community. The second referred to the relationship to the nation, which was described and invoked as love of and loyalty to the fatherland or conversely betrayal of it. Added to this was the nationalisation of honour and a religious charge to the concept of fatherland, which demanded inner unity as an absolute necessity. Banti paid no attention to the fact that it was not only democrats and liberals but also conservatives who made use of these semantic fields.

Banti's study, which focuses primarily on discourses around martyrs, honour, purity, courage, sacrifice and family ties, set a precedent. Countless studies adopted this or similar patterns of interpretation. In her study of Garibaldi, one of the most important revolutionary actors, Lucy Riall, for example, focuses on his 'invention' as a hero by the mass media. This kind of approach was combined with recent trends in research on emotions, such as that of Carlotta Sorba, an acknowledged expert in the history of music and opera. In spite of the brilliance of individual studies, the influence and contemporary reception of this constructed 'canon' are rarely questioned.

When historians leave the level of discourse and examine the actual reception of art works, their results are sobering. Axel Körner, for example, was able to show that the chorus *Va pensiero* in Giuseppe Verdi's opera *Nabucco,* also known as the *Chorus of the Hebrew Slaves*, only gained its status as an anthem of liberty after the founding of the nation state and Verdi's stylisation as the national 'bard'. The reaction of the public at its premier in La Scala in Milan in 1842 was not to greet it with ovations and agitation for the nation state as is often reported. The police in attendance would have immediately prevented this. Similarly, historical paintings and portraits by Francesco Hayez, the most famous painter of Italian Romanticism, were only able to have an impact after 1861, as they had previously hung in private aristocratic palaces. It has to be added that Hayez did not only paint portraits of Milanese patricians who were in the opposition. He painted portraits of the Austrian general Radetzky and Emperor Ferdinand, for whom he had also painted a magnificent cycle of frescoes in the Hall of Caryatids in Milan, to Ferdinand's great satisfaction. Hayez followed the wish of the emperor by making the praise of rulers his subject. Alberto Banti and many others adopt the works of both Verdi and Hayez as important media for the struggle for a democratic, liberal nation state before unification unquestioningly. But are songs, poems, romantic tales, pictures and opera sufficient to motivate people to fight for a nation state? How many of them actually went to fight voluntarily? And did all the elites want the nation state in the form it took, which was then teleologically celebrated by state-biased historiography as without alternative? The majority of Italians were faced with more existential problems and would scarcely have been motivated to leave their house and home to fight for an abstract idea. What was the role played by economic and power-political motives? Who were the winners, who the losers in this complicated process?

The authors of studies with a discourse analysis approach also tend to gloss over the question of what was actually understood by nation or nation state. Was it really the unification of the whole of the Italian peninsula or did the people in Sicily, Tuscany, Piedmont, Lombardy and Venetia dream of smaller nation states? During the nineteenth century, the concept of nation or *patria* oscillates between narrow, urban and regional connotations and the idea of a nation or a united nation state. However, even if there was not necessarily agreement over the ultimate political goal to be achieved, the revolutionary potential on the side of the elites was great enough for them to rebel against the monarch again in 1820.

## 3.3 The southern European revolutions of 1820, 1821 and 1830

Five revolutions broke out in southern Europe in 1820–1821 and a sixth was crushed at the outset in Milan. In Spain, in the Kingdom of the Two Sicilies, in Portugal, in the Kingdom of Sardinia-Piedmont and in Greece, officers, nobles, members of the intelligentsia and sons of the wealthy bourgeoisie were ready to fight for a constitutional state. Although these revolutions, with the exception of Greece, stopped short of overthrowing the monarchs, the failure of Metternich's prevention policy was evident. This wave of resistance began in January 1820 in Spain, where officers triggered a revolution with the aim of forcing the re-introduction of the Cortes constitution, thus establishing a constitutional monarchy. This liberal constitution had been drawn up by the Spanish Parliament in Cádiz in 1812, that is in the most southern part of Spain, which was not occupied by French troops. It was an eclectic mixture of French, British and American models, but took Spanish traditions into account. Sovereignty was with the nation, legislative power was shared between the king and the Cortes and government had to answer to parliament, which met in a single chamber. The Catholic faith was recognised as the only true religion.

Events in Madrid had a signal effect and in the next few months, officers and nobles called out revolutions in the Kingdom of the Two Sicilies, in Portugal and in Sardinia-Piedmont. On mainland southern Italy, the Carbonari and Freemasons had been agitating for a constitution on the Spanish model since March. On 1 July, the officers Michele Morelli and Giuseppe Salvati deserted from the cavalry regiment in Nola to the east of Naples with a hundred and thirty men and twenty officers. Both men came from rural aristocratic families and had enjoyed stellar military careers under Murat. During the Napoleonic period, Morelli had been a member of the elite mounted Veliti Guards regiment. The uprising gained momentum in Avellino and Salerno, supported by activities of the Carbonari, who were amongst the most determined supporters of the liberal movement. On 3 July 1820 the Constitution of Cádiz was officially proclaimed by the officers in Avellino. Over the next few days, this action led to a genuine uprising that spread throughout the kingdom and spilled over into papal territory in Benevento and Pontecorvo. By 5 July, the Carbonari had already raised the red, blue, and black flag on public buildings in Benevento and forced the papal representative to flee. With the arrival of the charismatic General Guglielmo Pepe, another of Murat's former aristocratic aides-de-camps, and his assumption of command, the Carbonari revolution began to take on a new and threatening dimension for the Bourbons. The king, Ferdinand I, was urged by his advisers to accept the constitution and form a new government before handing over the regency to his eldest son Francesco. Pepe and his troops were enthusiastically welcomed when they marched into Naples on 9 July and only four days later Ferdinand was compelled to swear an oath to the constitution. Elections were held for the first time and on 1 October 1820 parliament convened in the Church of the Holy Spirit in Toledo Street. Male spectators were admitted regardless of their class but women were excluded. The newly gained freedom of the press permitted lively public discussion. Journalists did not limit themselves to debates on the constitution and reforms, rather they tried to exert overall influence by means of their publications. In contrast to the 1790s, the moderate constitutional elites now succeeded in integrating the lower classes into a kind of secular religion in support of the constitution using persuasive practices traditionally employed by the church and the court. These included political catechisms, communal anthems and imposing ceremonies.

These revolutionary achievements in Naples immediately found a widespread echo in Sicily. The Sicilians had been united with the Kingdom of Naples as the Kingdom of the Two Sicilies against their will since December 1816. They had seen their own constitution of 1812 suspended and had been forced to give up their flag, both of which were proud institutions and signs of their independence. With the unification of the two kingdoms, Napoleonic reforms were also implemented in Sicily, which led to the abolition of old legal and economic privileges. The unification of the administration also resulted in Palermo losing its function as a capital city and being demoted to the level of other provincial cities.

In the summer of 1820, a separatist movement in Sicily profited from the uprising of the Carbonari and supporters of Murat on the mainland. They exploited the power vacuum to demand autonomy and the re-introduction of the old constitution of 1812. There was, however, no great interest on the island in creating opportunities for debate and discussion in the public sphere. The old elites rejected the Constitution of Cádiz because it had been adopted in Naples without their consent. Dissatisfaction was also voiced as to why their own constitution, the Bentinck constitution of 1812, had been disregarded.

In contrast to the revolution in Naples, where the general mass of the people remained calm, the rebellion in Palermo immediately assumed the character of a popular uprising similar to those in the *Ancien Régime*. Alongside the separatist aspirations of the traditional nobility, a grassroots revolution of the urban lower classes erupted in Palermo. Incited by the old nobility, they stormed the prisons, destroyed the royal coat of arms and plundered the royal palace. This was not least a reaction to years of economic decline after the withdrawal of the British from the island. By August the independence movement had spread across the whole island and outright civil war developed between those in favour of independence, as in Palermo, and those who were against it, as in Messina and Catania. Peace was only restored when in September General Florestano Pepe, a brother of Guglielmo and also a supporter of Murat, landed in Sicily with Neapolitan troops. After the bombardment of Palermo on 5 October 1820, the insurgents capitulated. In this way, prominent representatives of the Neapolitan revolution themselves became agents of oppression in order to protect the unity of the state against the reactionary ambitions of the Sicilian people. This Sicilian 'episode' contributed towards weakening the effect of the revolution on the mainland and making the capital Naples even more hated in Sicily.

Ultimately, it was not internal disputes that led to the failure of the revolution in the Kingdom of the Two Sicilies. Once again, it was Austria that ended the political experiments in the shadow of Vesuvius and Etna by force of arms. Before and during the revolutions, those monarchs who had come under pressure turned to the major European powers. They met after the Congress of Vienna for four consecutive congresses, first in Aachen (1818), then on Austrian territory in Troppau (1820), in Ljubljana (1821) and in Verona (1822). After the last unresolved issues of the Congress of Vienna had been negotiated, the main purpose of this congress diplomacy was to prevent future revolutions. Domestic political crises in individual states were treated as international affairs, since the major powers were of the opinion that there was a danger of revolutionary conflagration.

The southern European revolutions at the beginning of the 1820s confirmed these fears only too well. For this reason, the congresses established the principle of intervention. Ferdinand I had barely signed the constitution in Naples when he hurried to the congress in Troppau to seek military support. Austria, Russia, Prussia and France decided to apply the principle of intervention against revolutionary Naples, opposed only by Britain. Since his brutal suppression of the republic in 1799, Ferdinand had not been popular with the British. During the consultations in Troppau, the emperor, Metternich and the tsar invited him as the King of the Two Sicilies to Ljubljana, where the next congress was planned for January 1821, to decide the fate of the rebels. The Holy Alliance refused to recognise the constitutional governments and with Ferdinand's consent, Austrian troops invaded the Papal States and the Kingdom of the Two Sicilies, defeating General Pepe's troops at the beginning of March. All the legislation introduced by the constitutional government was revoked.

Once again repressive measures followed. The level of violence used in Sicily in January 1822 was even greater than during the suppression of the mainland revolution. The leaders of the revolution were either sentenced to death or exiled, mostly in absentia. More than fifteen hundred people stood trial between 1821 and 1826. Hundreds were sentenced to imprisonment, countless defendants were deported to Austria and seven hundred were forced to leave the kingdom. This time, however, only two death sentences were carried out. The public execution of the two officers who had sparked the revolution in Nola, Michele Morelli and Giuseppe Salvati, took place in the capital on 12 September 1822, with a mass of spectators.

In the Kingdom of Sardinia-Piedmont, just as in Naples, student unrest was followed by a conspiracy of high-ranking officers and members of the Carboneria from both aristocratic and bourgeois circles. They initially demanded the introduction of a constitution modelled on the French *Charte* of 1814. Under pressure from the Carbonari, however, they ultimately decided in favour of the liberal Constitution of Cádiz, as in the Kingdom of the Two Sicilies. They had come to an agreement with the heir to the throne, Charles Albert, who made no secret of his sympathy towards the liberals. He was the only member of the House of Savoy who had not followed the king into exile in Sardinia. Charles Albert had spent part of his youth in Napoleonic France and after 1815 had maintained friendly relations in liberal circles and with the Carboneria. He now presented the prospect of supporting the insurgence. On 10 March 1821 the garrison in Alessandria revolted and raised the green, white and red flag. Their leaders demanded that Victor Emmanuel I adopt the Constitution of Cádiz, but despite the appeals of his nephew, Charles Albert, he refused. The revolution spread and the insurgents conquered the cities of Asti, Casale and Ivrea whilst in Turin soldiers and students fought side-by-side for the constitution. On 12 March, the king sent a dispatch to Charles Albert telling him to negotiate with the rebels. At the same time, he abdicated in favour of his absent younger brother, Charles Felix, and appointed his nephew Charles Albert as regent.

The following day Charles Albert proclaimed the Constitution of Cádiz for the whole of the kingdom and attempted to quell the Carbonari riots. However, Charles Felix disapproved of these measures and rejected the constitution. After some hesitation, the crown prince Charles Albert gave in to his uncle, the new king, and turned his back on the liberal revolution, announcing that he would relinquish the regency on 23 March, before being forced to leave Piedmont for Tuscany. He ultimately submitted to the reactionary measures of his father in order not to lose his claim to the throne. The liberal elites naturally accused him of being a traitor. The troops supporting the constitution were declared rebels by Charles Felix and were defeated on 8 April 1821 by the royal troops in all three rebel cities, Turin, Alessandria and Casale. The final battles took place near Novara where, with the support of the inevitable Austrians, the regular Piedmontese troops were victorious.

Less than a few weeks after it had begun, the constitutional revolution in the Kingdom of Sardinia-Piedmont ended in a repressive climate comparable to that in Naples. Between May and August, the property of any supporters of the constitutional movement was confiscated. 180 individuals including 82 officers were put on trial by the Royal Court and 71 rebels from the nobility were sentenced to death, 69 of them in absentia. However, only two death sentences were carried out in Piedmont – on the bourgeois cavalry captains Giacomo Garelli and Battista Laneri, both protagonists in the uprising in Alessandria. Thanks to the military support of the *Tedeschi (Germans),* the common name for the Austrians, Charles Felix was able to enter Turin in October. On 13 October, the king addressed the public with a proclamation: 'There will be a return of the happy times when the treacherous and preposterous theories of our days will be despised and religion, good manners, the paternal affection of the king and the obedient devotion of his subjects will be understood to be the only basis of the happiness of the people'.[3] From then on the universities in Turin and Genoa were kept under even closer supervision than before. After the suppression of this uprising, the opposition regarded the House of Savoy with deep distrust.

The majority of the rebels from the liberal elites were deliberately allowed to flee, since they were members of those families that had been the mainstay of the royal family in the military and administration for centuries. Amongst them were members of the oldest and most wealthy families, such as Prince Emanuele dal Pozzo della Cisterna, whose family tree could be traced back to the thirteenth century. His father had held distinguished posts in local government during the Napoleonic period and secured his son a position as chamberlain at the court of Princess Borghese. On Emanuele's return to Turin from a trip to France at the beginning of March 1821, the police searched his carriage and found not only banned books and pamphlets, but also compromising letters, proving that the prince and other liberal aristocrats in France and Italy's neighbouring states were well connected with the most prominent figures of European liberalism. The Austrians then demanded to see the records of this investigation in order to find information about Conte Confalonieri and others involved in the planned uprising in Milan. Among those incriminated by the material that was found were Marquess Demetrio Turinetti di Priero from a diplomatic family and the Napoleonic officer Baron Ettore Perrone di San Martino. Both belonged to the younger age-group that researchers call 'generation Napoleon'. They were also sentenced to death in absentia. Despite sequestration, that is the state confiscation of his assets, Prince Emanuele dal Pozzo managed to salvage part of his fortune and live in Paris until 1848, apparently incognito. The French police did in fact know his identity but did not arrest him; there seems to have been no great pressure from Turin to extradite him. When he returned to Turin in 1848, this high nobleman was immediately made a senator by Charles Albert, and his wife, Louise, was appointed lady in waiting. His daughter eventually married a prince from the House of Savoy. The majority of other exiles were also by no means bourgeois radicals, but conservative liberal actors, most of whom advocated a constitution modelled on that of the *Charte* in 1814 or the Constitution of Cádiz.

While the Austrians were able to quell the revolutions and rebellions in Naples and Turin during the Restoration using military strength, they were careful to prevent anything similar developing on their own doorstep. In Milan the police struck before the liberal opposition could bring itself to act. They had in any case been under observation for a long time, particularly those connected with the counts Frederico Confalonieri and Luigi Porro Lambertenghi, who had been financing the magazine *Il Conciliatore* (*The Reconciler*) since 1818. The aim of this literary and economically liberal publication was to 'reconcile' Neoclassical and Romantic ideas of art. As the older trend, Neoclassicism was equated with Austrian positions, while Romanticism stood for France and liberal values. The best-known writers and poets of northern Italy published in the *Conciliatore,* including Silvio Pellico, Giovanni Bercher and Marquess Ludovico di Breme. Liberals in other cities in Lombardy were included by means of a network of correspondence. The majority of the total of 240 subscribers came from patrician circles. However, constant pressure from the censors and political repression forced those responsible to abandon the project and stop publishing the paper in October 1819. They also followed the outbreak of constitutional revolutions in Spain, southern Italy, Portugal and Turin with a sense of excitement and hope. In retrospect, they can be seen to have re-interpreted the Napoleonic era. They assumed that the changes of the previous twenty years could not be reversed, particularly as far as the liberal reforms and experiences of a larger national unit were concerned.

It proved to be impossible tor the Austrians to realise their ambition to de-politicise the population; the lessons of the French era continued to have an effect. The slogan now was 'under Napoleon, we were students, under Austria we are slaves'. However, in contrast to Turin, Naples and Sicily, an uprising in Milan was suppressed from the start. The spies had done excellent work and the protagonists planning the uprising were arrested. There was also no support from the military in Milan. The Habsburg judiciary took harsh action against the rebellious social elites. Whereas Porro Lambertenghi and Marquess Giuseppe Arconati and some others were able to flee, Conte Frederico Confalonieri, Giorgio Pallavicino, Conte Francesco Arese and dozens of other patricians were sentenced to death. The emperor eventually commuted the death sentences to decades of imprisonment in the Špilberk fortress in Moravia. These were extremely harsh sentences for a conspiracy that was only sketchily planned and never actually took place.

There was a wide response to the trials amongst the European public, and later in historiography, not least as a result of the numerous memoirs of those concerned, which often drifted between real life experience and literary fiction. The most well-known of these was Silvio Pellico's *Le mie prigioni (My Prisons),* in which he described his imprisonment in a dungeon and fortress in Venice and on the Špilberk and which became a best seller. This book, together with the memoirs of other protagonists, created images of martyrs to liberty in the battle against the Austrians. After 1821, if not before, liberal patricians saw themselves as penalised, condemned and suffering under 'foreign rule'. Naturally there were also supporters of Austrian rule, often denigrated as *austriacanti.* However, it was more than just memoirs that the liberal patricians used to style themselves as political martyrs and revolutionaries. They also commissioned the most respected and expensive painter at the Academy at the time, Francesco Hayez, to create the pictures they required. Their self-conception is depicted most impressively in an unusual portrait of Conte Francesco Arese, showing him as a prisoner on the Špilberk. Pardoned in 1827, he commissioned a portrait by Hayez that showed him as a martyr in prison. Hayez himself noted in his memoirs that, as with many other of his paintings, this portrait was never publicly exhibited.

Fig. 4 Francesco Hayez, Sicilian Vespers, 1846.

Among Hayez' most famous paintings are the portrayals of the *Vespri siciliani*, a subject depicted by him three times in large-scale paintings between 1822 and 1844. They are based on a historical episode from the distant past which, due to various literary and historical adaptations, increasingly became a liberation myth during the first half of the nineteenth century. Sicilian Vespers was the name given to the uprising against French rule under Charles I that broke out at the time of evening Vespers on 30 March 1282, Easter Monday. It began in Palermo, but quickly spread across the entire island and eventually led to the expulsion of the House of Anjou from Sicily. In 1822 the painting was commissioned by Marchioness Visconti d'Aragona, whose husband had also been imprisoned the previous year for his involvement in the uprising against the Austrians. Hayez painted a second version for Conte Arese. The central topic in all the versions is the struggle for freedom and honour. Hayez skilfully brings the topic up to date by portraying members of the liberal aristocracy in the paintings. In all three versions, the background is filled with scenes of unrest and revolt following this event. The focus of the action is on honourable resistance to foreign rule. The Milanese nobility commissioned compositions from Hayez which, with the appropriate education, could be interpreted as patriotic resistance to foreign masters. However, the fatherland they desired bore no resemblance to the nation state which was to come into being in 1861. The liberal patricians wanted an independent Lombardy, possibly also a kingdom of northern Italy, but above all, an enhancement of the political standing of their own caste. The main aim of the nobility in Lombardy and Tuscany alike was to cement their own position as the elites in early European liberalism.

In the period after 1821 and these repressive measures, a deathly hush seems to have covered the political landscape in the Italian states. Thousands of political suspects were in exile in neighbouring European states, in North Africa, in America or in Italian prisons. Nevertheless, revolutionary movements and liberal ideas continued to exist. In 1830 it was once again the echo of European revolutions and insurrections that led to demonstrations by liberals and patriots in Italy. At the end of July, after the famous *Trois Glorieuses* when, within three days, a largely bloodless revolution ended the rule of the reactionary Bourbons in France, and the more liberal Louis-Philippe, from the House of Orleans, came to the throne, there were student demonstrations in Ferrara, publicly celebrating the political coup in Paris.

Louis-Philippe, the so-called Citizen King, immediately granted fundamental political rights. In contrast to the Bourbon kingdom, his monarchy had not been established at the Congress of Vienna. The new system in France threatened to undermine the order established in 1815. The first concrete outcomes of the change of ruler were the strengthening of the constitutional monarchy and replacements in government offices. The ultra-conservative aristocracy was ousted by liberal members of the nobility and the bourgeoisie. The effect of events in Paris were felt most where the politically active elites had not come to terms with the restorative turn of events after the Congress of Vienna, that is in Belgium, Poland, the German Confederation and on the Italian peninsula. Here, patriotic conspiracies and revolutionary projects sprung up once again, clearly influenced by France. Many Italians lived in France in exile, and Louis-Philippe himself had pledged to support the patriots in Modena were the Austrians to intervene. In Paris, the Jacobin Filippo Buonarroti, for example, agitated repeatedly for a republican revolution in Italy.

This time, however, Milan and Naples remained calm. One explanation for this is the efficiency of the political repression, but another might also be the two changes on the throne. The liberals in Naples were hoping for a change of political course after Ferdinand II assumed power in 1830. In Turin, it was not yet clear how Charles Albert would behave after his accession to the throne in spring 1831. The most serious conflicts took place this time in the smaller duchies and the Papal States. In Modena, the wealthy merchant Ciro Menotti, who with his brother Celeste was well connected with the political emigrants in France, came forward at the end of 1830 with a manifesto setting out a programme that was both moderate and national. It was entitled *Ideas for organising the consensus of all cities in Italy to be united in their support for its independence, unity and liberty.* Duke Francis IV initially appeared to support it because he hoped to extend his power, but on 3 February 1831, took action against a conspiracy meeting in Menotti's home. As leader of the movement, Menotti was executed in May 1831 and the liberal movement gained a further martyr. Garibaldi was to name his first son after him.

In Rome, a conspiracy of the Carbonari supported by medics, students and artisans and abetted by Bonapartists under Louis Napoleon, later Napoleon III, failed as early as December 1830. Shortly afterwards there were uprisings in Bologna, Imola and Reggio-Emilia and riots in Forlì. The papal governors left their posts and on 8 February 1831, a provisional government in Bologna, headed by the lawyer Giovanni Vincini, declared the end of the temporal power of the Pope. Five out of eight members of the new government had served as civil servants under Napoleon and the Napoleonic *Tricolore* fluttered from the rooftops. Other cities followed the example of Bologna and provisional governments were set up in Modena and Reggio. They all acted in complete isolation and the political actors were once again nobles and very wealthy members of the bourgeoisie. The rural population, who were completely disregarded in the theoretical texts of the liberals, remained wholly passive.

With the exception of Tuscany, the whole of central and northern Italy was affected by the revolutionary movement, that is, Umbria and the Marche as well as Parma, which Duchess Marie Louise of Habsburg had been forced to leave on 15 February. The failure of the papal troops resulted more from their own weakness than from the strength of the opposition, although the revolutionaries had for their part completely overestimated their own strength. They had put all their hopes in Louis-Philippe, but in vain, since he refused to support them. In 1831, he adopted a conservative approach and came to an agreement with Austria. Law and order were restored by means of foreign intervention in the same way as it had been ten years earlier. The Pope and the sovereigns of the smaller duchies called the Austrians for help and they quickly put down the uprisings, marching into the Duchy of Modena on 4 March 1831 and just fourteen days later into the Papal States. Ancona capitulated at the end of March and the Papal States resumed control of the Marche. Again, repressive measures were implemented in Bologna, Rome and Modena. Further attacks were carried out on the papal troops after the Austrians withdrew in 1832, but again the Austrians intervened successfully. This time, Louis-Philippe, in rivalry with Vienna, also sent troops into the Papal States to support the Pope. From then on Austria was no longer the only major European power to have a strong military presence in central Italy.

Paris and Vienna attempted to persuade the newly elected pope Gregory XVI to adopt a measured response towards his political opponents in the Papal States, but to no avail. Once again many either managed or were forced to flee. Although a joint memorandum was drawn up by European diplomats in Rome urging reforms akin to those of Consalvi to be implemented at long last, in order to ameliorate the untenable situation in the Papal States, even this led to no more than a few insignificant administrative reforms. The course subsequently followed by the Roman Curia was even more authoritarian and defensive. The Pope reacted to the events with his first grand encyclical, *Mirari Vos* (*That you wonder*) in which he condemned rationalism, religious indifference, freedom of conscience and expression, and any attacks against legitimate governments. It was the first in a series of ultraconservative, intransigent encyclicals which were to poison discussions and deepen the gulf between the Catholic hierarchy and more liberal forces.

The revolutions of 1831 had a long-term effect on public opinion in Italy and internationally. On the one hand, their lack of success was associated with the failure and weakness of the Carbonari movement, and on the other, these renewed uprisings were interpreted as a significant step towards a liberal nation state. This time the promotion of liberal political and national demands and a patriotic struggle against the Austrians was less equivocal. Revolutionary slogans in Bologna supported the 'United Italian Provinces'. At the same time, from a European perspective, the Papal States were seen increasingly as an obstacle to independence and national unity.

## 3.4 Italians in exile

After the first wave of revolutions in 1820–1821, an estimated two thousand Italians were living in exile. Several thousand joined them after the attempts at political revolution in 1830–1831 had failed. Individuals and smaller groups in political exile were not a novelty in the nineteenth century but now it assumed new dimensions and a new significance. In his biographical study of one of the best-known Italian exiles, the Venetian poet Ugo Foscolo, Carlo Cattaneo wrote the memorable phrase: 'Foscolo gave Italy a new institution: exile'.[4] The poet left Milan immediately after the Austrians came to power. As a supporter of the French Revolution and a volunteer in the Cisalpine army, his odes had initially celebrated Napoleon as a liberator, but later he turned away from him in disappointment. In 1816 he went via Switzerland to London, where he was revered as a poet and moved in the highest social circles. Right up until his early death he was one of the many exiles who drew political and emotional attention to the situation in Italy.

Foscolo's fate was by no means an isolated case. After conservative powers successfully crushed both the repeated attempts at revolution in the former Napoleonic Empire and the effort of democrats and liberals across Europe to reverse the internal political consequences of the Congress of Vienna, hundreds and thousands of opposition members fled the countries concerned. Polish, German, Spanish, Greek and Italian refugees met in places where they appeared to be safe from imprisonment or death sentences. These European exiles were typically mostly wealthy and educated. The transnational political experience they gained in Britain, Switzerland, France, the Ottoman Empire and North and South America was to shape their subsequent political culture profoundly. Historian Maurizio Isabella argues that political ideas of importance to the Italian nation state movement were born in the context of European and American debate. Political circles emerged that exploited all the available media and means of communication to mobilise the global and international public. The most popular refuges were Paris, London, Zurich, Geneva and Brussels. Until the passing of the Aliens Act in 1905, Britain was the most generous host country in Europe. No foreigners were refused entry, certainly no suppressed liberals from the continent, and nobody was later expelled for their political activities in Britain.

After the failure of the revolutions and conspiracies in the Kingdom of the Two Sicilies, Austria, Lombardy and the Kingdom of Sardinia-Piedmont, most exiles initially made their way to Spain, which was favoured as a destination after 1820–1823 because of its liberal monarchy. Agostino Bistarelli was able to identify around 850 Italian exiles in Spain in the 1820s. Those fleeing northern Italy were given financial and organisational support by the governor of Genoa and shipped to Spain with the governments' knowledge. The majority, up to 60 per cent, were military personnel, followed by young students and those in the liberal professions. They were mostly born after 1789 and a surprising number were not urban citizens but had previously lived in the provinces. Whereas bourgeois exiles went to Spain to fight for the constitutional state against the interventionist troops of Louis XVIII, who overthrew the *Triennio* in 1823, the nobility from Piedmont and Lombardy chose to live in France or Britain, particularly attracted by the British form of government and its political stability. When Spain turned back towards restoration, revolutionary Italians and their Spanish counterparts fled to France.

A great deal of attention has been paid to political exile in France, especially for the period after 1830, not least because the liberal July monarchy introduced the right to political asylum in 1832. However, the fact that hundreds of Italians were already resident in France under the Bourbons is frequently overlooked. They were closely monitored by the police and, as a consequence, we are comparatively well informed about them. Several hundred exiles from southern and northern Italy were under surveillance by the French Ministry of the Interior. Paris was considered to be a place of political subversion and they were generally not tolerated there. As a result, Conte di Morozzo and Marquess de Prié, for example, had to take up residence in Bourges where the prefect had them put under close observation. The police reported on their everyday lives in minute detail. The few who lived in Paris were under even stricter military and police control to prevent any further political involvement. If the exiles contacted the French opposition in any way, they were made to leave the city they had been assigned to or were immediately expelled from the country.

Not all the exiles remained political agitators. Isidore Palma, for example, one of the leading rebels from Alessandria, whose comrades in arms had been executed in Piedmont, lived a completely unremarkable existence. Others, on the other hand, such as Santorre di Santarosa, continued to lead the life of one of the many Italian 'professional revolutionaries'. Born in 1783 Santarosa, who came from the Piedmontese civil service and military elite, was mayor of his home town Savigliano during the Napoleonic period and served as sub-prefect in La Spezia from 1812–1814. He was influenced politically and culturally by Rousseau, Foscolo and Vittorio Alfieri. After 1815 he joined the army in Piedmont and became a member of a secret political society. Santarosa was at the centre of those responsible for the revolution in the Kingdom of Sardinia-Piedmont in 1821 and when Charles Albert fled the country, he became minister of war in the short-lived provisional government. He escaped persecution by fleeing to Switzerland where he published a well-received memoir, *De la révolution piémontaise,* purposely written in French to reach a wider audience. He then moved to France where he spent some months in jail and from there to Britain where he survived by teaching languages. Together with Giacinto Provana di Collegno, a former aristocratic officer under Napoleon, and other key revolutionary figures from Piedmont, he rushed to Greece to support their struggle for independence against the Ottoman Empire and was killed in combat. His fate was typical of the dedication of Italian exiles, many of whom had to move from country to country and used both numerous publications and force as weapons to fight against contemporary authoritarian regimes.

Foscolo may have 'founded' Italian exile very early on, but Italy's best-known and most influential political exiles worldwide were undoubtedly Giuseppe Mazzini and Giuseppe Garibaldi. Following failed attempts at insurrection, Mazzini moved to Marseille where he founded *Giovine Italia* in 1830. He was inspired by contacts with other exiles and the democratic, republican atmosphere in France and was now ready for open political struggle with the clear aim of founding a republican nation state. After the defeat of all the previous isolated, uncoordinated local and regional uprisings, he worked together with young exiles towards a national rebellion. The number of Mazzini's supporters grew rapidly in Liguria, Tuscany, Romagna and a little later in Piedmont and Lombardy. They built up networks and tried to spread his ideas within Italy. In the middle of 1832, Mazzini was accused of conspiracy by the French, Austrian and Piedmontese governments and the police attempted to arrest him, so in 1833 he fled to Switzerland. He and his political friends were planning a military expedition to Piedmont, an attack that Mazzini hoped would trigger an international conflict. His plans earned a good deal of sympathy from supporters of democracy in Europe and in February 1834 Polish, French and German republicans also in exile in Switzerland took part in the famous

Savoy campaign. Approximately 200 men were involved in this military offensive, including 140 Poles who had fled from Russian persecution after the failure of the revolution. The campaign ended in disaster. The Piedmontese line infantry swiftly routed the insurgents. Mazzini had clearly overestimated the amount of support they could expect from wider sections of the Italian population.

After this painful defeat Mazzini again fled to Switzerland where he transformed his idea of the liberation of Italy into a concept for the whole of Europe. 'Young Italy' was transformed into 'Young Europe'. Together with representatives of the German and Polish exiles, Mazzini signed a declaration of solidarity, an act of fraternity, *Atto di Fratellanza,* on 15 April 1834 in Bern. German and Polish exiles had already formed 'Young Germany' and 'Young Poland' respectively. Now their joint aim was the liberation of 'enslaved' nations from their 'tyrants', and a federative European democratic order under a united leadership. Their motto was 'liberty, equality and humanity'. Their founding members were seven Italians, five Germans, and five Poles, all of whom had fled from their home countries after failed insurrections and attempts at revolution. However, the celebratory act of foundation in Bern in April 1834 remained no more than a noble gesture. Circumstances prevented the group from having any political influence, let alone becoming a threat. There was huge diplomatic pressure on Switzerland, particularly on the part of Austria. After further public protests, the founding members were forced to leave the country. Mazzini decided to go to London where, apart from his involvement in the 1848 revolution as head of the short-lived Roman Republic, he remained as a journalist and writer fighting for a republican nation state until shortly before his death in 1872.

If Mazzini was the 'brain' of the movement for a democratic Italian nation state, Giuseppe Garibaldi adopted the role of its 'sword'. Born as a merchant's son in 1807 in what was then French Nice, he became a sea captain and was influenced early on by Mazzini's ideas. He joined the *Giovine Italia* movement and fought beside Mazzini in the Savoy campaign of 1834. Threatened by a death sentence in Piedmont, Garibaldi fled to South America and took part in various revolutions and uprisings in Brazil and Uruguay, always on the side of the revolutionaries and democrats. The famous redshirts with which Garibaldi equipped his troops originated at this time. The red material had been produced for a slaughterhouse in Montevideo that had gone bankrupt and was being sold off cheaply. From a military point of view, this choice of colour may not have been ideal, but the shirt became a symbol of the will to sacrifice and of a certain fanaticism of Garibaldi and his supporters. He achieved greatest military renown when he and Mazzini put up a spirited defence of the Roman Republic against papal and superior French troops in 1849 and when he conquered Sicily with volunteer forces in 1861. His indefatigable commitment for the cause of democratic nation states, and his charisma made him a 'hero of both worlds', Europe and America. International press coverage and Garibaldi's own stylisation of himself as a death-defying gaucho in a poncho contributed substantially to this image of the fearless folk hero.

Fig. 5 Henri Lehmann, Cristina di Trivulzio di Belgiojoso, 1843.

Female exiles were a rarity. By far the best known was *La prima Donna d'Italia*, Cristina Trivulzio di Belgiojoso. Born in 1808 in Milan, this immensely rich patrician was no doubt one of the most important female intellectuals to campaign for a liberal nation state during the Risorgimento. Her family belonged to the circle of elites agitating against Austrian authority throughout the *Vormärz* (pre-1848). Her stepfather, Alessandro Visconti d'Aragona, was involved in the thwarted conspiracy of 1821, charged and sentenced to jail. Like so many of her like-minded friends, both male and female, state repression forced Cristina Trivulzio di Belgiojoso to spend many years of her life in exile in Paris. She was served a summons to appear in court in Milan for treason. After 1831 she remained in Paris where she worked as a journalist for the liberal paper *Constitutionnel*, reporting on the situation in Italy. Although she was a writer, her main commitment was as ambassador of the Italian national movement and advocate for the numerous refugees to whom she also lent financial support after the sequester on her estates in Lombardy was lifted. She used her fashionable salon to build political networks. The groups she hosted were comprised of the elite of exiled Italians and liberal French politicians and historians, including Adolph Thiers, François Mignet, Terenzio Mamiani and Niccolò Tommaseo. There was also the occasional conservative liberal guest such as Benso di Cavour, who happened to be visiting an agricultural trade fair in Paris. Her popular salon was also visited by members of the European artistic intelligentsia, among them Heinrich Heine, Honoré de Balzac, Frédéric Chopin and Franz Liszt. Together with her friend General Lafayette, Princess di Belgiojoso founded a relief agency to support the numerous Italian exiles in France. At the beginning of the 1840s, a general amnesty enabled her to return to Lombardy and she subsequently commuted between her old and new homes. Cristina Trivulzio di Belgiojoso was an example of the women from the Italian social elites who used both their money and their pen to campaign for the nation state. In her case, however, political commitment went far beyond the norm.

It was a notable exception for a woman to go into exile alone. The majority were accompanying their male relatives who were fleeing from political persecution. Surviving correspondence provides valuable information about the lives of Costanza Trotti Bentivoglio Arconati and her sister Margherita in exile. Costanza's husband was one of the aristocrats sentenced to death in absentia in Milan in 1824 for his participation in the conspiracy of 1821, and she decided to follow him into exile. Arconati had inherited not only a townhouse in Brussels but also Gaasbeek Castle not far from the city. This swiftly became a meeting place and refuge for Italian liberals. Giovanni Berchet and Vincenzo Gioberti were among the guests. On a visit to her sister, Margherita met Giacinto Provana di Collegno, whose life was typical of that of an exile. A young Piedmontese aristocrat, he had been trained in Napoleon elite school Saint-Cyr and served as an officer under Napoleon. After 1815 he joined the Savoy army and belonged to the liberal aristocratic circle around Prince Charles Albert. Both Giuseppe Arconati Visconti and Giacinto Provana di Collegno were connected to secret societies in Milan and Turin respectively and called for constitutions based on the Spanish model. When the revolution failed in 1821, Provana fled to the preferred countries of exile, initially to Switzerland, then to France and Britain. There he joined fellow Turin conspirator Santorre di Santarosa as a volunteer fighter in the campaign for Greek independence. He met Margherita in Gaasbeek in 1827 and married her in Bonn in 1836. In private, both sisters were involved in the political debate, they supported networks and campaigned for an Italian nation state, liberated from the Austrian 'yoke'. Costanza Trotti Bentivoglio Arconati was impatient for the Kingdom of Sardinia-Piedmont to finally take up arms against the Habsburgs.

During their years in exile, but particularly after the foundation of the nation state, the exiles created heroic and romantically idealised images of their lives, through memoirs, poems, novels and biographies. Their experiences as politically persecuted migrants played a key role in patriotic discourse. Exile permitted them to boast superior ethics and virtues: they had suffered for the fatherland far from their families. Foscolo was celebrated by Mazzini as the exile par excellence. He stood for a life in exile marked by sacrifice and poverty but also by the consistency of his principles and his love of the fatherland. The freedom to choose to leave one's homeland became a noble duty when liberty was robbed by a despot. Exile and even martyrdom became matters of political and romantic honour. Apart from Mazzini and Foscolo, it was mainly the poet Vittorio Alfieri whose poems and dramas extolled liberty, the fatherland and heroic rebellion against despots. The adventure of political migration was elevated to a moral imperative in his works. Authors drew willingly on the example of Dante Alighieri. They saw him as the founder of political exile and thus their forerunner. The tragic figures of Italian exiles populated contemporary romantic novels in France and Britain. In the liberal-conservative cultural magazine *Revue des Deux Mondes,* exile was described as a type of national tradition south of the Alps and voluntary or enforced exile as a key element of politics, frequently evoking romantic emotions and intense suffering.[5] A further influence on this emotional idealisation was the image of the fatherland as a metaphorical equivalent of the mother. Exile ruptured an individual's close connection to the nation, that is to their natural or even biological family. The discourse was, however, not only emotionally but also religiously charged. Political exiles were seen as martyrs, their travels as pilgrimages and their propaganda activities as a political apostolate. Giuseppe Mazzini was foremost in drawing comparisons with the disciples of Jesus.

In the second half of the century, thousands of exiles from the noble and bourgeois elites were to occupy key positions in the liberal kingdom of Sardinia-Piedmont and the young Kingdom of Italy and were thus paramount in shaping their substance. Their transnational, political, military and cultural experiences in neighbouring European countries, sometimes over decades, influenced their political activity after 1848–1849. However, it should also be noted that this 'generation Bonaparte' was mainly made up of frustrated aristocratic officers who, after the *Gloire* in the *Grande Armée* and the restrictions imposed by restoration policies, joined the opposition. The majority of exiles were soldiers and not intellectuals and most of them aspired to a liberal-conservative monarchy. After the events of 1820–1823 in Spain, the 'people' were for them no longer a valid political force. Since the lower classes had supported the counter revolution their political competence was seriously questioned. Giuseppe Pecchio, a senator in the former Kingdom of Italy, was of the opinion that it was the backwardness of the people in southern Europe that was the problem. The right to vote should be reserved for competent citizens. Their goal was now a state led by a king and a small elite without the sovereignty of the people and the 'liberation' of the nation. The chief enemy was in Vienna. The experience of exile, therefore, led not only to utopian, but also dystopian theories. There were of course still the famous democrats such as Mazzini, Garibaldi and even Buonarroti who campaigned most loudly and effectively, but they were a minority and were thus far unable to mobilise the masses for their political plans. Democratic aristocrats such as Conte Carlo Angelo di Bianco di Saint-Jorioz remained the exception. Later most democrats were quite prepared to become part of the liberal state, accepting positions of responsibility. The Constitution of Cádiz continued to lose its appeal while French bicameralism became more attractive. An Italian nation state comprising the whole of the peninsula was now not necessarily the ultimate goal. General Giacomo Durando, for example, wanted two kingdoms: a northern kingdom under the House of Savoy and a southern kingdom ruled by the Bourbons.

In general, care should be taken in portraying the exiles as a harmonious, consensual political family. Even in exile, there was frequent animosity and disagreement over the political future of Italy. Costanza Trotti Bentivoglio Arconati, for example, the mistress of Gaasbeek Castle, was a bitter rival of Cristina Trivulzio di Belgiojoso in Paris who, for her part, fell out with Mazzini because he accused her of not giving sufficient financial support to his operations like the Savoy campaign. In fact, Mazzini quarrelled with many exiles who he thought were not fighting for the sacred cause of the nation with sufficient vigour. The amnesties at the beginning of the 1840s led to many exiles returning home. Those who were not pardoned, however, rushed to Italy in 1848 to fight once again with words and weapons for liberal or democratic states on the Italian peninsula. Those who did not have to live in exile, however, also went in pursuit of transnational impulses and an exchange of ideas. Conte Camillo di Cavour, Conte Cesare Balbo, Baron Bettino Ricasoli and many more, travelled for years in Europe, preferably in France and Britain, in their quest for the best political system, for industrial progress and cultural exchange.

## Notes

1 Massimo d'Azeglio, I miei ricordi, Sesto San Giovanni 1915, p. 88.
2 Amerigo Caruso, Nationalstaat als Telos? Der konservative Diskurs in Preußen und Sardinien-Piemont 1840–1870, Berlin/Boston 2017, p. 158.
3 Carlo Felice di Savoia, Proclama 13 ottobre 1821, Turin 1821.
4 Carlo Cattaneo, Ugo Foscolo e l'Italia, Milan 1861, p. 34.
5 Charles de Mazade, Une vie d'émigré italien – Giacinto de Collegno, in : Revue des Deux Mondes, XXIX (1859), p. 460.

# 4. The Economy

## 4.1 Agriculture as king

At the end of the eighteenth century, Italians lived off agriculture. Although some produce was traded, the majority served to supply the domestic population. Depending on the region, more than 80 per cent of the population was employed in agriculture, a percentage that was similarly high in other European countries such as France. By the mid-eighteenth century, Italy had reached the end of a long-term economic decline. Between the eleventh and sixteenth centuries its economic and political core had been formed by its prospering cities. This was mainly due to trade with spices from the East and cloth produced within Italy, as well as the credit market and commercial dealings with the Levant. Eastern trade had been controlled mainly by the maritime republics of Venice and Genoa but also by smaller Italian ports. However, the discovery and expansion of transatlantic trade routes led to the Mediterranean cities dramatically losing their significance. Not only was trade with the East stifled by the more successful expansion of Portuguese, Spanish, French, Dutch and British trade relations but also, during the eighteenth century, Dutch and British shipping companies became established along the trans-Mediterranean routes and in the Italian ports.

In the early modern period Italian cities showed very little willingness and inclination to invest into proto-industrial projects. They preferred to seek more reliable profits in agriculture, even if they were lower. Here their investments were guaranteed by feudal jurisdiction and the dominant patrimonial ownership structures. In contrast to the mediaeval period, early modern Italian cities, therefore, ceased to be centres of manufacturing and finance. They were home to the wealthiest families of the feudal aristocracy and patricians, who lived off their investments and were essentially consumers. The urban bourgeoisie tended towards the liberal professions and the civil service rather than entrepreneurship. The largest cities in Italy were now seats of government and administrative and political centres and, in the case of Rome, also a religious centre. At the beginning of the nineteenth century, 141,000 people lived in Milan, in Venice it was 135,000, in Rome 138,000 and in Palermo also 141,000. Naples was still by far the most important Italian city and, with its 330,000 inhabitants, the third most populous in Europe after Paris and London. Italy had the highest proportion of people living in cities of more than 5,000 inhabitants in Europe. No other European region around 1800 could boast more than five cities with a population of more than 100,000.

A further European phenomenon can be observed in the Italian states during this 'saddle period', namely demographic change. Whereas 15.5 million people lived in Italy in the middle of the eighteenth century, within a century its population had expanded to 24 million, bringing with it an 80 per cent rise in the demand for food. The rapid growth in population was due to a significantly lower rate of mortality, which can be explained by improved hygienic and sanitary conditions and improvements both in the quantity and quality of the food supply. The cultivation of new high-calorie crops, such as maize, made it possible for the poor to change their patterns of food consumption. In spite of the sharp rise in the population, the increase in agricultural production was able to prevent famines. The only exceptions were the crises during the war years, the famine of 1772–1774 and the global crisis caused by the eruption of Mount Tambora in the South Pacific. Researchers consider this the most powerful volcanic eruption of the last 10,000 years and it caused a climate catastrophe in 1816–1817. After the violent explosion in April 1815, huge amounts of ash and aerosols made their way into the stratosphere and were dispersed around the world blocking the sun's rays. This resulted in a so-called 'volcanic winter' in which average annual temperatures dropped by three to four degrees. The eruption led to lower temperatures over several years, failed harvests and years of famine. Contemporaries were naturally unaware of the connection between the eruption and the ensuing catastrophe. Since existential problems were and still are frequently blamed on governments, this posed the reinstated rulers their first serious test at the beginning of the Restoration. Apart from a few major crises, however, agriculture in all the Italian states in the second half of the eighteenth century, and particularly in the first half of the nineteenth century, went through a process of dynamic transformation. The effects of this were long-term and exacerbated the already existing imbalance between the north and the south of Italy.

For international economic historians, nineteenth- and even twentieth-century Italy was only of interest as an example of a particularly difficult and flawed path towards a modern industrial society. Numerous studies concluded that the modern image of Italy was determined by clientelism and corruption, centralised bureaucracy, and an inefficient state economy. The factors they cited as obstacles to economic growth included the absence of an agricultural revolution, the inadequacy of infrastructure and a pronounced north-south divide. It is true that the Italian peninsula had practically no natural resources, especially no coal, and its geographical circumstances meant it could not be united into a single economic area. These were not ideal conditions and meant that Italy's economic take-off was delayed until around 1900.

However, economic historians always found it difficult to explain why Italy rose to become one of the fastest growing and strongest exporting industrial countries in Europe after World War II, in spite of these difficult beginnings. As a result, in the last two decades more historians have been exploring the long-term causes of this development and questioning the established paradigm of economic backwardness. Giovanni Federico and Jon Cohen have pointed out the paucity of statistical sources for the nineteenth-century Italian economy and highlighted data from the *Banca d'Italia* which testify to an overall higher economic growth than previously calculated. This sheds a somewhat more positive light on the agricultural sector. The authors emphasise the fact that in several regions modern methods of cultivation had been customary since the late nineteenth century and that landowners were by no means as hostile to innovation as had been previously assumed.

Yield and profits in agriculture were naturally significantly determined by soil conditions, the climate and ownership patterns. Three major systems can be roughly distinguished: one in the north of Italy, one in the centre and one in the south. In Lombardy and Piedmont in the north, large capitalist-run estates were predominant in the Po valley. Technically advanced irrigation systems were used and dependent day labourers were employed and socially-controlled by their mostly aristocratic owners. Among the most prominent was undoubtedly Conte Camillo Benso di Cavour. After trips to explore France and Britain, where he was fascinated by the railways, modern infrastructure and technical progress, Cavour became an aggressive, risk-taking manager of his inherited estates. With his friend, the banker Émile de la Rüe, he founded a company for the production of fertiliser, supported engineers who were developing mechanical threshing machines and speculated so successfully with grain that behind his back he was called a usurer. He was constantly on the lookout for successful business deals. In 1847, he wrote to de la Rüe: 'This year we've traded with guano and rice and maize. Next year it will be the turn of the banks and the railways'.[1] He constantly interfered in his tenants' work, not permitting them any independence. Cavour was no exception. Others, such as the Tornielli and Leonardi families from Novara, the Beraudo di Pralormo, Ferrero della Marmora and many more, increased their profits considerably by investing huge sums of money in canals and irrigation and drainage systems, and experimented with different methods of cultivation and animal breeding. These measures as a whole resulted in the agricultural regions of Piedmont becoming the most productive in Italy after 1850. In the hilly areas of northern Italy, on the other hand, the number of bourgeois landowners increased at the expense of church property. This process was not only the result of secularisation during the French period but had begun beforehand and continued after 1815.

Central Italy, for its part, was characterised by the *mezzadria* or sharecropping system, not only in the early modern period but also well into the twentieth century. In Tuscany, Umbria, the Marche, Romagna, Venetia and on the foothills of the Apennines in Latium, tenant families lived on farms that were supposed to sustain them. The balance of this sharecropping system was based on the struggle – the landowners would naturally have called it cooperation – between the families of the patron and the tenants, the *famiglia colonica.* While the tenant families had to organise the work to be done, the patrons controlled what was produced and what was handed over to them. Relations between the families were by no means limited to economic matters. The patron was also a figure of authority for the tenant families in many other matters of life. Half of what they produced was handed over in kind to the patrons as rent. Although this division of produce remained, orientation shifted towards the market during the 'saddle period'. This refutes the earlier theory that the *mezzadria* stabilised the system and inhibited agricultural development. Before 1800 the principle was to feed the tenant family, but as demand from the market increased, pressure was placed on productivity and more intensive new technologies were employed. This often met with fierce opposition from the tenants, who complained that they were being forced to work harder. Eventually, however, it also meant that the tenant families were producing increasingly for the market and less for their own consumption.

Towards the end of the eighteenth century, a new system became established in central Italy: the *fattorie.* These were large estates that coordinated the activities of several small manor houses or farms called *poderi.* In 1830 there were approximately 50,000 *poderi* operating in Tuscany with the sharecropping system, of which 12,000 were run by approximately 1,000 *fattorie*, all of which were established in the eighteenth century. The spread of this system is indicative of increasing market orientation, since they produced mainly for the neighbouring cities.

The suth, the islands and the plains of the Papal States, i. e. Latium, were dominated by large arable estates, smaller farms on the coastal strips and herds of cattle grazing in the hills. Since the Middle Ages enormous flocks of sheep had been driven to graze on the higher, less fertile mountain areas. This transhumance was found especially in the Apennines, in the south and on the islands. Here, the number of bourgeois landowners also increased to an unprecedented extent, although the estates of the aristocracy remained largely unaffected. The bourgeoisie acquired land as a result of the reduction in church and feudal property and the dispersal of common land. This correlated with population growth and an increasing demand for food. The reform measures introduced after the end of the eighteenth century and during the Napoleonic period also transformed the southern Italian barons from feudal lords to landowners. The most backward conditions persisted on Sardinia. In 1850, 50 per cent of its agricultural land still consisted of communal property and demesnes.

The situation was quite different on Sicily, where although 90 per cent of agricultural land was still in feudal ownership in 1800, a reversal in property structures over the next 40 years led to 90 per cent then being privately owned. However, there was no change in the economic dominance of the nobility and hardly any in the composition of the ruling elites. Nor did increases in agricultural production benefit the bulk of the poor peasant population. Their living conditions were wors-

Fig. 6 Giovanni Fattori, The Rest (The Red Cart), 1887.

ened by the mounting loss of common land *(usi civici)*. Day labourers worked for the *gabelloti*, large tenants whose focus was grain production. The situation of the rural underclass was hardly better when they worked for bourgeois estate owners rather than for the nobility. Like the figure of Calogero Sedara in what is probably the best-known novel on social and political conditions in Sicily, Giuseppe Tomasi di Lampedusa's *Il Gattopardo*, the bourgeois estate owners in the story of Prince Salina turned out to be even more mercenary and unrelenting than their aristocratic counterparts. Bourgeois entrepreneurs in particular introduced progress in the countryside with new initiatives, such as the cultivation of citrus fruits. The aristocracy also eventually adapted to the new situation and adopted new business practices. This was an inevitable process in the course of the desired boost in production.

Everywhere in Italy, not only in Sicily, increasing productivity can be observed in the 'saddle period'. It resulted from the dissolution of the social and economic orders of the *Ancien Régime*, the rise in the labour factor and the application of new techniques and new crops. There were wide regional differences, which depended not only on property structures but also on climatic conditions and soil quality. While cereals, maize and grapes for wine were grown everywhere, the individual regions specialised in particular crops. In the foothills of the Alps, the productivity and techniques for the cultivation of maize advanced most significantly. Its high yield meant that it became the preferred food of the poorer sections of the population. Maize became for Italy what the potato was for Northern Europe. However, the malnutrition stemming from this unbalanced diet caused a disease known as *pellagra* which could lead to skin complaints and diarrhoea and eventually damage the nervous system. The name of the disease comes from its main symptom *pellagra* which means rough skin. Rice, in contrast, was still far too expensive as a staple food for the masses. It became a popular food only for the urban upper and middle classes.

By far the most profitable export article was raw silk from northern Italy. It was considered to be the best available on the international market. The care of silkworms in the mulberry trees was entrusted to the tenant farmers in the hills on a sharecropping (*mezzadria)* basis. Mulberry trees were grown in Piedmont, Lombardy, Venetia, the Papal Legations, Tuscany and Latium. There was also significant silk production in certain locations in the south. In 1861, 20 per cent of Italian silk came from Campania, Calabria and Sicily. However, enormous increases in exports of silk in the first half of the century were mainly attributable to Lombardy and Venetia, where approximately 1.5 million kilograms of silk were produced in 1815, 3.5 million in 1841 and around 4.4 million mid-century. Two-thirds of this was produced in Lombardy. Initially their main customer was Britain and it was only after the price of Italian silk in Britain was undercut by Chinese and Indian goods that the merchants began to sell raw silk to France, chiefly Lyon, Germany and Russia. The government in Turin had hoped to generate higher profits by selling the end product, but its efforts to prevent the export of raw silk were unsuccessful, since it was instead smuggled into the neighbouring states.

Whereas raw silk was the most important commodity in the north, in the south, besides grain, olive oil became the most important export in the first half of the nineteenth century. Demand for it came mainly from the British, French and Dutch, who, if they did not use it for lamps or soap production, used the oil in industrial processes to make fabrics more supple. The figures for the rise in exports of olive oil from the Mezzogiorno are remarkable. In the 1830s and 1840s olive oil was exported to the sum of five million ducats, but this rose to nine million by the end of the 1850s. This increase can only be explained by the expansion of olive plantations. The main areas for the cultivation of olives were in Apulia, Terra di Bari and Otranto, as well as in Calabria. Production in Apulia experienced a significant upswing after the 1840s, since its oil was now no longer exported in its natural state but was enhanced by technological improvements in its refining and preserving. Growing demand was satisfied not only by extending the areas of land cultivated, but also in the case of oil and wine by the targeted use of sulphur.

Further goods in demand for export from the nineteenth century onwards were citrus fruits and almonds from the south and particularly wine, which was constantly improving in quality. Although Marsala wine had more or less disappeared from the international market before the unification of Italy, excellent wines from Tuscany and Piedmont became increasingly popular. And in this sector, it was once again primarily the aristocrats prepared to experiment and invest who developed the best wine-growing estates. At the Castello di Grinzane, Camillo Cavour cultivated a Barolo which is considered one of the best Piedmont wines to this day. Baron Bettino Ricasoli, his successor as Italian prime minister, made a similar contribution towards improving quality wines in Tuscany. After the failure of the revolution in 1850 he inherited his father's estates which were completely bankrupt. An income of 100,000 lira was not sufficient even to pay the interest on the debts. Ricasoli shut down his residence in Florence, moved to the countryside and taught himself chemistry and agriculture. During the next decades, he succeeded in producing an excellent Chianti in the Arno valley using the Tuscan sharecropping system. Like Cavour, Ricasoli intervened in the production process, oversaw the selection of grape varieties and the work in the vineyards and dismissed incompetent tenants and their families. The traditional autonomy of the tenants disappeared also as a result of having to renew leases annually. Ricasoli perfected production and marketing. On his death in 1880 his lands were free of debt and his family inherited a handsome fortune. As in the case of Cavour, Ricasoli's involvement in Tuscany was by no means an exception. He is merely a prominent and well-researched example of a new type of aristocratic entrepreneur who introduced capitalist methods into agriculture. Further examples of the old Tuscany nobility are the Peruzzi family, famous as powerful bankers in Florence during its mediaeval heyday, and the family of Cambray Digny. Both Luigi Guglielmo Conte di Cambray Digny and Ubaldino Peruzzi combined their offices as mayors of Florence and ministers in the young nation state with particularly successful involvement in the modernisation of the production of wine. Peruzzi, who happened to be related to Ricasoli and to be the grandson of the last member of the Florentine Medici family, by no means confined himself to agriculture, but like Cavour enjoyed speculating, including in the railways.

## 4.2 Manufacturing and the beginnings of industry

In comparison to the early industrialised countries, Italy is often accused of economic backwardness whereas Britain and the German states in particular are cited as shining examples during the 'saddle period'. Is there any sense in making such comparisons and what parameters are they based on? Was heavy industry the only means to becoming a modern society? The industrial zones of northern and central Europe were still islands in an ocean of agriculture well into the nineteenth century. The leading German and British industrial areas emerged where there were large coal deposits, that is in the Ruhr area, in Silesia and the Saar basin, or in Wales, Yorkshire and Scotland. In Italy, on the other hand, this black gold was only to be found at smaller sites in the Apennines. Iron ore deposits were limited to Aosta and Vercelli (Piedmont), southern Tuscany, Elba and Sardinia. Developing an economy based on the exploitation of large coal deposits as happened north of the Alps was simply impossible. A further factor was a certain scepticism in the attitude of members of the wealthy upper classes towards industry. They distrusted swift, aggressive industrialisation, since on their travels to Britain they had been able to observe its social consequences: pauperism and the development of a proletariat. Even Cavour, whose approach to the economy before the foundation of the nation state was extremely dynamic and liberal, assumed that industrialisation in Italy was only desirable in the so-called 'natural' sectors, i. e. in foodstuffs and textiles. In his opinion, these sectors should advance gradually and without state intervention.

Comparing Italy with its Mediterranean neighbour states, rather than with northwest Europe, shows that its role as far as manufacturing, mechanisation and industrialisation are concerned was even pioneering. The number of factories during the *Ancien Régime* was still small, but there were some highly esteemed production sites. One of the earliest European porcelain factories, that of the Ginori family in Tuscany, certainly enjoyed international renown. Porcelain had first been successfully manufactured in 1710 in Meissen and previously had to be imported from China. The first Italian porcelain factory was founded by Marquess Gino Ginori in 1737 in Doccia, his country estate northwest of Florence. On a diplomatic trip to Vienna, he had visited the porcelain manufacturers Du Paquier in Vienna and recruited porcelain painters there. Doccia produced luxury tableware for the Italian nobility, who had their coat of arms burnished on it, but beyond that it manufactured Baroque sculptures in the Florentine style, large-scale sculptures depicting classical and biblical themes, and chinoiseries and exuberant figurines as table centrepieces. In a period of conspicuous luxury consumption, these kinds of high-quality artefacts made of 'white gold' could earn a fortune. Apart from the respected porcelain painters, Ginori employed members of his tenant families in Doccia, whom he recruited as and when required. This permitted the porcelain to be produced at a relatively low cost. The resulting specimens were and still are sought-after prestige objects and collector's items in Europe.

Meanwhile in the neighbouring Papal States, paper production experienced a remarkable boom in the Marche. In Fabriano, a small city near Ancona, paper had been produced since the Middle Ages but had been squeezed out of the market at the end of the eighteenth century by more high-quality products from France. In 1782, an employee of one of the numerous small production sites in Fabriano by the name of Pietro Milani founded a paper manufacturing company together with Conte Antonio Vallemani. The Conte made his paper mill available and provided the financing while Milani contributed entrepreneurial spirit and technical expertise to their joint venture. After a short time, Milani's machines were producing paper more efficiently and in much better quality, which was able to challenge the competition from abroad. This success was crucially driven by numerous experiments and the consistent use of the most up-to-date techniques. Milani was alone in the Papal States to succeed in producing so-called silk paper, whose chief characteristic was its uniform transparency and fine texture. He bought up one mill after the other

Fig. 7 Gionori Porcelain Manufactory, The Lamentation over the Dead Christ, 1745/46.

in Fabriano and managed to rise from being a dependent worker to becoming the owner of an entire business empire. In 1817, he passed on his life's work to his three sons, who continued to expand the business in the nineteenth century. Both Milani's company and that of the Ginori in Tuscany went on to produce paper and ceramics respectively well into the twenty-first century, albeit in modified forms and under different ownership.

In the kingdom of Naples Ferdinand IV himself took the initiative in promoting the production of the popular silks. His father, Charles III, had already set up a porcelain factory on Capodimonte outside the gates of Naples in 1743. This involvement put the Bourbons on equal footing with numerous other rulers of the *Ancien Régime* who supported the manufacture of porcelain, glass, ceramics, tapestries and wallpapers throughout Europe. In 1776, a silk factory modelled on the French royal factory was set up near Caserta, Ferdinand's huge summer residence. Here in San Leucio, he had his hunting lodge transformed into a centre for silk manufacture. The process was technologically advanced using looms imported from Piedmont and the Languedoc for the first time. Machines were used to throw and reel the silk thread which was then woven into fabrics by the workers in the factory. There was a strict hierarchy amongst employees and their work was regulated by a charter stipulating duties and schedules. This imposed rigid discipline on worker families, for whom, in return, a settlement of terraced houses was purpose-built. Silk and woollen cloth had previously been produced in southern Italy by means of the putting-out system. The silks manufactured in San Leucio were of the highest quality and sold well. Whether they would have been able to hold their own on the market without the support of the royal family is an open question. There are further examples of successfully functioning factories during the period of the French revolution such as the wool-spinning mills in Piedmont (Biella) and Tuscany (Prato).

Many factories in Italy came under considerable pressure at the beginning of the Coalition Wars, and as a result of Napoleon's Continental System, even though modern liberal legislation had an essentially positive influence. However, the effect of Napoleon's protectionist economic policy, which was intended to safeguard French goods from competition from abroad, was to weaken the economies of its neighbouring states. A trade agreement with the Kingdom of Italy enforced by the emperor favoured the import of raw materials to France and conversely the sale of French manufactured products to Italy. Naturally these conditions did not encourage large-scale investment in early industrial projects in northern Italy. The situation was different, however, in the annexed Italian regions, since they profited from Napoleon's protective tariffs. The huge demand for army supplies further fuelled the demand for cloth, sulphur, gunpowder, iron and weapons. After the collapse of the Empire, most of the businesses that had produced goods under these favourable economic conditions were plunged into a crisis.

The situation was similar in the kingdom of Naples. Its rulers Joseph Bonaparte and his successor Joachim Murat had succeeded in confidently and vigorously promoting industry in the interests of their state and against the wishes of Napoleon. However, since Murat rejected any kind of protectionism in the form of custom duties, most of the southern Italian companies had to compete with superior quality goods from abroad. For the first time, foreign capital flowed into the country on a significant scale, and in the manufacturing sector the south gained the edge over the north. Overall, it can be said that, apart from in the production of iron and silk, the origins of the mechanisation of work processes in manufacturing date back to the Napoleonic period.

After 1815, businesses had to find their way back into dealing with more and smaller Italian states and new systems of customs duties. Since the majority of exports went abroad and very few to the neighbouring states, however, domestic tariffs did not play a particularly important role. Nevertheless, Italian producers found it difficult to conquer new markets. After the end of Napoleon's Continental System, cheaply produced cottons from Britain flooded the continent. As in Britain, the textile sector in Italy was the first to exhibit the typical characteristics of industrial production, namely, concentration, mechanisation, the use of energy and no use of seasonal labour. As far as early industrial development is concerned, it can be said in general that those locations which had been producing for a long time in whatever form, whether the putting out system or early manufacturing, were where the roots of early industrialisation and modernisation processes sprouted. All the companies introduced machines from the pioneering industrial regions of Europe, copied them, refined them and recruited technical experts.

In the early nineteenth century, Biella in Piedmont and Prato in the Duchy of Tuscany became the absolute world leaders in wool and cloth manufacturing. Success in early industrial development depended on location factors and family dynasties with entrepreneurial skill. Bella lies in the foothills of the Alps and is inextricably linked to the name of Sella, a family that had been engaged in textile production since the sixteenth century. In 1817, Pietro Sella, who had first trained in Britain, was encouraged by the minister of the interior, Roger de Cholex, to set up a textile machine workshop in his home town. Local coal deposits could be exploited in the area and the first mechanical spinning machines were imported from the famous Cockerill works in Seraing in Belgium. Belgian technicians were also recruited. Later, mechanical looms were imported and the family set up a company generating hydroelectric power. The most prominent scion of the family in the late nineteenth century was Pietro Sella's son, Quintino. Having studied engineering in Turin and Paris at the *École des mines*, he initially pursued a career as a mineralogist. In 1860 he resigned from his professorship in Turin in order to help shape the young nation state as an economic politician sympathetic to industry and finance as for the *Destra Storica (Historical Right).*

Another family whose involvement shows striking parallels to the economic and technical activities of the Sella family in Piedmont were the Mazzonis in Prato not far from Florence. Wool and textiles had also been produced here in Tuscany since the early modern period. Giovanni Battista Mazzoni, a member of one of the local cloth manufacturing families, was in the first cohort of students in the *Scuola normale superiore* founded by Napoleon in Pisa. After the change of rulers, the Habsburg Grand Duke Ferdinand III recognised the young man's extraordinary talent and gave him a grant to continue his academic studies in Paris. When he returned to Tuscany in 1820, he used a former monastery to set up a factory whose machines were driven by hydraulics. He also perfected a spinning frame for carded wool yarn and co-founded a bank. After 1850 Mazzoni succeeded in applying a new technique to recycle bulk imported fabric remnants and discarded clothing and mix them with new fresh wool to produce much cheaper textiles that were in high demand abroad. As *gonfaloniere (mayor)* of Prato, he campaigned for the creation of a trans-Apennine railway that would connect his hometown with Florence and Bologna.

There were also similarly successful textile and wool producing centres in Venetia, Lombardy and the Papal States which all had the same characteristics, namely, traditional families of entrepreneurs who recognised the signs of the times, local hydropower at their disposal and the ability to rely on craftsmen who had long since acquired technical skills and thus provided a kind of potential workforce reserve. In Schio in Vicenza province, for example, wool had been produced since the fifteenth century. Here in the Leagro valley, Alessandro Rossi built one of the largest textile factories in the country. In 1873, his company *Lanerossi* made the leap from a family business to a public limited company. In the neighbouring town of Valdagno, meanwhile, the Marzotti family set up their factories. The workers who had been previously working in isolation in the putting-out system were brought together in Luigi Marzotti's company. His son Gaetano gave up trading with finished products and concentrated wholly on production. He was raised to nobility as a count and went on to represent the interests of the province in the national parliament. As a patron Marzotti invested his wealth in contemporary art. Like Mazzoni, he was also a champion of local railway construction. In London in 1879 he recruited support to found a railway company, the *Province of Vicenza Steam Tramway Company,* which enabled the transport of raw materials and commuting workers. In Lombardy the numerous production sites for silks and textiles in the Alps and in and around Milan are particularly noteworthy.

In the south of Italy, it was unusual for factories to be concentrated in one area as they were around Biella, Schio and Milan. Centres of early industrial production emerged in the Papal States in southern Latium. In Isola del Liri with its great waterfalls and in nearby Sora and Arpino, hydraulically powered wool and paper manufacturing developed, employing several thousand workers between 1820 and 1860. The introduction of Dutch machines meant that eventually sufficient paper could be produced to prevent further dependence on expensive imports. In the Kingdom of the Two Sicilies, various products including profitable silk fabrics were manufactured in Cosenza. A further important location was Salerno, not far from Naples, where again favourable conditions were provided by hydraulic power from the Sarno and Irno rivers, sufficient wool and low labour costs, combined with a population traditionally employed in the textile industry. Nevertheless, before unification only very few companies existed in the south which could be called industrial.

In the first half of the nineteenth century, some early progress was made in the chemical industry. However, the shortage of coal made itself sorely felt in this sector, since most of it had to be imported at great cost and could only be partly compensated by hydro power. There was insufficient coal for the treatment and processing of iron ores, copper and zinc, and for the extraction of sodium carbonate, chlorine and magnesium. There was also insufficient iron ore and sulphur in Italy to support a significant chemical industry. The only place where there were large sulphur deposits was in Sicily where in the 1840s sulphur exports made up 20 per cent of its total export volume. Sulphur mining in Sicily continued to use traditional methods and employed 16,000 workers in conditions that were inhumane and a health hazard. In the north the chemical industry stagnated, for example in the areas of fertiliser and soap manufacture.

The mechanisation of the cotton industry was followed by the manufacture of machinery and eventually by the railways. Industrialisation gradually spread, whereby the development in northern Italy was conspicuously more dynamic than in the south. Growth was mainly concentrated in Piedmont, Lombardy and Liguria and its centres Milan, Turin, and Genoa with their rich elites, their industries, transport links and opportunities for technical training. They created the triangle that has remained instrumental to economic modernisation and industrial production to this day. Milan became the most important base for mechanical industries entering the Italian market. Around the middle of the century more than ninety workshops were active in Milan, creating the framework for the development of the metal industry in this, the most powerful economic region of Italy. Money from the production of silk poured into new industrial projects in the area. The enormously lucrative trade with silk had provided the nobility, particularly in Lombardy, with huge amounts of capital.

The most popular legal form of founding companies in Milan was limited partnerships. These comprised of a managing director who had a public role and the limited partners who simply signed the contract in front of a lawyer, and in this way, invested their surplus funds. They brought together business capital and technological know-how and extended entrepreneurial networks. Due to the fixed duration of the contract the limited partners were also unrestricted in their mobility. The most important business newspaper in Milan, *L'Eco della Borsa,* commented on this system in 1838: 'A man who is a skilled worker does not usually own the capital he needs: through limited commercial partnerships the lawmakers aim to combine capital and entrepreneurial spirit'.[2] The Elvetica foundry and machine factory, for example, which manufactured turbines, steam engines and machines for processing agricultural products, was founded in 1840 by Bouffier and Schlegel, members of the bourgeoisie, but its capital came from eight limited partners, nearly all from the urban aristocracy of Milan. Marquess Leopoldo D'Adda invested over 120,000 lira alone as a partner in Elvetica in 1850. Five years later, the company was employing between 350 and 400 workers.

*La Grondana,* a company in Milan that produced rolling stock for the railways, also provided forward-looking impulses. Rich Milanese notables gradually attempted to increase their assets by diversifying and investing outside their traditional focus on land, the silk trade and government securities. They became involved in machine factories, infrastructure projects and public service companies, such as the *Società del gas.*

While Milan as the capital of Lombardy developed into the centre of metal production and processing, they also gathered pace in other traditional sites such as Brescia, Bergamo and Dongo on Lake Como, where European know-how and old capital were similarly combined. In 1840, the Rubini family recruited an engineer from Alsace called Georges Henry Falck. Together they founded a company, Rubini, Falck, Scalini & Co., which was the first to use blast furnaces and the puddling process in the production of metal. This drastically reduced the amount of energy required. Meanwhile, Piedmont's metal industry was also consolidating in the Aosta valley and one of the leading metal factories in Liguria was established in Sampierdarena, nowadays part of Genoa. It was founded in 1846 by the British engineer Philip Taylor and the entrepreneur Fortunato Prandi and sponsored by the state, with the aim of providing the material required for the railway between Genoa and Turin. Taylor and Prandi, however, went bankrupt in 1852. The company was then taken over as a limited partnership by Italian bankers and the engineer Giovanni Ansaldo and was enthusiastically backed by the prime minister, Conte Camillo Cavour. It initially produced parts for the railway and then, as from 1854, the first Italian locomotive, the Sampierdarena. Raw materials came from the considerable iron ore deposits on the nearby island of Elba. Other metalworking towns and factories of note were Follonica in Tuscany, the *Mongiana* ironworks in Calabria which employed 1,000 workers in 1860, and the *Oretea* iron foundry in Palermo, which at this time employed 200 men.

All in all, these were significant beginnings which created the necessary basis for further industrial development in the second half of the nineteenth century, particularly in northern Italy. The shortage of coal was offset in many places by technically advanced hydro power using the plentiful rivers. And yet it must be stressed that compared to northern Europe, the iron and metal production industries in Italy never really flourished due to the overall lack of natural resources. While 3.7 million tons of iron were produced in Britain in 1861, Italy produced just under 30,000. Wealth and affluence continued to be acquired primarily from agriculture and the production of silk. In the middle of the century, Italy was populated by people working as peasants or day labourers, numerous artisans, merchants who were often also entrepreneurs, bankers and those employed in public administration and in the liberal professionals.

However, as in other areas of Europe, profits were increasingly likely to be made by speculation in rail company shares and through bank or insurance transactions. On 3 October 1839 the first railway line to Granatello di Portici along the Gulf of Naples was opened by King Ferdinand II in a grandiose ceremony. The line was 7.6 km long and its purpose was to take the king from Naples to his summer palace and European tourists on their Grand Tour to Herculaneum. In spite of these early beginnings in the south, progress in the north was much more dynamic. At the beginning of the 1860s, the south had 126 km of railways that had cost around one million lira. This was in contrast to 1,400 km of railway in Piedmont, Liguria, Lombardy and Venetia, enabled by investments of over twelve million lira, resulting in the north with its canals and railways being comparable to the other advanced regions of Europe in terms of infrastructure. In Turin Charles Albert was an energetic supporter of railways, whereas Pope Gregory XVI prevented similar investment in the Papal States. Immediately after the election of his successor Pius IX in 1846, however, it was possible to establish the first railway companies there too. Again, it was the rich, landed nobility that invested capital. At the head of the various railway companies were members of aristocratic Roman families, Borghese, Caetani, Corsini, Odescalchi and several others. Railway company shares were overall a popular form of speculation and helped to generate further wealth. The railway companies remained in private hands until the beginning of the twentieth century. Any attempts to nationalise them were thwarted by parliament.

The banking and insurance businesses were dominated by the same players but moneylending methods changed fundamentally in the nineteenth century. At the beginning of the century western European banking was completely haphazard by today's standards. The only exception was in the large trading cities such as London, Paris, Cologne and Florence, where even before 1800 large banks had been established. They granted loans to select business customers, but only to them. This meant that anyone seeking credit in western Europe had to depend on the private market. Throughout the whole of the nineteenth century, loans were granted by means of family, business and social networks, and these were only gradually supplanted by institutional financial transactions. The credit system in Italy worked through agriculture and trade in products from the primary sector. Private banks and savings banks then began to emerge during the long nineteenth century. In the 1830s and 1840s, the savings banks became a model for success. They were established in all major cities in Italy and were used to save modest sums of money. The purpose of the savings banks was essentially to protect people from poverty in old age – they did not provide risky loans for starting up new businesses. Another means of borrowing money was offered around 1860 by the approximately 1,000 *monti di pietà*, pawn shops, which were mostly directly or indirectly controlled by religious institutions. For a long time, the finance for founding new companies came from private capital by means of the limited partnerships mentioned above, in which family networks played a significant role. After the 1840s banks such as the *Banca di Torino* and the *Banca di Genova* were set up in the larger trading centres. They financed infrastructure projects and industrial enterprises on a large scale. Milan naturally developed into a first-class banking centre and the *Banca Nazionale* of Tuscany, founded in 1857, financed the iron industry in Follonica with private and international capital in order to accelerate modernisation processes.

## 4.3 European business networks

The growth of the Italian economy owes a great deal to the transnational activities of European immigrant merchants and entrepreneurs. However, the significant role played by Italian merchants in other countries should not be overlooked. It can be said in general that wherever business opportunities opened up in Europe, they were often grasped by foreigners who had certain technical training or capital at their disposal. According to Monika Poettinger, the proportion of foreign businesspeople in all major central European cities was around 30 to 40 per cent until the 1830s.

These economic migration patterns had a long tradition. In the late mediaeval period merchants, artists and bankers had already begun to make their way from the urban landscape of northern Italy to the most important European centres, but also to southern Italy and the Mediterranean and Black Sea regions. One of the most successful of these groups were the moneylenders, demonstrated by the fact that the word *Lombard* was a synonym for an exchange banker. Originally from the wider region around Asti, they were present in many European regions and highly valued for their expert mathematical skills. Still today their activities can be traced in the countless occurrences of 'Lombard Street' and *Rue de Lombards*. Even in the Middle Ages, people were generally prepared to accept particularly capable merchants and craftspeople from other countries. The 'Italians' were active everywhere, in the same way as the Armenians and the Jews. Apart from bank dealings, they traded in fabrics, spices and slaves. It was important to these new citizens to retain and cultivate their contacts back home, which led to the emergence of family networks with younger male relations following established entrepreneurs abroad. In the early modern period, economic migrants were joined by whole armies of painters, sculptors, architects and musicians devoting themselves to the service of the European courts and aristocracy.

In the eighteenth century, Italian merchants from the north of the country, sometimes disparagingly referred to as 'lemon and bitter orange merchants' by their German colleagues, made up an extremely successful group of Italian economic migrants. Those identifiable around 1800, particularly in south-west German cities, originated most significantly from the immediate or wider surroundings of the three lakes in Lombardy: Lake Maggiore, Lake Lugano and Lake Como. By far the largest groups lived in Mainz, Cologne and Frankfurt/Main and smaller cities such as Bonn, Trier (Trèves) and Koblenz located on navigable rivers. New branches of the business were established by male family members in neighbouring cities who traded in products from their northern Italian homeland, including citrus fruits, and within a short time managed an extraordinary rise into the leading bourgeois-aristocratic families of their adopted cities. They married daughters of the local merchant and civil service elite and were rapidly integrated into local politics. During the *Vormärz* (pre-1848) period they tended to be on the side of the liberals. In the following are just a few examples of the most famous Italian migrant families who proved to be true masters of integration. In Frankfurt there was the well-known family of the writer Clemens Brentano, and the wealthy merchant family Guaita from Codogna, a small town above Menaggio on Lake Como. In 1822 Georg Friedrich von Guaita became the first Catholic mayor in Frankfurt, a strictly Lutheran city. A branch of the Guaitas settled in Aachen as needle manufacturers and held the office of mayor there doing the French and Prussian periods. In Cologne, meanwhile, the Farina family had created the famous *Eau de Cologne.* It was a huge commercial success and is still produced to this day by the family business using the same recipe. And around 1800 the Puricelli family built up a successful ironworks empire in the Hunsrück region, west of the Rhine.

In the meantime, British, French and Swiss merchants and bankers settled in the Italian states. One of the most brilliant ascents was undoubtedly achieved by the Torlonia family. They came from the Auvergne and had settled in Rome in the mid-eighteenth century. They made an immense fortune from trading in cloth and grain and investing in cotton manufacturing, sawmills and mines, and later especially from art dealing and banking transactions. After 1800 they were the leading bankers in Rome. During the French period Giovanni Torlonia speculated successfully with army supplies and credit transactions and during the Restoration he and later his son Alessandro acted as bankers to the Pope and the European aristocracy visiting Rome. Giovanni and Alessandro accumulated aristocratic palaces, estates and titles, first that of a *Marchese di Romavecchia* and later a *Principe.* Alessandro, in particular, used his wealth to present himself in the style of Renaissance popes as a patron of the arts, sponsoring palaces, residences, art collections, theatres and archaeological excavations. A luxurious reception with more than 4,000 guests included Pope Gregory XVI and King Ludwig I of Bavaria. For another festival with music and fireworks, Alessandro invited twenty thousand Romans to his Villa Torlonia outside the city. The Roman poet Giuseppe Giacomo Belli, well-known for his biting sonnet about Roman society, wrote about this spectacle, praising the prince, saying he had made himself a name among the Roman people with this celebration. Stendhal's travelogues also contain long passages about the cultural and social antics of the Torlonia family, whereby the remarks relating to banking are extremely disrespectful.[3]

When Alessandro inherited his father's immense fortune after his death in 1829, he increased it and, like Cavour and Ricasoli, diversified his business. He was extremely successful in the banking and railway businesses throughout Europe and had close connections to James de Rothschild. At the same time, he continued to invest vast sums in agricultural engineering ventures and purchasing land. His largest undertaking was the draining of an entire lake, Fucino, south of Rome, an extraordinary project from a technical, cultural and social point of view, which enabled twenty thousand hectares of farmland to be reclaimed. In this way, the Torlonia succeeded in rising to become part of the landowning aristocracy in Rome. In 1870 nearly half of the Roman Campagna (91,000 ha) still belonged to only twenty-five noble families. The ten richest owned 75,000 hectares between them of which 26,000 were the property of the Torlonia family. They also owned large estates in more distant areas of the former Papal States.

A similarly illustrious example of elite economic migration is provided by the most powerful and influential European finance company, the Rothschilds, in Frankfurt/Main. The founder of this banking empire, Mayer Amschel Rothschild, sent his sons to carefully selected European centres, Paris, London and Naples, to establish branches of the company there. Karl Mayer von Rothschild established the family's fifth bank in Naples in 1820. In 1814 he had organised supplies to Wellington's troops and in 1821 financed the Austrian troops that assisted King Ferdinand I to put a swift end to the liberal revolution in Naples. In contrast to Torlonia, the Jewish banker Rothschild did not attempt to become integrated in his new location but commuted between Frankfurt and Naples. He also knew how to make a show of his new wealth. His magnificent Villa Pignatelli was situated on the Riviera di Chiaia coastal road with a view of Vesuvius in the vicinity of the palaces of the Italian aristocracy and provided accommodation for his elite European clientele when they were visiting the Gulf of Naples. After the death of Karl Mayer von Rothschild, his son Alphonse took over the branch in Naples. The bank always remained in close contact with the parent company in Frankfurt. When Alessandro Torlonia, in his capacity as treasurer to the Pope, attempted to restructure the heavily indebted Papal States with the aid of a huge state loan and his own funds were insufficient, he did not turn to the Rothschild bank in the neighbouring state, but to James de Rothschild in Paris. Following intensive negotiations, they concluded a contract for a huge issue of bonds, the first of a whole series. For more than twenty years after that, James de Rothschild was not only the most important banker in the Papal States but also in the other Italian states before unification. After the founding of the nation state, the Rothschild bank assumed the same function in the Kingdom of Italy. One of Rothschild's most powerful competitors in Naples was the Mörikhofer family, originally from Switzerland, who had initially been silk traders in Lyon. Towards the end of the seventeenth century, they moved their business to Naples and changed their name to Meuricoffre. They invested their profits from trading into the foundation of one of the most well-funded banks and, after 1815, in the same way as the Rothschilds, they became involved in managing the sovereign debt of various Italian states through banks in Paris and London.

The stories of these families, the Torlonias, the Rothschilds and the Meuricoffres, may seem to be isolated and outstanding examples of success stories, but they are in fact only particularly impressive examples of a complex transnational system of migration on the Apennine peninsula, in which the Swiss, Germans, French, English, Belgians and Greeks were the largest groups. Whereas migration was previously only studied in one direction, that is migration to the host country, there is nowadays increasing focus on circular paths with remigration processes, as in the case of the Rothschilds in Naples. The fact that some migrants returned home makes it difficult to measure the extent of migration. Official statistics did not yet exist and the borders were porous. One consistent phenomenon, however, can be observed whenever foreign companies were established, namely the enormous importance of family networks creating the trust essential for sometimes very risky business dealings. There was also an astonishingly high level of mobility.

The bankers and merchants mentioned here still represent the type of migration common in the eighteenth century. The largest cities and ports of the states in the *Ancien Régime* were home to numerous companies that traded in imports and exports on a commission basis. One business model that attracted foreign capital before 1800 was the close link between the establishment of a bank and the silk trade. Milan, for example, was the preferred location for German and Swiss entrepreneurs, whereas in neighbouring Bergamo around twenty business families from the cantons of Grisons, Zürich and the French Cevennes can be traced back to silk production during the 'saddle period'.

In the nineteenth century, a new type of business model emerged, namely entrepreneurs founding workshops and factories in collaboration with engineers who had the urgently required technical know-how. We have already encountered them in the context of both the numerous textile and paper factories and the ironworks and engineering companies in all the Italian states. At first glance, these migration processes seem to be similar for the individual cities, but a closer look at the periods in which the families settled reveals differences between the north and south of the country which mirror the processes of early industrialisation. The first evidence of these new types of foreign entrepreneur and engineer can be found in Lombardy, Piedmont and Liguria. They contributed particularly to the acceleration of industrial development in the textile sector, constantly importing new technologies and testing new organisation processes. Locally they competed and cooperated with traditional domestic companies.

Similar phenomena can be observed in the south: Naples, Messina, Palermo, Catania and Bari all attracted merchants, bankers and entrepreneurs from Switzerland, the German states, Britain and France, who played a leading role in the economic activities of the kingdom. The waves of migration can be categorised chronologically as follows: first there was a major influx after the middle of the eighteenth century. This was interrupted during the French revolutionary wars, only to increase again noticeably during the Napoleonic decade. In the 1830s numbers rose significantly when, in addition to the various initiatives in trade and banking, foreign companies invested massively into the cotton industry. In this sector, the unusual involvement of Swiss Protestants is striking. However, this last wave only affected Naples and Solano, and Bari marginally, whereas a steady stream mainly of merchants continued to enter the Sicilian cities.

Migration of foreign entrepreneurs to Italy has been generally well researched, with Protestant migration analysed most thoroughly. This is because there were both many Protestant migrants and they left easily recognisable traces, since for reasons of their denomination, they were unable or unwilling to integrate into the mainly Catholic society. These migration processes have been researched for Bergamo, Genoa, Milan, Turin and Naples. Daniela Luigia Caglioti has published in-depth studies on Naples, exploring the history of German and Swiss merchants and company owners through several generations. They brought with them capital and technical know-how, were well integrated into local information networks and skilfully exploited their superior resources. In Naples new social contacts were always limited to other Protestant families. The Germans and Swiss lived in a parallel society, family networks excluded Italian Catholics from their private lives, so that they always only married within their own circles. After the outbreak of World War I, this segregated status led to their internment and expulsion.

The situation was similar in Genoa, which was particularly popular with the Swiss and the British. As in Naples they felt compelled to maintain their own school, Protestant church, cemetery and hospital. They established a separate system of social organisations with a benevolent society, elite clubs and social clubs. The Protestant migrants in Bergamo and Milan, on the other hand, proved to be less isolationist. They acquired new citizenship, learned Italian, married locals, conducted business with Italian companies and participated in local and national politics. They also shared the social life of the Catholic majority. Nevertheless, they continued to cultivate their own language and their ties and solidarity with their own society in a very special way. Life was made easiest for the minority in Turin, where they encountered Protestant Waldensians, a religious minority that enjoyed widespread acceptance there. Far less is known about the thousands of Catholic entrepreneurs coming to Italy from France, Belgium, the German Confederation and the Habsburg Empire in the long nineteenth century, since they were much more easily assimilated into mainstream society.

## 4.4 Mobility and Migration

This considerable extent of mobility was by no means limited to the European merchant elites. It was a central element of economic and social life. As such it has received a great deal of attention in Italian historiography and has become institutionalised in research centres and specialised archives. Italian migration research owes its boom primarily to a current domestic political problem, namely the flow of migrants into Italy from poorer Mediterranean countries and Africa, who are seen increasingly as a burden, and which encourages historical comparisons. It also profits from the popularity of cultural history, whose favoured types of sources – diaries, memoirs, letters, photographs and songs – provide an almost unmanageable amount of material on this topic.

In Italy, thousands of people left their homes each year to earn their living elsewhere. Italian migration researchers focussed for a long time mainly on the huge number of migrants who left the country between 1870 and 1970. The highest estimates suggest that twenty-six million Italians left their home country during this period in exchange for an uncertain future abroad. The sheer extent of this phenomenon explains why various historians have referred to the migration of Italians as a veritable diaspora. However, this type of migration process is by no means peculiar to modern or recent history. Migration has a centuries-old tradition, not only in Italy. Although the figures for the huge Italian migration between 1870 and 1970 suggest that its character was different from that of earlier centuries, similar structures of individual and collective behaviour can in fact be found before 1870, particularly if we look at the micro-historical level. Migration was not only an escape from oppressive poverty, but also an important component of economic activity. There is no doubt, nevertheless, that the majority of people migrated because the place they lived in could not provide them with an adequate livelihood.

A determining factor for Italians migrating in the early modern period was the geographical location of their home. In the eighteenth century, people migrated from the countryside to the cities, particularly from poor mountainous areas to the plains and the coast. In the Alpine regions migration was the rule, not the exception. Around 1800 the proportion of those seeking work in the northern and central mountain areas – the Alps, the Apennines and the Abruzzi – had risen, depending on the season, to 14 or more per cent. This is the highest figure in any data on labour migration for this period. These people moved to the wider areas of the Mediterranean region but also crossed the Alps towards the north. Transitions between different types of mobility were fluid. Some mobility transformed into emigration but there was also a different kind of mobility to places nearer or further away that proved temporary. This was often the case for mountain dwellers and harvest workers who had strong roots in their home villages and yet only spent a few weeks in a year or a few years of their lives there. This complexity can be somewhat reduced by dividing migration into various categories.

The first category comprises the majority of the rural poor, who quite simply offered their own physical strength both in the cities and the countryside, as porters, servants, and unskilled and day labourers. The flow of migrants to the cities tended to take place in winter, whereas in the spring and summer, reapers and harvest workers looked for work in the country. The second category is made up of skilled itinerant artisans: carpenters, bricklayers, basket weavers, boilermakers, chimney sweeps and glaziers. A well-researched example is the large number of Italian pewterers or tinsmiths who worked in the Rhineland and Westphalia in the eighteenth and nineteenth centuries. Most of them originated in a small area west of Lake Maggiore with its centre in Valstrona, where they lived in a few neighbouring upper Alpine valleys before setting off across the Alps. As in the case of other migrant groups, not all those who left their homeland intended to settle abroad permanently, but around 40 per cent of the pewterers became de facto immigrants. The first phase of their migration was to learn a craft or trade; children and adolescents moved to areas of Germany between the ages of twelve and twenty. They had access to a well-functioning network of family relations and acquaintances connecting their homes with the migrants in Europe and this enabled them to find apprenticeships and jobs. If the market was favourable, the apprentices moved up into the role of job providers, recruited their assistants in turn from the same area and thus encouraged migration specific to a certain group and occupation. This worked particularly well with a moderate number of migrants in less popular occupations. To be only trading in pewter and not producing it was, however, more of an exception. On the other hand, to be doing both, i. e. combining craftsmanship and trade, also typical in other artisan occupations, was extremely popular, especially in itinerant trades. The Italians were apparently more adept at this, particularly at business affairs, than their German competitors. They also had a higher level of literacy and did not isolate themselves socially from the local population or self-segregate when choosing where to live. The majority of those who had not brought their marriage partners from home married local women. As the demand for the production of pewter declined towards the end of the nineteenth century, the pewterers gradually abandoned their profession. The system of migration through family chains outlined here can also be traced for other itinerant craftspeople.

The third category of migration includes peddlers or hawkers – travelling salespeople who sold a variety of goods such as haberdashery, seeds, papers, pamphlets, books, barometers, thermometers, stucco figures, lemons and wooden objects. Musicians with tamed animals and people in show business fall into a fourth category. Diplomatic reports reveal countless Italian organ grinders, pipers, fiddlers and bagpipe players who populated the streets of Paris and London and were repeatedly banished. This kind of migration, a daily spectacle for Giuseppe Mazzini and his comrades in the British capital, did not evoke solidarity with their compatriots, but rather a sense of shame. The first travelling players in America were recorded in the middle of the 1830s but it was not until the 1850s that this means of earning a living became more widespread. They were generally known as 'Savoyards'. The image of poor organ grinders accompanied by performing monkeys and dogs became a popular motif in genre painting.

Fig. 8 Friedrich Anton Wyttenbach, Savoyard Boy with Monkey and Dogs, c. 1840.

The fifth and last category of migrants is that of beggars – also a Europe-wide phenomenon. The numbers are difficult to verify as beggars were anxious to evade any intervention by the authorities. It can be assumed, however, that it was a problem of considerable proportions, depending naturally on economic cycles. Concrete figures are available for Genoa in 1809 which show that with a population of 70,000, approximately 10,000 beggars lived in and around the city. Italian street children gained sad notoriety, although some of them can be categorised as migrant workers. In western Europe they appeared mainly as chimney sweeps, street musicians and beggars. The action urgently needed on the part of the state was triggered by the world exhibition in Paris in 1867, where hundreds of Italian children were found begging. The reputation of the nascent Italian state was at stake. It was, however, years before a law was passed criminalising the employment of minors in itinerant trades. Children were either given away by their families or in some cases even sold, since their parents were not in a position to feed them. Some families were motivated by the hope that they were providing their children with a better future, but mostly it was a matter of sheer survival.

Reliable information on the numbers of migrants before 1870 can only be obtained from micro-studies. Other figures frequently come from the clergymen who were required to count the souls in their parishes in the spring. It is, however, possible to draw conclusions about migration from the first official statistics on Italians abroad compiled in 1871.[4] The data suggests that in the late 1860s 100,000 people migrated from Italy annually. This was mainly migration across the 'green borders' to France, Switzerland, Belgium, the Habsburg Empire and the states of the German Confederation. The only notable transatlantic migration was to the eastern states of South America. People from Liguria, Lombardy and Piedmont preferred to migrate to Argentina, where between 1830 and 1950 there were 3.5 million resident Italians. These were on the one hand poor migrants, but also merchants who went to seek their fortune in the New World. Excellent research has been carried out on chain migration from the small city of Cuneo in Piedmont. The analysis is based on a large collection of private documents, letters, short narratives and memoirs, as well as on conversations with protagonists and their descendants. Very few of them were able to rise to economic success in their new South American homes and the majority struggled to survive. The letters are impressive documents of the trials of everyday life and the strength of ties to the old homeland, often lasting for decades.

Argentina was considered the Italian Australia. Statistics for Liguria in 1854–1863 show that the destination of 65 per cent of migrants in South America was first Argentina and then Uruguay. There they took over control of river navigation and related activities such as trade and shipbuilding. The migrant families from the Ligurian coast did not move to the countryside as farmers but settled in the cities. In 1853 they made up 10 per cent of the total population of 100,000 in Buenos Aires. By the mid-nineteenth century, the majority lived in modest prosperity in their own neighbourhoods but were well integrated into the rest of society. The children of a number of them who had made a name for themselves as merchants and ship owners married into the Argentinian elite, were permitted to take up liberal professions such as journalism, or even embarked on a civil service career.

However, the Italians were welcome as new citizens not only in Argentina. The Emperor of Brazil launched a remarkable settlement project that specifically recruited immigrants. Peter II was married to a princess of Naples, Teresa Maria Cristina from the House of Bourbon, and she in turn was friendly with Adelina Malavesi from Modena. Due to her political involvement during the revolutions of 1848–1849, Adelina Malavesi was forced to flee and went to Brazil. There, at the request of the empress, she founded a colony of fifty Italian families. The migrants, most of whom came from Modena and its surroundings, settled in Porto Real not far from Rio de Janeiro. They were extremely successful economically, initially broadly in agriculture before gradually specialising in the production of sugar. These more affluent migrants later moved to São Paulo or Rio. However, this kind of link between political exile and economic migration seems to have been an exception rather than the rule. The exiles Giuseppe Garibaldi, Conte Livio Zambeccari and Giovanni Battista Cuneo are not known to have had any significant contact with their compatriots. From the USA, it is also known that the relatively small number of Italian intellectuals, musicians and merchants in New York were either oblivious to the masses of their poor and uneducated fellow Italians arriving after 1870 or gave them a very cool reception.

## Notes

1 Camillo Cavour, Epistolario, ed. Narciso Nada, Florence 1978, vol. IV, p. 86.
2 Del sistema delle azioni nella società in accomandita, in: L'Eco della Borsa, 15 February 1838.
3 G. G. Belli: Sonetti, 1623, 3 vols., ed. Carlo Muscetta, Milan 1965; Stendhal, Promenades dans Rome, Édition établie et annotée par V. Del Litto, Paris 1997 (1st edn. 1829).
4 Statistica generale del Regno d'Italia, Censimento degli italiani all' estero (31 December 1871), Stamperia Reale, Rome 1874.

# 5. Culture and Society

## 5.1 Social issues

One of the main features of Italian society in the eighteenth and nineteenth centuries was the unequal distribution of goods. In contrast to the relatively small rural and urban middle-class and a very wealthy elite, the majority of Italians suffered from extreme and oppressive poverty which persisted until the time of the post-World War II economic miracle. It can be safely assumed that the powerful images of wretched living conditions in the Basilicata under twentieth-century fascism portrayed in such novels as Carlo Levi's *Christ Stopped at Eboli* and Stefan Andres' *Positano* are similarly valid for the nineteenth century.

According to statistical surveys, approximately one-fifth of the total population could be classed as permanently poor or in need. The number of poor in the Mezzogiorno in 1832 was given as 237,000 but this excludes Naples, where they were not even recorded. In Lombardy, from a total population of 2.5 million in 1848, 500,000 were considered poor, i. e. one fifth. The situation in the cities was no better. Of the 24,000 inhabitants of Luca, 5,000 were classed as poor, and in 1844 the substantial figure of 13,000 of the total of 75,000 inhabitants of Bologna were defined as beggars or people in need of poor relief.[1] Historical analyses attribute rural poverty primarily to the agrarian structures that had a considerable effect on land ownership and consequently on living conditions, as mentioned in the previous chapter. In every region of Italy there were day labourers and small farmers who owned either no land or very little. Although they and the urban poor already lived in paltry conditions, the crises caused by the two historic famines in 1815–1817 and 1846–1847 led to even greater hardship. The effects of successive historic crop failures in the first restoration years were already well-known and familiar and were felt throughout the country. They led to a rise in underemployment, public unrest, the looting of markets and bakeries, an increase in mortality and widespread hunger. On 7 July 1815, a police inspector in the border town of Chiavenna in northern Lombardy reported that those classified as in need, which was the majority of the population, were no longer able to feed themselves. They were eating wild herbs which caused serious illnesses. A priest from Udine reported on 6 June of the same year that the people were eating ground maize stalks seasoned with herbs, without any salt and in some cases mixed with dung. A few years later a contemporary witness from Ancona described how the majority of the population were surviving off acorns but that unfortunately there were not enough to go round. In these circumstances it is hardly surprising that pamphlets were distributed to the peasants exhorting them to intensify the cultivation of potatoes as a nutritious crop. One of these numerous pamphlets was written by a doctor in the Marche, Giuseppe Casagrande, who was doing his best to alleviate the misery. In his *Manuale di carità* he suggested not only eating acorns, but also the peel of citrus fruits, dried melons and herbs and even cats, dogs, vipers and other snakes. However, he did warn against consuming worms and cicadas.[2] Governments generally responded to the scourge of famine with well-tried methods such as fines for withholding grain, community work for the unemployed, more public relief efforts and appeals to private donors.

In spite of the differences arising from people's status as day labourers without land or as small tenant farmers, it can be assumed that malnutrition was widespread. The meals eaten by the poorer classes were deficient in proteins, vitamins and calories and therefore led to constant and widespread undernourishment. In northern Lombardy, for example, the staple diet lacked variety as it consisted mainly of maize. In the mornings there was bread made of maize, rye and millet that began to go mouldy within a couple of days. It was eaten without any spread and dunked in salted water or in oil. Lunch was maize with beans or cabbage, seasoned with oil or rashers of bacon, and accompanied by a small piece of cheese, and in the evening the meal was again maize in the form of polenta with a meagre side dish. Fresh meat was a rarity that most people could only afford at Christmas. The north had the advantage of chestnuts and the successful attempt to spread the cultivation of potatoes.

The diet of the urban poor was no different from that of their rural counterparts. They both contained a preponderance of cereals and vegetables. In Rome, however, they were able to enjoy a slightly more varied diet. Their breakfast was made up of bread with fruit, cheese or cured meat, lunch was vegetable soup with a little bacon and bread, fruit and cheese. The main drink was water or, in the evenings, some wine to go with a meal of bread and salad. In the south the middle classes ate pasta dishes on six out of seven days a week, but the day labourers and ordinary artisans were only able to satisfy their desire for macaroni on feast days. The consumption of meat was rare and restricted to a little pork in the winter and mutton in the spring and summer. There was also no fresh fish on the menu for the poor but only dried cod (*baccalà*) and salted anchovies. In the south on the other hand, there was always plenty of fruit and vegetables.

It is hardly surprising that those who were so undernourished frequently fell victim to the epidemics and plagues rampant in the nineteenth century. These included typhoid in its various forms, diphtheria, influenza and tuberculosis. The transmission of malaria was also assisted by the numerous marshes and lakes in central Italy and the cultivation of rice in the north, both ideal environments for mosquitoes. There are estimates for Tuscany around the middle of the nineteenth century which paint a drastic picture of the extent of malaria. In 1844, it was thought that 54 per cent of the population of Orbetello, 59 per cent of Grosseto and 66 per cent of Gavorrano had malaria. In the north of Italy, this sad spectrum of poor health was exacerbated by a disease called *pellagra*, caused by a concentration of maize in the diet. It led to skin complaints and diarrhoea and eventually damaged the nervous system. In 1816, 10 per cent of the population in the region of Vicenza alone were suffering from *pellagra*. Italy was also naturally not spared by the Europe-wide cholera epidemic which claimed thousands of victims in the mid-1830s. Poor hygienic and sanitary conditions meant that this epidemic mainly hit the poorest section of the population. In Naples, of the 30,000 cases registered, 17,500 died. Such epidemics had a massive impact on economic life. They led to a decline in trade, unemployment amongst artisans and labourers and rising living costs.

The housing situation in the cities also significantly impacted hygiene and sanitary conditions. These miserable conditions can be illustrated by the situation in Brescia, a town in the more affluent north of Italy. Its main characteristics were a high density of the population within the city walls, narrow streets, a lack of open spaces, damp and dirt in the buildings and streets, the disastrous state of the sewage system and polluted water in the wells. The result of all this was a high rate of mortality. In nearby Milan, there were numerous neighbourhoods with houses unfit to live in. If they were demolished and replaced by new buildings, the poor could no longer afford to live there. The situation in Genoa was no better. Even as late as 1855, most of its population lived in cramped quarters, in damp, unhealthy houses adjoining each other, with insufficient fresh air. In Naples, families lived in a single dirty room with a well shaft in segregated areas in the lower town, especially near the port and in the *Mercato* district. These neighbourhoods were considered dangerous and had a high concentration of prostitution, which rose to alarming levels in the second half of the century.

A further depressing problem was posed by the plethora of abandoned children, whose number rose steadily during the second half of the nineteenth century. Before 1800 in Brescia, for example, fewer than 400 children a year were abandoned, but by the 1830s it was around 600. In Cremona more than 22,000 children were abandoned between 1800 and 1850. Constantly rising figures can also be established for Milan. While no more than 800 children per year were abandoned there before the French Revolution, between 1841 and 1850 an annual average of 3,000 children were handed over to its church institutions and after 1850 this figure rose to 4,300. Even considering the fact that the orphanage *Santa Caterina alla Ruota*, for example, accepted babies from the surrounding area as well as from the city, these figures are still dramatic. During the Restoration the numbers increased equally drastically in the Kingdom of Sardinia-Piedmont and in Tuscany. The mortality rate amongst these abandoned children was shockingly high. While 23 per cent of all the children in Lombardy died during the first year of their life, the catastrophic hygienic conditions, the lack of breast milk to feed them and the extent of neglect meant that between 80 per cent and 90 per cent of children in orphanages did not survive longer than twelve months. To add insult to injury, these children suffered from social stigma. Until the Napoleonic period they were all given the same derogatory surnames, *Colombo* in Milan and *Esposito* in Naples, meaning 'dove' and 'exposed' or 'abandoned' respectively.

Contemporaries were naturally concerned and disturbed by this phenomenon of pauperism. Governments, civil servants, clerics and intellectuals produced numerous papers, documents, pamphlets and books with suggestions of how to solve the problems. Their vigorous debates were part of a wider European discourse whose content and ideas were broadly similar. While in the mediaeval period, paupers were still regarded as representatives of Christ on earth and therefore to be given support as a matter of course, the attitude towards them had begun to change fundamentally after the beginning of the early modern period. Paupers began to be seen as lazy, incorrigible, work-shy and detrimental to the prestige of the state. They were thought to cause social tensions and transmit diseases and were considered overall a threatening and hostile presence to be countered with repression and segregation. This image became entrenched in numerous nineteenth-century publications. The anonymous author of the paper *Qualche cenno sulla mendicità e sui mezzi di estirparla (Some observations on begging and how to eradicate it)* described the odious forms of begging to be found mainly in the streets of the wealthy. For Genoa in 1838, the publisher Felice Isnardi described scores of beggars roaming around and crowding the squares, streets and promenades and even the churches.[3] In Venetia it was alleged that begging had become a profession. Saverio Scrofani described similar scenes in Naples in 1816: 'Can there be a single person who hasn't seen swarms of men and women in Naples every day going round begging with their purses open praying on Monday for the souls in purgatory, on Tuesday to the archangel Raphael, on Wednesday to the Blessed Virgin of Carmine, and so on?'.[4] In addition, there was constant debate about how to tell genuine poverty from fake or dishonourable poverty. Misdirected charity, it was said, led to idleness, encouraged vice and even increased need. The poor were assumed to be lacking in self-control and therefore incapable of leading a responsible life. They should also, it was thought, be prevented from entering into ill-advised marriages.

This picture of the poor as lazy and detrimental to society corresponded to the measures used by Italian states since the *Ancien Régime* to try and counteract this evil, namely coercion, draconian penalties and imprisonment. Strict regulations concerning begging had already been imposed in the eighteenth century. These punitive measures were maintained during the revolutionary period and under Napoleon beggars were supposed to be systematically registered in each department and detained in workhouses (*ateliers de charité).* This harsh 'pauper policy' was continued during the restoration period. In Lombardy-Venetia begging for charity was forbidden and incurred a punishment of up to three months' imprisonment. Repeat offenders received additional sanctions of floggings and reduced rations. In the Duchy of Parma begging was also forbidden by law as it was in the Kingdom of the Two Sicilies. But this legislation was unrealistic and had correspondingly little success. The frequent publication of different laws against begging basically demonstrates how ineffective they were.

The policy of attempting to 'cleanse' towns and villages of beggars and paupers of both sexes and all ages and to banish them to specially designated institutions was implemented throughout Italy. The practice of segregating and locking away the poor and needy, typically symbolised by the English workhouses, was in fact extended during the nineteenth century. The poorhouse in Genoa was particularly remarkable for its dimensions – between 1830 and 1840 up to 2,000 people were incarcerated there. It was, however, surpassed by the pauper hospitals in Turin and Naples, which took in up to 6,000 'guests' every day. In 1860, the well-known Neapolitan hygienist Marino Turchi noted in this context: 'the common people detest this place more than prison, they call it the cage, a kind of shelter for criminals and beasts'.[5] In Lombardy-Venetia where they were jointly financed by the state and the municipalities, this kind of institution was organised in a more extensive and decentralised manner. Workhouses were established, not only in the capital Milan, but also in Pavia, Mantua, Como and Monza. In the Kingdom of Sardinia-Piedmont, pauper asylums were also established, driven by private and municipal initiatives, such as in Chambéry, Vigevano and Novara. There were comparable institutions in the other Italian states, although there was no clear-cut distinction between workhouses and poorhouses. Clearly none of these measures succeeded in solving the social problem. It can therefore be said in conclusion that in the period we are studying here, (1770 to 1870), little or nothing changed for the lower classes.

## 5.2 The small middle class and the dominant elites

There was no association between the poor of Naples, who lived in the gloomy alleyways of the lower town, and the middle classes, who were concentrated in a different world, the upper town. This was an area of luxury and extravagance, with cafés and the San Carlo theatre, famous throughout Europe, where those who could afford to rode out in their own carriages as a symbol of affluence. Around 1870 the upper classes comprised less than 10,000 of a total population of 450,000.[6] Rich nobles and wealthy bourgeois citizens were linked by a common lifestyle. In actual numbers, Italian nobility was of greater significance than it was, for example, in the German territories. In terms of the percentage of the total population, the aristocracy north of the Alps comprised one per cent compared to between five and seven per cent of the educated and economically active middle class. In Italy it was one per cent of nobility to no more than about two per cent of the well-to do bourgeois and educated middle classes. This small group, known as the *ceto medio* or *borghesia* was made up of merchants, civil servants, high school teachers, solicitors, pharmacists, doctors, lawyers and the self-employed who admired and imitated the cultural and social values of landowners and the aristocracy. The bourgeoisie also cultivated the idea of living off private means as rentiers in order to set themselves apart from the lower classes and petty bourgeoisie. They resided in spacious apartments occupying entire floors of townhouses. By wearing high quality clothes, eating white bread and beef and drinking expensive wine, as well as employing servants, an unmistakable line was drawn separating them from the rest of a predominantly impoverished society. Lawyers and doctors were particularly well respected. In the south of Italy there was one doctor or lawyer to every 1,000 inhabitants and as a result the proportion of students was higher than in the north. This middle class ensured its survival by means of education, careers and family networks and even managed to hand down their social circumstances and professional activities to the next generations. Sons of civil servants endeavoured to find employment themselves in the administration or the military. Lawyers took over their fathers' practices, which had in turn been inherited from their fathers. There was a high level of socio-professional homogeneity between marriage partners and marriage witnesses and very few people married outside their own professional circle. Of course, not all civil servants and bank employees were wealthy and although many of them in the lower ranks were distinct from the poor, they still had to struggle to survive.

The urban bourgeoisie were able to create local, regional and eventually even national power groups based on shared communication, social practice and specific interests and values. The concentration of lawyers in parliament in Italy was higher than anywhere else in Europe. In the cities, politicians, intellectuals and lawyers met in exclusive cafés at tables reserved for them alone and discussed the politics of the day. In Naples the bourgeoisie met at the *Gran Caffè* (now *Gambrinus*) on the Piazza del Plebiscito, in Florence it was the *Caffè Paszkowski*, and in Turin the *Caffè Fiorio* in Via Po. It was rumoured that every morning King Charles Albert asked: 'What are they saying in *Caffè Fiorio*' so as to gauge the mood in the city. Belonging to the bourgeoisie, however, did not only depend on profession, wealth and potential participation in power, but also on education and culture, where it shared numerous points of contact with the nobility.

The nobility dominated Italian politics, society, economy and culture until well into the nineteenth century. In the previous chapters, we have encountered its representatives many times as prominent actors in all these areas. Yet we cannot legitimately speak of Italian nobility as a whole. As in all other European countries it is necessary to differentiate between various types of regional aristocracy with respect to wealth and status. In the south, their extensive estates meant that the feudal nobility of the Mezzogiorno was probably the richest in the whole of the Italian peninsula. Their privileges were reduced in the nineteenth century, but this had little effect on their wealth and probably none on their social status. The situation was similar in the Papal States where the scene was dominated by clerics and the high nobility who derived their income from their land. Until the Napoleonic period the Papal States could still be described as an aristocratic monarchy, but reforms after 1815 largely drove the aristocrats out of the state administration. Although the nobility in Rome was connected to other European countries through marriage, this did not seem to result in them being particularly open to new cultural influences or economic innovations. On the contrary, with a conservative, church upbringing, very few nobles attended university, for example. It is probably fair to say that Roman nobility had a pronounced lack of education. One Leopoldo Torlonia, who gained a degree (*laurea*) in law, is cited as one of the few exceptions that proves the rule – and he did not come from one of the traditional families.

The situation was different in the neighbouring north, where in Tuscany, the Marche, Umbria, Emilia Romagna, Lombardy and Venetia an urban patrician class could be found. During the Renaissance, they dominated trade and banking, but gradually withdrew from this kind of business in the early modern period and invested primarily in land. If they were wealthy enough, they owned an impressive town palace for the winter and various estates in the countryside for the summer, which were at the same time the source of their wealth. During the Napoleonic period these patricians became more active economically and after 1815 no longer confined themselves to agriculture but attempted to increase their wealth in more modern sectors. At the same time the nobility in Tuscany was systematically excluded from the administration, the military, diplomacy and the court by the Habsburg Grand Dukes. The nobility in Lombardy and Venetia met a similar fate. They had no chance of a career at court or in the military, at least not in Italy. The northern Italian nobility, however, were able to retain their enormous wealth in the form of landed property and its influence based on kinship and patronage. They tried to make up for their loss of political power by effectively exploiting their social connections in the cities and achieving economic success. Furthermore, since Habsburg rule had generally prevented the northern Italian aristocracy from holding important positions in the military since the early modern period, there was no tradition of appropriate military training and career openings in their own country, as would be the case with other groups of nobility in Europe. If at all, sons were sent for that type of military training to Turin. Overall, landed property and credit transactions remained their main sources of income.

We can conclude this brief overview with the nobility in Piedmont, which was alone in the early modern period in being able to have a career at court, in the military, in administration, or in the diplomatic corps of the Italian monarchy. In contrast to the other regions, we have here a kind of *ministeriales,* that is, nobles in the service of their overlords, a group that expanded especially in the early modern period due to the bestowal of noble titles. While conventional theories assumed there was a gradual decline of the nobility in the nineteenth century as it gradually mingled with the bourgeois elites and thus lost its identity, new research on Piedmont reveals a completely different picture. In contrast to other regions in Italy, the nobility here was largely able to maintain its position as an elite ruling class. There was also a bourgeois elite that became rich as a result of industrialisation. However, at least until World War I, these two groups had hardly any contact with each other. Unlike in Milan, Florence, Genoa and Rome, the nouveau riche and the old aristocracy in Turin very rarely intermarried; on the contrary they were distinctively endogamous. The aristocracy was also notably traditional in its economic behaviour. Its wealth continued to be based on the ownership of land and the resulting rental income, although it was increasingly invested in an agrarian capitalist manner.

The number of large bourgeois landowners increased steadily in the whole of Italy after the Napoleonic era. This was partly due to the sale of secularised church property, and partly because profits from manufacturing and industry were invested in land. Large scale landownership no longer distinguished the wealthy middle class from the nobility, who also lost their privileges in the course of the century. As was the case north of the Alps, the nobility developed from being a social and political status to being a group defined by cultural and political memories. If there was anything, however, that made the nobility in the nineteenth century appear, at least outwardly, to be a homogenous social class, while at the same time distinguishing it from other classes, it was the persistence of its former social influence and standing in the sense of it being a normative model, or to put it more simply, *noblesse oblige*. The lifestyle and culture of the nobility was made up of a conglomeration of the most diverse ethical and social norms and ways of thinking that had been handed down for centuries. These conventions were transmitted primarily and most forcefully within the aristocratic families. As a result, it was the family unit as such that remained their primary point of reference.

A further important feature which distinguished the aristocracy from the middle classes, apart from its actual titles, was its awareness of its history, manifested in family trees and chronicles. For generations the aristocracy had developed as a closely connected entity made up of family traditions and memories, and it is not for nothing that in sociology it is considered the cornerstone of collective memory. The nobility also created new myths during the long nineteenth century and these were cultivated within aristocratic clubs and family groups. Quality based on social status was replaced by a belief in shared aristocratic values. 'Nobility' became all the more important, the more its privileged legal status faded.

Fig. 9 Pietro Ayres, The Marchesi Ferrero della Marmora Family, 1828.

This image of nobility was presented to the public in grand style, most impressively though not exclusively in the cultural sphere. At the beginning of the 1980s in his much-discussed book on the European nobility, Arno J. Mayer showed that official high culture was an important ideological instrument of domination for those in power.[7] It was not only public buildings, monuments and squares whose purpose it was to sing the praises of the *Ancien Régime* – painting, music, literature and history were also used as instruments of self-promotion.

In the nineteenth century, aristocratic traditions made increasingly high demands on the capacities of the nobility in terms of charity, religious commitment, military courage and the maintenance of considerable patronages. The nobles were masters at promoting their prestige in the political field. Studies on encounters with monarchs, royal festivities, weddings and funerals show how the nobility exploited the space offered by those contexts to the full as opportunities for self-promotion. A cultural history of the political is well suited to revealing new perspectives on competing perceptions and contemporary experiences beyond apparently objective power structures, written procedural rules and explicit discourses. Overall, however, in contrast to its counterpart north of the Alps, the nobility here had focussed since the mediaeval period to a very significant degree on the city as a stage for displaying their prestige and political power.

## 5.3 Salons and societies

Social and cultural interests led to the foundation of private salons, casinos, Masonic lodges, and numerous scientific, charitable, and musical societies where the urban elites gathered. Even in the early modern period, these institutions influenced the semi-public life of the nobility, and gradually also of the middle classes. In the course of the nineteenth century, they also became increasingly diverse. During our period of study, the salons and clubs were also used by the aristocracy and patricians to disassociate themselves clearly from the middle classes. The various models used by the urban elites to intermingle or distance themselves were characterised by both tradition and innovation. They contributed towards the specific character of urban centres both in Italy and in the rest of Europe.

There had been a *casino nobile* in many Italian cities since the second half of the eighteenth century. Its sole purpose was for the recreation of the aristocracy. The first of these casinos were in Pisa (1754) and Florence (1761), followed by the *Casino San Pietro* in Trieste (1763), and the casino in Bologna (1766). The *Patriottica nobile società* in Turin was opened a little later (1784) followed by the casino in Milan another three years later. By the 1790s this phenomenon had also reached the south with the founding of a casino for the nobility in Palermo, the *Grande conversazione della nobiltà* (1796). Finally, the establishment of a similar meeting place in Ferrara (1803) has to be mentioned. During the revolutionary period their activities were frequently interrupted, but at the same time the first wealthy members of the bourgeoisie were admitted. After the Congress of Vienna they resumed their activities, for example in Naples, but were subject to rigid police surveillance. In Milan in 1817 three such institutions coexisted: the re-established *Casino dei nobili*, the *Società del Giardino*, and the *Concordia*. The casinos were, on the one hand, less exclusive than the salons and the academies which only admitted a limited number of people but, on the other hand, this openness generally applied only to the aristocracy. In principle, this was the place where men socialised outside their family, with wine, tobacco, billiards, card games and conversation. The presence of their mothers, wives and daughters was only desired at balls, particularly the carnival balls, where they provided the necessary glamour. Private balls and festivals were used by the aristocracy to promote their public image and standing. Stendhal writes enthusiastically in his Italian travelogue about the luxurious balls held by Prince Borghese in his palace every Saturday in 1827. He comments that the balls to which Borghese and the banker Torlonia, who had been raised to the rank of prince, sent out invitations, surpassed those of the emperor Napoleon and anything else he had seen in the north.[8]

In the salons the situation was quite different and women were able to play a crucial role. The movement began with the founding of a literary salon in Paris in the seventeenth century in the Palais Rambouillet. In contrast to the formal, orchestrated ceremonies at the courts, the focus of the salons was on stimulating and witty conversation. While courtly culture remained restricted to the nobility, their salons were open to prominent representatives of the *res publica litteraria*: musicians, writers, artists, and philosophers. In the eighteenth and nineteenth centuries there were salons in every major city in Italy, which meant that not only were class barriers overcome, but also the barriers between the sexes. The salons were a symbol of intellectual Europe and also served as preparation and practice for the emancipation of women. In Turin, Florence, Pisa and Milan they were initially regular meetings of several larger families who felt they belonged together because of their shared language, culture and manners. This habitus included the dress and the dignified bearing of a gentleman (*galantuomo*) and their refined language, used to distinguish themselves from the 'hoi polloi'. Some salons were dominated by the hostess who received her *habitués* on a certain day of the week. The *salonnnière* enjoyed uncontested authority, and it was her job to create a cultivated atmosphere in her family palace, in whose rooms, magnificently decorated with artworks, the participants discussed art, music and literature. The history of Italian salons is inextricably linked to the enterprise of extraordinary female personalities, a veritable parade of intelligent women.

During the Restoration, luxury salons increasingly became meeting places for the opposition, such as in Milan for members of the nobility who were not admitted to the courtly society of the Habsburgs. The salon of the Countess Clara Maffai in the Via Tre Monasteri, for example, became a particularly attractive venue and was regularly frequented by artists of European rank, including Massimo d'Azeglio, Honoré de Balzac, Alessandro Manzoni, Giuseppe Verdi and Francesco Hayez. Of comparable importance in Florence were the salons of the Marchioness Marianna Ginori Lisci, Marchioness Teresa Bartolommei and the so-called red salon of Emilia Peruzzi de' Medici, who on Mondays received not only established artists but also the most famous politicians from moderate liberal circles on her red velvet sofas. In the summer, her salon was moved to the villa suburb of Bagno a Ripoli, to the cooler Villa La Torre all'Antella which the Peruzzi family had owned since 1299. As it was, many of the regular visitors to the salons accompanied the nobility in the summer months to their summer resorts, to the *villeggiatura*, where eminent guests from other European countries were also welcome. Peruzzi's salons provide a prime example of increasing politicisation during the Risorgimento. The salons provided a safe space beyond the reach of press censorship and police surveillance for the free exchange of information and ideas. Young aristocrats in particular made contact there with European politicians and artists who were travelling in Italy. Thus, for example, when Ubaldino Peruzzi and Lorenzo Ginori Lisci went to study in Paris, they used the connections they had built up in the local salons to meet leading political figures such as Adolphe Thiers, Alexis de Tocqueville, Alphonse de Lamartine and Louis Auguste Blanqui there. However, the only contact the young noblemen had with democratic revolutionaries in the coffee houses was during their time in the French capital, if at all. When they returned to Italy, they were socialised in the private salons as moderate liberals or conservatives.

In Rome, the Marchioness Boccapaduli and Countess Ersilia Lovatelli Caetani opened the doors of their palaces to members of international intellectual circles who were staying in the city. Naturally, there was not only one fashionable salon in every major city, but several, where groups, networks and political circles of every persuasion developed. In Turin after 1814 the set around Juliette Colbert, the wife of the Marquess Falletti di Barolo, in her eponymous palace was of a more conservative nature. Conservative Catholic circles met at the home of Cesare Taparelli d'Azeglio until 1830, while at the same time the moderate liberal camp met at the home of Prospero and Catherine Balbo, complemented by foreign diplomats and bourgeois academics. After the 1848–1849 revolution, the liberal salon of the Marchioness Costanza Trotti Bentivoglio Arconati, who had returned from exile, was particularly popular. Various travel reports suggest that the idea of socialising in the salons was also hugely popular in Naples and that, as in Paris of the Restoration, the social life of the Neapolitan elites was conducted in salons and cafés. The most highly esteemed were the private gatherings at the residences of Principessa Francesca Pignatelli di Belmonte, of Pauline Craven née de la Ferronnays and the musical salon of Countess de la Feld. Although members of the bourgeoisie were permitted into these circles by personal invitation, the ideal of equality for all participants remained elusive, if only because of the enormous disparity in wealth.

Despite the fact that aristocratic women were frequently the driving force and focal point of the salons, for a long time they were unable to become members of a club or society. Since the beginning of the nineteenth century, a widespread culture of societies developed in cities across Europe with a focus on various cultural or intellectual matters or with the purpose of collectively furthering involvement in civic society. Societies emerged as a panacea for every social crisis. There was probably no social or cultural field that did not invite associations or societies, whether it was education, poor relief, the care of orphans, the building of monuments or classical music. In addition, there were academic and economic societies that were devoted to the study of geography, antiquity or the improvement of infrastructure. They could be closely monitored or even prohibited by the authorities, since each of these initiatives had to be personally approved by the local sovereign. As a result, associations can be taken as a measure of the extent to which the ruler's politics were liberal or authoritarian. Compared to Britain, France and the German

Confederation, Italy was late to develop societies, but this was not due to a lack of interest. Rather, such initiatives were rejected out of hand. The most restrictive policy was to be found in the Papal States where, until they were conquered by the troops of the young nation state, there was not one single society of any kind, not even a casino for the nobility. In the Kingdom of the Two Sicilies, a casino was permitted, but the establishment of other societies was similarly forbidden.

In Lombardy-Venetia, on the other hand, the social scene experienced a period of invigoration at the beginning of the Restoration. The *Società di incoraggiamento delle scienze, lettere e delle arti (Society for the promotion of science, literature, and the arts)*, founded in Napoleonic times and reserved for bourgeois citizens and civil servants until 1814, was continued, but it swiftly became aristocratic. Further initiatives were introduced by Conte Federico Confalonieri, inspired by what he had experienced on his travels to France and Britain. He enthusiastically promoted four projects simultaneously: a society for the dissemination of the Lancaster school model (*Società per il mutuo insegnamento*), whose purpose was to draw gifted, but impoverished pupils into education, further an *Ateneo* (academy) for the promotion of science and culture, a society for the support of a national theatre and a society for the establishment of an industrial bazaar. The Conte had been able to mobilise his aristocratic networks for all these projects and succeeded in gaining several hundred members who were prepared to subscribe to costly stocks and shares. First, he approached his close friends, then his wider acquaintances and they, in turn, recruited further supporters. The whole system was based on co-optation: new members were selected by existing members. However, the only society that was actually recognised by the government was the society for the promotion of school teaching. Since many of its members, however, were involved in planning the uprising of 1820 and consequently pursued by the police, it had to close at a time when the first schools had only just begun to operate.

Between 1821 and the end of the 1830s, no new societies were permitted. It was not until three years after the death of the Emperor Francis I in 1835 that there was an amnesty under Ferdinand I the 'Benign' and the founding of societies was once again permitted. The extraordinary commitment of Confalonieri may have been an exception, but in the 1840s the idea of the enormous value of societies spread and numerous texts were published about it. In Lombardy-Venetia, Tuscany, and the Kingdom of Sardinia-Piedmont, there was a veritable wave of society founding. They were now seen as an expression of civic progress and stood for an ethos of the general good. With combined force they promoted intellectual, economic and moral improvement. At the same time, they were also seen as a crypto political arena for practising civic virtues and as virtual shadow parliaments in an authoritarian state, defying rules that prohibited political discussion as a matter of principle. For urban elites, societies were an instrument of liberal social policy. The call for collaboration, however, was only directed at the rich and educated who recognised the social situation of the lower classes and strove to help them by means of philanthropic societies, while at the same time stabilising the existing social order and supporting their own authority. Whereas in the Germanic states, the landscape of flourishing societies was strongly determined by the bourgeoisie and civil servants working together with the nobility, in the Italian cities the scene was completely dominated by the nobility. They claimed the leadership of societies for themselves and by selecting the founding members, ensured further growth from their own ranks. In addition, the membership fees for the societies were very high. Calculations for Florence show that approximately 800 people were engaged in elite societies, equivalent to two per cent of the population. It was common for people to be members of more than one society and sometimes many more. Leading liberal politicians, such as Marquess Cosimo Ridolfi and Marquess Gino Capponi are known to have been members of over a hundred agricultural, botanical, statistical, philanthropic and historical societies.[9] It was not the purpose of every society to serve science or the common good – at times it was to gain distinction. In 1841 Principe Emilio Belgiojoso founded a jockey club in Milan, the kind of exclusive society he had encountered during his time in exile in Paris. The thirty founding members paid 1,000 Austrian lira and were mainly recruited from members of the nobility critical of the government. At exactly the same time Conte Camillo Cavour founded the *Società del Whist* in X, another exclusive gentlemen's club.

Whereas the police and ministers of the interior watched the societies with suspicion, monarchs attempted to exploit them to stabilise their power. The Turin historical society is a particularly clear example of this phenomenon. In 1834, King Charles Albert of Sardinia founded this first Italian historical society in Turin. It was an institution directed from above by the state. The admission of members and the choice of topics of this *Deputazione di Storia Patria* were strictly controlled by the king and the main initiators, Conte Prospero Balbo and Conte Luigi Cibrario. High-ranking state and court officials, leading archivists and librarians, culture ministers and conservationists, all ardent supporters of the Piedmontese monarchy, gathered here to work on the source editions and topic areas prescribed by the king. During the whole period of this study, Turinese history was fashioned according to the motto *Dio, patria, famiglia* (*God, fatherland, family*). The king and his senior civil servants only entrusted the material and the writing of this history to a handpicked and select number of aristocrats and civil servants with the appropriate political stance. Its purpose was to provide historical legitimisation for the successful rise of the House of Savoy. The Turinese *Deputazione* did not produce popular biographies or monographs for a wider readership. Its task was to produce collections of historical sources needed for studying the state and legitimising the monarchy and to publish relevant standard academic histories. Given these circumstances there was no question of a critical examination of the topics. The authors or their ancestors had been part of the Piedmontese success story for generations and, as senior representatives of the civil service, they showed undivided loyalty to the royal family.

German monarchs in Dresden, Munich, Berlin and Stuttgart also encouraged and instrumentalised historical societies in a similar way, but apart from in Turin and very much later in Parma-Piacenza (1854) this was not the case in the royal capitals of Italy. This may well have been because here it was not possible to write a joint success story of the regional nobility and the monarchy. Apart from the early societies, the true phase of society founding did not take place until after Italian unification. Although there had been initiatives towards founding historical societies in Naples and Rome as early as the 1840s, they were prohibited by the state. The members recruited by Carlo Troya to the first Neapolitan historical society (*Società storica napoletana*) in 1842, for example, were moderate and loyal notables who were also closely connected to the Bourbon court in a variety of ways. This society was nevertheless placed under police surveillance, classified as ultra-liberal and dangerous and soon dissolved. Censorship and police surveillance made it impossible to found any societies in the Papal States.

## 5.4 Opera, the fine arts and literature

Due to the authoritarian and repressive climate, the elites in southern Italy and the Papal States were unable to build up a network of clubs and societies comparable to those in northern and central Italy. Instead, it was the salons and especially the opera houses that became the meeting places for the elegant world. Internationally renowned opera houses were built everywhere in the eighteenth century: the *Teatro Valle* (1727) and the *Argentina* (1732) in Rome, the *San Carlo* in Naples (1737), the *Teatro Regio* in Turin (1740), the *Comunale* in Bologna (1763), the *Scala* in Milan (1778) and the *Fenice* in Venice (1791). In the nineteenth century new buildings in the neoclassical style with monumental facades sprang up in nearly every large or medium-sized city. The Marche was particularly prominent in the new construction and furnishing of theatres and opera houses subsidised by the local nobility. The result was elegant temples of art, some of which were out of proportion to the size of the cities they served, which rarely had more than 15,000 inhabitants, even including the surrounding areas. In 1868 a ministerial survey revealed a remarkable ninety-one active opera houses in the Marche, making up one tenth of the total in Italy. In the same year there were 942 opera houses in 650 municipalities nationwide, a number unrivalled internationally.

The opera scene was particularly vibrant in Naples. In the San Carlo, the Teatro del Fondo and the Fiorentini there were 100 productions every year between 1809 and 1844 and in the 1824–1825 season it was even 138. Observers from abroad noted that the main purpose of attending the opera was not to enjoy the spectacle, but to socialise. According to Madame de Staël, people in Italy did not go to the opera to listen but to meet and converse with their best friends in their boxes.[10] Her compatriot Stendhal described evenings in the *Scala* mainly devoted to conversation. He described how people would greet each other from one box to another and pay each other visits in the same way as they would in a salon.[11] He himself had rented a box during his stay of several months in Milan in 1816 and spent his evenings there.

The theatres and opera houses were financed by the nobility and the city administration. The old-established families bought or rented their boxes over many generations, conspicuously attaching their crests and fitting them with their own furniture. For the nobility who had lived in a city for centuries, visiting the opera regularly in their own family box was a firmly established part of their tradition. Every autumn the aristocracy returned from their country villas and presented themselves at the opening of the main opera season. There was an evident hierarchy between the boxes and the seats in the stalls where the middle classes sat, thus clearly mirroring the internal structures of high society in the opera houses. The performances in the autumn featured not only an *opera seria*, the serious style of Italian opera, but also specially staged ballet performances that were not part of the opera, so that an evening at the opera could stretch to five hours. The auditorium was fully lit and there was a constant hum of conversation in the background. On the ground floor of the opera house, cafés, restaurants and gaming tables offered drinks, food, and entertainment. In the shorter seasons during carnival and in the spring, the programme usually only presented an *opera buffa*, a style of opera involving more everyday topics, with no separate ballet performances. The leading opera houses had a monopoly on the most fashionable balls during the carnival season. Being able to attend these exclusive balls was again a sign of social distinction.

The gatherings of hundreds of operagoers were closely monitored by reactionary rulers in all Italian states. First, the texts in the libretti had to be approved in advance by the censors. Then, every performance was attended by police officers, since there was always the danger that dissident ideas could be disseminated by means of changes to the text, gestures and facial expressions. The audience was repeatedly instructed not to communicate with the actors and singers by applauding, calling out or gesturing. In spite of this, people in the stalls continued to interact with those on the stage.

From 1770 to 1870, theatre or rather opera was seen as the quintessence of Italian culture. Its subject matter and music reflect the philosophical and literary topics of the time. During the eighteenth century, two types of opera developed. The first was the *opera seria*, a courtly genre which served to represent and legitimise the aristocracy and the sovereigns. Its narratives were based on history and mythology, and its characters represented gods, heroes and rulers. The other type of opera was the *opera buffa*, which developed in Venice and Naples and whose roots came from the *commedia dell'arte*. Towards the end of the eighteenth century, plays and operas began to incorporate the ideas of highly esteemed Enlightenment figures such as Diderot and Lessing. At this time, a new type of opera called the *opera semiseria* began to replace the strict forms and sequences of the *opera seria*. Bourgeois characters were now no longer seen as comedy figures and other characters were portrayed more realistically. The intention was that by visiting the theatre, the audience would be morally reformed. This tendency continued during the Napoleonic period. In Milan, the philosopher Melchiorre Goia took the view that theatre was the school of virtue.

With the Restoration, romantic, melodramatic operas from Italy began to conquer the world. In 1816 the *Barber of Seville* by Gioachino Rossini was premiered in the Teatro Argentina in Rome. With this innovative piece the composer achieved a spectacular success at the age of only twenty-four. It was enthusiastically acclaimed by the national and international world of opera and paved the way for the great popularity of romantic opera. As well as Rossini, the composers of *bel canto* who ushered Italian opera to world fame and whose works still belong to today's standard repertoire were Gaetano Donizetti and Vincenzo Bellini. Rossini had already composed sixteen other operas before the *Barber of Seville*, including for the Teatro Valle, the *Scala*, the *Fenice* and the *San Carlo*. It was the *opera seria Tancredi* performed in Venice in 1813 that brought him his first major success, but his *opera buffa L'Italiana in Algeri* was even more highly acclaimed when it was premiered there in the same year. Following further compositions for various different northern Italian opera houses, Rossini was appointed director of both the *San Carlo* and the *Teatro del Fondo* in Naples. Later he enjoyed resounding success with performances in Vienna, London and Paris. In 1824, he became director of the Italian opera in the French capital Paris, the cultural metropolis of Europe. For the coronation of Charles X in Reims, Rossini composed *Il viaggio a Reims,* which was performed with a sensational cast of star performers. A year later he was appointed composer to the French king. With the outbreak of the July Revolution in 1830, however, Rossini lost all his offices and status in Paris and returned to Italy. By then his period of greatest creativity was over. He had composed thirty-nine operas within just twenty years, making him one of the most famous composers in the world, on both sides of the Atlantic.

Rossini's two contemporaries, Donizetti and Bellini, were also seized by an explosion of creativity in their early years and composed dozens of operas in a very short space of time. In many ways their careers were similar to that of Rossini. Gaetano Donizetti came from a modest background in Bergamo, made his debut in Venice and, after initial successes there, moved to Italy's opera capital, Naples, where he composed up to four operas a year. His breakthrough to international fame, however, only came with the performance of his *opera seria Anna Bolena* at the *Scala* in Milan in 1830. In the next few years, he composed two more world-famous works, the melodramas *L' elisir d' amore* (1832) and *Lucrezia Borgia* (1833). In 1840 he moved to Paris where his new operas were enthusiastically received and in 1843, he accepted an offer from Emperor Ferdinand to relocate to Vienna as his musical director (*Kammerkapellmeister*) and court composer. However, only two years later in 1845, he returned to Paris seriously ill and died three years after that in his home town in Lombardy.

His friend and rival Vincenzo Bellini grew up in a family of church musicians in Catania. Sponsored by the Duke of Sammartino, he studied at the royal college of music in Naples. He made a promising debut at the conservatoire theatre with his opera *Adelson e Salvini*, which brought him to the attention of the director of the *Teatro San Carlo*, who had previously backed Rossini. For *San Carlo* Bellini composed the opera *Bianca e Ferdinando* which prompted the young artist's international breakthrough. He created further operas for the great opera houses of Italy, travelled to London where he met with spectacular success, and for the Italian opera in Paris he composed his final work for the stage. With works such as *Norma* and *La sonnambula,* Bellini is considered one of the architects of romantic opera, whose works were a major influence on Giuseppe Verdi. The biographies of these three composers and the venues where their works were performed show clearly that opera was a transnational art form and a worldwide business. Their works were performed not only in Europe but also in New York and South America.

Giuseppe Verdi, who was born roughly ten years later in Roncole in the province of Parma, continued this series of successes and took it to new heights. Coming like Donizetti from a humble background, his remarkable early talent was backed by a wealthy merchant in Busseto, Antonio Barezzi. In 1838, Verdi moved to Milan where four years later he scored a resounding success with his opera *Nabucco.* Like his predecessors, Verdi produced a series of operas that were premiered at the best opera houses in Europe: at the *Scala*, the *Fenice, San Carlo, Teatro Argentina*, in London, several times in Paris and in Saint Petersburg. Finally in 1871, *Aida*, today probably his most famous work, was first performed in Cairo. Verdi attached great importance to basing his operas on sophisticated literature. Thus, the libretti of his *Ernani* and *Rigoletto* were based on plays by Victor Hugo, those of *Macbeth* and *Otello* on Shakespeare's plays and of *Luisa Miller* on *The Maid of Orleans, The Robbers* and *Intrigue and Love,* all three by Friedrich Schiller.

After the founding of the Italian nation state, Prime Minister Conte Camillo Cavour persuaded Verdi to run for parliament. However, he soon relinquished his mandate. His fame gave him the freedom to work at different international opera houses and he even composed music for a text by Arrigo Boito, *Inno delle Nazioni,* to be performed at the world exhibition in London in 1862. Financial independence was vital to him and for that reason he consistently invested his profits in a country estate, San Agata, in his birthplace Roncole. Living there enabled him to demonstrate his financial independence to his local native environment. He also founded a retirement home in Milan, *Casa Verdi*, for impoverished singers and musicians, which today still provides places for sixty residents. Verdi's grave can be found in the chapel of this *casa di riposo*.

In autobiographical sketches of the late 1870s after the foundation of the Kingdom of Italy, Verdi styled himself as the 'bard' of the nation state movement. One feature of this which has become embedded in cultural history is an anecdote suggesting that the opera *Nabucco*, which was premiered in the *Scala* in 1842, was a clear patriotic statement by Verdi and as such celebrated by supporters of the opposition in the audience. The chorus *Va pensiero* sung on the bank of the River Euphrates by Hebrews enslaved by the Babylonians was said to have opened the eyes of the people of Milan gathered there to their own fate under the foreign domination of the Austrians. It was believed to have been a kind of Italian national anthem, understood as a protest against Austrian despotism. There are, however, no contemporary sources to verify this interpretation. On the contrary, first, a libretto with any kind of allusion to the tyranny of the Habsburgs would never have passed the censors. Second, there is no evidence of the audience reacting in any particular way to the chorus *Va pensiero*, whereas what they evidently did react to enthusiastically was the preceding ballet performance. Third, Verdi had dedicated the work to the emperor's daughter. And fourth, the *Scala* worked very closely with the State Opera in Vienna, not exactly a judicious venue for Italians to be making blatant demands for a nation state.[12]

Verdi, the man and his works, were not alone in being appropriated by cultural historical narratives in recent years as committed protagonists of the nation state movement even before 1848. The fact that Rossini set Schiller's *William Tell* to music is considered another patriotic act. Bellini's *Norma* is also unashamedly regarded as part of the Risorgimento canon. Like *Nabucco*, it was premiered in 1831 in the *Scala* under strict state oversight. It is naturally always difficult to establish how art is received and interpreted, but it is clear that the composers we are dealing with here cultivated good relations with the conservative monarchs in France, Austria and Italy, who were their sponsors and whose commissions they carried out. In the 1840s, Verdi was not dreaming of any kind of nation state, only of his own country estate.

In 1848, Giuseppe Mazzini described the state of modern Italian painting from his exile in London as follows:

> The immense and glorious past of Italian painting fascinates and absorbs all those who do not have a well-founded faith in the future and wish to study the present. Three centuries of titans cast their shadows on all that is done today. Three centuries of art deemed magnificent by virtue of its concept and execution and the numerous masterpieces that were created – they appear as a threat to the forgotten, modest, isolated studios of modern

> painting and to the foreign travellers, amongst whom are too often young Italians. Who would want to stop in the studio of a Hayez or a Podesti in a country that can offer the Sistine chapel, Raphael's stanzas, the Camposanto, and galleries of Florence and Rome?[13]

Thirty years earlier, Napoleon had expressed the same sentiment even more drastically in a conversation with Canova: 'When it comes to painters, in Italy they are pretty poor, and the best of them we have here in France'.[14]

Both of these judgements sum up the state of European painting in the late eighteenth and nineteenth centuries. While in the field of opera it was Italy that produced first rate works of art that gained international recognition, for painting it was Paris that set the standards. In the Renaissance and Baroque periods, Rome, Florence and Naples with their royal and aristocratic patronage had been the undisputed centres of the fine arts, but during the eighteenth century the focus shifted to northern Italy. In Venice, Giambattista Tiepolo and his sons worked as sought-after, highly-priced painters of frescoes. The Prince Bishop of Würzburg commissioned him to paint a fresco for the ceiling of his bishop's residence for 40,000 guilders. Today it is considered his masterwork. Other artists in high demand were the view painters (*vedutisti)* Francesco Guardi, and Giovanni Antonio Canal with his nephew Bernardo Bellotto, both of whom used the same artist's name, Canaletto. Like Tiepolio, both Canalettos were in demand for their city panoramas, not only within Venice. Canaletto the elder worked for a long time in Britain, where he carried out numerous works for the aristocracy, while the younger Canaletto worked in the royal capitals of Dresden, Prague, Vienna and Warsaw. The now less well-known Rococo painter Stefano Torelli from Bologna was engaged for the elector's residence in Dresden. When Dresden became embroiled in the Seven Years War (1756–1763), he accepted commissions in north Germany, including the decoration of the audience chamber of the town hall in Lübeck with lavish frescos.

After the middle of the century, the Baroque and Rococo styles were increasingly replaced by neo-Classicism. This reversion to classical antiquity was prefaced by Johann Joachim Winckelmann's pithy phrase 'Noble simplicity, quiet grandeur' (*edle Einfalt, stille Größe)*. In his *Thoughts on the imitation of Greek works in painting and sculpture,* published in 1755, Winckelmann, a German archaeologist and art theorist, put forward his interpretation of the essence of Graeco-Hellenistic art, which was to influence the visual arts and contemporary taste throughout Europe. After Winckelmann had converted to Catholicism in 1763, Pope Clement XIII appointed him Prefect of Antiquities in Rome. The most important impulses for painting came from Paris and it was Jacques Louis David who was the first to break with traditional Baroque style with his painting *The Oath of the Horatii* in 1784. Although this painting was never intended to portray a conspiracy against tyranny, it was interpreted as such in the context of the French Revolution and secured

David's fame. His works were greatly admired in Italy and had a lasting influence on painting.

During the Napoleonic era, numerous neoclassical historical paintings were commissioned by the new rulers in Italy so that they could furnish their residences with art that represented the interests of the state. Andrea Appiani, the most influential official artist in Milan, owed his fame to the protection of Napoleon. He painted a portrait of the energetic young general in 1797 and for the royal residence of the Kingdom of Italy in Milan he created a highly acclaimed series of frescoes with an apotheosis of Napoleon. They glorified political and military milestones from the first Italian campaign to Napoleon's coronation with the crown of Lombardy in Milan. Other high dignitaries in the young kingdom had their portraits painted by Appiani. For Napoleon's stepson and viceroy, Eugène Beauharnais, he completed a series of frescoes in the dining hall of the royal villa in Milan. In 1805, he was named official court painter of the Kingdom of Italy. In Paris this office was held by Jacques Louis David.

Meanwhile, in Rome, the former papal palace, the Quirinal Palace, was being furnished with pomp and splendour for the emperor and his second wife. This major construction site provided work during the last years of the empire for artists of distinction as well as young talents who were staying in the Eternal City when it was annexed by France in 1809 after the abduction of the Pope. The palace was intended to serve as a residence for Napoleon when he was staying in Rome and the rooms were decorated with neoclassical history paintings. Three paintings with antique themes were created by Jean-Auguste-Dominique Ingres for the chambers of the empress. Vincenzo Camuccini, who was employed by the Pope both previously and again after 1814 as *Inspector General of Roman painting*, was also involved in decorating the imperial residence with neoclassical pictures. At the same time as Murat was promoting contemporary art and sculpture supporting the state in Naples, Elisa Bonaparte (Baciocchi), one of the emperor's sisters, was sponsoring Pietro Benvenuti in Florence as the first court painter. Since her ambition was not satisfied by being granted the principality of Lucca, she pressed Napoleon to permit her to reign over the Duchy of Tuscany as well. Napoleon, however, only made her governor of Tuscany with the personal title of Grand Duchess. The decoration of her ducal residence in Florence was nevertheless ambitious. In 1812 Benvenuti, who was not only a successful history painter, but also a sought-after portraitist, painted *The Court of Elisa Baciocchi in Florence with Antonio Canova*. It shows Canova presenting the Duchess with a portrait bust he has made for her. Since Canova was undoubtedly the best-known sculptor of the Napoleonic era, this portrait represented the duchess not only as a ruler but also as a patron of the arts. After 1815, Benvenuti painted portraits of the Austrian Grand Dukes and their families.

Fig. 10 Pietro Benvenuti, Elisa Baciocchi, Grand Duchess of Tuscany, at her Court in Florence, 1812.

Antonio Canova's rise in fame to become the most sought-after sculptor of the turn of the century began after studying classical antiquity in Rome. There his extraordinary talent was brought to the attention of the popes, who commissioned him to design and create funerary monuments. In 1798, during the first French occupation of the Papal States, Canova first travelled to Austria and Prussia. He then responded to a summons from Napoleon Bonaparte to come to Paris, where he was immediately accepted into the Academy of Arts. Murat and Josephine were the first in the family to frequently commission works from Canova. They both bought copies of *Amor and Psyche*, Murat bought a *Boxer* and Josephine a depiction of *Hebe*. On his way back from Paris to Rome, Canova stopped over in Lyon at the home of Cardinal Fesch, Napoleon's uncle and one of the keenest art collectors of the time. In Milan, he was the guest of Murat and the vice president of the Republic of Italy, Francesco Melzi d'Eril. After these visits, he was considered the official artist of the French regime. His return to Rome was celebrated in the house of Angelika Kauffmann, who had earned an international reputation as a portraitist. Kauffmann was born in Switzerland, trained by her father at Lake Como and, after a tour through Europe, had now returned to live in Rome as a painter of princes, aristocrats and artists. Her house was a popular meeting place for the high society in whose circles her clients were to be found. Her 1764 portrait of the art theorist Winckelmann secured her fame. She also met Johann Wolfgang von Goethe on his

Italian journeys and often visited art collections with him. He acknowledged 'her talent is phenomenal and, for a woman, quite remarkable'.[15]

Over the next few years, Canova created controversial, heroic sculptures of King Ferdinand in Naples, and an oversized one of Napoleon. Both of them were depicted in the nude, in keeping with Canova's ideals of classical beauty. They were never exhibited in public but found a lively echo in contemporary discourse. The art world celebrated his life-size sculpted portrait of Princess Paolina Borghese, another sister of Napoleon, as a masterpiece. He portrayed her with her own features as a semi-recumbent Venus, triumphantly holding an apple in her hand. Another sculptor who rose to comparable fame at this time was the artist Bertel Thorvaldson, a Dane who spent most of his artistic life in Rome. He was trained at the academy in Copenhagen, then travelled to the Eternal City on a scholarship to study classical antiquity. Like Canova, he received state commissions from Napoleon as well as from papal circles. In 1823, Consalvi commissioned him to design the funeral monument for Pope Pius VII. It was placed in Saint Peter's Basilica in the *Cappella Clementina* and is considered one of his most remarkable works.

With the decline of the Napoleonic empire, the enthusiasm for (neo)-Classicism also waned. Artists now turned to Romantic compositions, but history painting remained undefeated and, according to the tributes of the Paris Academy, the leading institution since the *Ancien Régime,* was still the most distinguished artistic genre. It was promoted by rulers until about 1800, and served to extol them, often as mythological figures. This trend continued in the nineteenth century, but with the added novelty that the painters' compositions were intended to be emotionally or morally moving. Art critics who discussed history painting now referred expressly to the *toucher*, i. e. the way viewers were moved by the paintings. In the 1820s, Francesco Hayez emerged as the uncrowned master of 'touching' Romantic history painting in Italy. Born in modest circumstances in Venice, his talent was discovered early. He spent his youth in Rome, where he was trained, and in 1818 he settled in Milan in the vicinity of the *Accademia di Brera*. This academy of art had developed during the Restoration to become the best address for contemporary painting in Italy. Hayez' breakthrough as an artist came in 1821, when his painting *Il Conte di Carmagnola* was exhibited in Milan. Its subject matter was based on a romantic tragedy published shortly beforehand by Alessandro Manzoni. At the beginning of his career, Hayez was able to find potential patrons amongst the wealthy Milanese patricians for his large-scale and correspondingly expensive compositions. He also reaped great success with his painting *Vespri siciliani*, which he produced three times. The version presented in 1822 is considered one of the most important works of Romanticism. It is also based on a historical episode from the distant past: the Sicilian uprising against the rule of the House of Anjou. Marchioness Visconti d'Aragona, who commissioned the first version, insisted on some of her best friends being immortalised in the painting. This established a principle and Hayez can be seen to frequently paint the portraits of his clients in his historical paintings.

The preference for historical dramas set in the Middle Ages or whose subjects were distant lands was also a pan-European phenomenon. One only needs to refer here to Paul Delaroche in Paris, or Alfred Rethel in Düsseldorf. Hayez' clientele was also by no means limited to the Milanese nobility – he painted for Genovese shipowners, Sicilian aristocrats, merchants in Frankfurt and Milan, and the King of Württemberg. Besides his history paintings he also produced hundreds of portraits. He did not only shine as the preferred artist of the moderate, liberal aristocracy in Milan, he also painted the ultraconservative Metternich and the Habsburg emperor. In 1835, he made his way to Vienna, and at the end of this journey, his book of commissions was full. On the one hand he painted portraits of the most important dignitaries in Vienna and, on the other, in Milan he was commissioned to produce frescoes whose purpose was to extol the existing political order. Hayez' career did not suffer from the extremely violent revolutionary conflicts in Milan in 1848. In 1850, the Habsburg governor, General Radetzky, appointed him professor at the Brera art academy and finally, in 1855, entrusted him with its directorship. He coped with the advent of the new political order in 1859 with no difficulty, becoming a member of the committee whose task it was to re-organise the Brera. This exceptional artist was awarded both the Habsburg and the Savoy orders of merit.

While top Italian artists frequently went to the European cultural centres in search of commissions, whole armies of painters, sculptures and architects from neighbouring countries made their way south. If at all possible, a sojourn in Rome to study there was part of their training. The Germans' desire to travel to Italy was strengthened by Goethe's autobiographical account, which was carried around like a bible in the pockets of many of those who wanted to relive the poet's journey. An annual Rome prize was awarded to artists and architects by the Academy in Paris which permitted the fortunate winner to rise to new heights. It enabled them to spend time at the French Academy in Rome, which, together with the papal *Accademia San Lucca*, had an excellent reputation. Artists of all kinds and from all European countries were drawn across the Alps, often financed by an allowance from their king or prince. Some only stayed a few months or a year, others their whole lives. Veritable colonies of artists were formed in Rome, Florence and Naples. A group of German artists around Johann Friedrich Overbeck and Franz Pforr, who had founded the Brotherhood of Saint Luke, had a defining effect on style in Rome after 1810. Living together in the monastery of San Isidoro according to monastic rules, they revered Raphael and Albrecht Dürer as their models and devoted themselves primarily to biblical subjects. Some of them converted to Catholicism because they saw it as a source of inspiration for their art. The Romans derided them as 'Nazarenes' because their long hair was reminiscent of Jesus and his disciples.

In Naples of the same period there was the School of Posillipo, which owed its origin to the Dutch painter Anton Sminck van Pitloo, who was sponsored by Napoleon. He trained in Paris and Rome and in 1820 founded a private school of art in Posillipo, now a district of Naples, where he developed and taught landscape painting with particular light effects. In this style countless view paintings (*vedute*) of the Gulf of Naples were produced, a subject that was in high demand by wealthy travellers to Italy. The style of painting developed by Pitloo and his pupils, Giacinto Gigante to name but one, is considered to be the most significant contribution to southern Italian art during the Restoration. Even without the School of Posillipo, landscape painting, together with genre painting and portraiture, was a particularly popular source of income for artists from everywhere in Europe living in Italy. Camille Corot, among others, stayed in Italy for four years, when he painted his much sought-after images of longing for the 'land where the lemon trees blossom'.

While the School of Posillipo changed the focus of painting in the south, at the time of the foundation of the nation state the same was being done in Tuscany by a different group of artists, the *Macchiaoli*. They shunned the academic style of romantic painting by artists such as Hayez and turned to more realistic, impressionist painting, often preferring smaller-scale scenes of bourgeois and rural life. Painting outdoors, they created pictures with bright luminous colours and spontaneous impressions. The name of the group was derived from the Italian word *macchia*, meaning a patch or blotch, and refers to their style of painting. The best-known *Macchiaoli* painters were undoubtedly Nino Costa, Giovanni Fattori and Telemaco Signorini.

Fattori made a name for himself not only as a landscape painter but also as a painter of patriotic battle scenes. There was a huge surge in depictions of episodes and battles from the wars of unification after the foundation of the Italian nation state in 1861. History painting turned to contemporary history and idealised nationalism, bravery and contemporary military heroism. The most popular subjects were the battles won over the Austrians, depictions of the troops of the Red Shirts, Garibaldi's irregulars, and the martyrdom of youthful volunteers. For a national painting competition organised by the government, Giovanni Fattori painted the large-scale battle scene *The Italian Camp at the Battle of Magenta* in which the French and Piedmontese had defeated the Austrians in the Second Italian War of Independence. He also painted pictures of troops and portraits of Garibaldi. Fattori and other painters of patriotic scenes were born in the middle of the 1820s in northern or central Italy and had witnessed the war themselves or fought as volunteers. This was true for Carlo Ademollo, who enthusiastically joined the royal troops in 1859 and the National Guard in Florence in 1866. He was appointed official war artist by King Victor Emmanuel for his pictures *The Breach at the Porta*

*Pia*, *Garibaldi in Rome*, *The Handshake of Teano* between Garibaldi and the king, *Garibaldi on Horseback*, and *The Death of Enrico Cairoli*. A further artist in this category was Girolamo Induno, who was trained as a genre painter at the Brera academy. In 1848 he took part in the famous uprising in Milan, the *Cinque Giornate*, in which the Milanese succeeded in driving the Austrians under General Radetzky out of the city in spite of their overwhelming superiority. He then hurried to Rome to help defend the Republic of Rome. Over the next few decades, he painted numerous episodes from the wars of unification. Works commissioned by the king include *The Departure of the Conscripts* and *Bivouac of Soldiers in Garibaldi's Army near Capua*. His depiction of the embarkation of Garibaldi's legendary thousand as well as numerous versions of Garibaldi's Alpine fighters and the *King's Entry into Venice* became particularly famous. Michele Cammarano, who was originally from Naples and whose father had written libretti for Verdi, was also fascinated by Garibaldi. He learnt his trade at the Academy of Art and the School of Posillipo and made his name as a painter of battles able to depict the action of war particularly dramatically. An example is his large-scale work *Breach at the Porta Pia*, in which the soldiers dash straight towards the viewer, even though this event was in reality fairly unspectacular. The mostly oversized paintings by Ademollo, Fattori, Induno, Cammarano and other war artists hung in municipal and state museums and were intended to help raise awareness of the glorious path to the Italian nation state.

In the field of architecture, in Italy – as in the rest of Europe – there was no significant innovation until after the fall of the Papal States. Buildings such as the numerous opera houses, villas, palaces and gardens had been constructed in the neoclassical style since the late eighteenth and early nineteenth centuries. The sixteenth-century villa style of Andrea Palladio still served as a model in Britain and the United States as well as in Italy. As the nineteenth century progressed, various 'neo' styles prevailed: neo-Romanticism, neo-Gothic and neo-Renaissance. There was no significant urban development in Rome until after 1870, nor in Turin where the royal residence and surrounding hunting lodges had largely been built in the early modern period.

The development of style in Italian literature was similar to that in the visual arts and music. Classicism dominated the last third of the eighteenth century but was replaced by Romanticism after the fall of the Napoleonic empire and was in turn supplanted by Realism after the middle of the nineteenth century. There was considerable synergy between the various art forms, so that novels, plays and poems often inspired painters, librettists and composers of operas, and vice versa.

The most influential Italian dramatist in the Enlightenment period was Conte Vittorio Alfieri d'Asti. Born in 1749, he was sent as a boy to be trained at the military academy in Turin in accordance with his rank but dropped out. Restless journeys through Europe as far north as Scandinavia followed from 1766–1772, made possible by his parents' considerable fortune. Alfieri then returned to Turin, lived as a dandy and wrote his first tragedy *Antonio and Cleopatra*, but because he had grown up in both French language and culture and the Piedmontese dialect, he settled in Florence in order to learn the best Italian. Subsequently all his plays were written in Tuscan, considered the purest and most beautiful variant of Italian. After a longer sojourn in Rome, he moved to Paris in 1787, where, as a convinced republican, he enthusiastically supported the outbreak of the French Revolution. When the radical Jacobins came to power in the summer of 1792, however, and the civil war and acts of terror began, he fled France. His assets in Paris were confiscated, his government bonds lost value, and his former enthusiasm turned to hatred of all things French. This was reflected in his play *Misogallo*, which deals with betrayed love, lost hopes and shattered illusions. Alfieri wrote twenty-two melodramatic tragedies in all, many of which could not be performed until 1789 in Paris. The early drama *Filippo,* written in 1775, was the first to elaborate the theme that became central to his works, namely the fate of a ruler who is obsessed with the pursuit of power and responds to growing resistance with ever-increasing despotism. A later example is *The Avenged Etruria* in which the despot Alessandro de' Medici is murdered by his cousin Lorenzo. Lorenzo was extolled by Alfieri as a hero of liberty for having avenged the tyrant's wrongdoing and wickedness. The other tragedies also return repeatedly to the feeling of hatred against any kind of tyranny and servitude. Alfieri appears to have had a huge influence on the following generations. Massimo d'Azeglio, for example, reports in his memoirs that as a young man he memorised entire dramas by Alfieri in his study and recited them effusively.[16]

Ugo Foscolo, who was thirty years younger, is often mentioned in the same breath as Alfieri and considered the last important Classical poet. He was, like Alfieri, initially an enthusiastic supporter of the French Revolution and the young Napoleon. For this reason, he volunteered to join the French Cisalpine legion and fought in the Battle of Marengo. However, after 1800, Napoleon's authoritarian style of government forced him into literary resistance. Like those of Alfieri, Foscolo's tragedies such as *Ajax* (1811) focus on the struggle for a free fatherland. Although they were set in ancient Greece, it was impossible to ignore the veiled criticism of Napoleon and his minister of police, Fouché. Foscolo wrote not only tragedies but also the first ever Italian epistolary novel *Last Letters of Jacopo Ortis* in 1802. It was influenced by Rousseau and Goethe and also deals mainly with contemporary political topics. In desperation over the appalling state of the nation under French and Austrian rule in northern Italy, the hero takes his own life. In his popular poem *From the Graves*, Foscolo calls on his fellow countrymen to be inspired by past heroes and rise up against tyranny and bondage. During the Napoleonic era his neoclassical works were frequently censored. At the beginning of the Restoration, he immediately left Italy and went into exile in Switzerland and then London, thus boosting his reputation as a principled patriotic resistance fighter.

If Alfieri and Foscolo were the most respected poets of Classicism in Italy, Conte Giacomo Leopardi and Conte Alessandro Manzoni enjoyed the same esteem for the Romantic period. They both played a crucial role in the revival of literary Italian in the nineteenth century. Leopardi was born in 1798 to an ultra-conservative noble family in provincial Recanati. Although he tried his hand with tragedies and as a translator of Greek epics as a young man, he eventually became most famous for his collections of poetry. His *Canti* (songs) were a masterly expression of his prevailing mood of world weariness *(Weltschmerz)*, pessimism and nihilism. They reflect a yearning for a fulfilled life of youth, beauty and love while also demonstrating that all present hopes and desires cannot be fulfilled. As a melancholy Romantic poet, he shunned contemporary faith in progress and saw the Italian nation in a state of decline. Besides his masterful poetry, Leopardi published *Operette morali (Small Moral Works)*. These were dialogues and essays in which he painted an imaginative, sarcastic picture of the vanity and futility of existence, portraying the pursuit of love and fame and the longing for death.

Giovanni Berchet was also one of the most important patriotic poets alongside Leopardi. He had taken part in the preparations for the Milanese uprising in 1821 and subsequently lived in exile in Belgium, which meant that his poetic works *I profughi de Parga (The Fugitives of Parga)* (1821), *Romance* (1822–1824) and *Fantasy* (1829) did not immediately reach Italy. Nevertheless, the theme of *The Fugitives of Parga* enjoyed great popularity. It was not based on a heroic historical epic but on a topical human drama that had played out in the distant eastern Mediterranean. In 1814 the island of Parga was declared a British protectorate and in 1819 handed over to Ali, the Pasha of Janina. The Greek islanders were expelled and resettled in Corfu. This deportation also served as a topic for a historical painting by Hayez, who remarked in his memoirs that the fate of the islanders of Parga was well known to everyone and that it was accompanied by large public demonstrations of support for the victims.[17] Another popular writer, Cesare Cantù, a grammar-school teacher, was able to stay in Milan until the 1848 revolution, when he too was temporarily imprisoned and fled to Piedmont. In his previous historical works and romantic novels, he had attacked Austria, but when his novel *Margherita Pusterla* was published in 1838 after thorough scrutiny by the Austrian censors, it became a bestseller. Cantù used the novel's main protagonist to convey conservative Christian values, as did the protagonist in his popular novel *Carlambrogio da Montevecchia*, who returns to religion as 'the true and eternal power'. He was a prolific Romantic writer and, as a staunch, even orthodox Catholic, believed in the inviolability of the family and the autonomy of the Church. As such he saw himself in the role of impartial educator of the Italian people.

Conte Alessandro Manzoni was also among the most prominent and widely read Italian authors. His novel *I Promessi Sposi (The Betrothed)*, was a resounding success far beyond the borders of Italy. It's second, revised edition was published in 1827 and earned him instant fame. When Manzoni sent a copy to Goethe, he greeted it most enthusiastically and strongly advocated a German translation. Manzoni reworked the Italian version, deleting any traces of Lombardian dialect, and this new edition in standard Tuscan was published in 1840–1842. Although its subtitle *A seventeenth-century Milanese story discovered and rewritten* labels the novel as a mere retelling of an existing source to lend it authenticity, it was in fact the first modern Italian novel and is considered the most significant work in Italian literature after Dante's *Divine Comedy*. It is set at the time of Spanish foreign rule and the first five chapters describe historical events and conditions without introducing a single character from the actual plot. These detailed descriptions of historical events and social conditions are based on Manzoni's intensive research of the sources. A young couple, Lucia and Renzo, from the village of Lecco at the southern end of Lake Como, are at the heart of the novel. They are engaged to be married but Don Rodrigo, a nobleman notorious for his brutality, bets on a whim that he will have Lucia. His *bravi (paid thugs)* browbeat Don Abbondio, the priest, into not marrying the couple, at which point they flee with Lucia's mother Agnes. The two women go to the monastery of Monza while Renzo goes to Milan where he gets involved in a bread riot and is accused of being one of the ringleaders. He is arrested and freed again, whereupon he flees to Bergamo, which at that time belonged to the independent Republic of Venice. Meanwhile Don Rodrigo has Lucia kidnapped and taken to his castle. But she, the pious young fiancée, is able to bring about his spiritual conversion; he finds faith and sets her free. After overcoming several bewildering hurdles in plague-ridden Milan, the two lovers are reunited, marry and start a family in Bergamo.

Contemporaries did not only read *The Betrothed* as a historical novel; they also interpreted it in the context of their own political situation. Its panorama of the times is menacing and oppressive, reflecting a jurisdiction undermined by corruption, whose threats of severe punishment stood in marked contrast to its lack of efficiency. The masses, the ordinary people, are at the mercy of state despotism. Manzoni is portraying Lombardy suffering under Spanish foreign rule and more or less enslaved, which discerning readers could compare with contemporary Habsburg rule if they so wished. What was new and modern here was that for the first time in Italian literature a novel's heroes are simple, pious people. Lucia is threatened by sexual violence and Renzo represents the youthful hero.

Similar patterns can be found in other more or less well-known works of Italian Romanticism – novels, poems and tragedies that appeal to shared emotions. A free fatherland and independence were the fundamental aims of every patriotic supporter of the Risorgimento. There were, however, other even more profound values to be defended – the violation of personal honour and also honour violated by the tyranny on Italian soil and by attacks on the chastity of Italian women.

Typical, gendered categories supply the framework for these melodramas within which the heroes are faced with obstacles on their path to happiness. Romantic love was likened to patriotism. Male heroes challenged established conventions and defended their wives from armed threats from outside. Private emotions, public passions, family ties and patriotic loyalties became inextricably linked and were joined by the nationalisation of honour and a religious charge to the concept of fatherland. A combination of all these elements can be found in Alessandro Manzoni's historical novel, Leopardi's poems, Verdi's operas and Francesco Hayez' historical paintings.

## 5.5 Schools, universities and academies

During the eighteenth century, public schooling became increasingly a matter for the state and not, as in the Middle Ages, controlled by the cities. Measures for reforming the school system were introduced in central and northern Italy during the Enlightenment period. They began in the Kingdom of Sardinia-Piedmont under Victor Amadeus II, who decreed several reforms in 1717 and 1727 and placed schools under state supervision. Other Italian states also introduced steps towards secularising schools so as to reduce the powerful social normative influence of the Catholic church. The first public, non-church schools were opened in the Duchy of Parma and Piacenza by Ferdinand I. Reform efforts went furthest in Lombardy under the Habsburgs where Maria Theresia introduced compulsory schooling for children between six and twelve years of age. In 1786 a comprehensive network of schools began to be set up, divided into three types: 'trivial' for each municipality, 'intermediate' for each city and 'normal' for the provincial capitals. Just two years later the first state teacher training centre opened in Milan. Public education was introduced at the same time in the Duchy of Tuscany under the Habsburg Leopold I, divided into primary and secondary schools. The rulers in the south and the Papal States were, however, much more conservative in their actions. Schools in the Kingdom of Naples remained mainly in the hands of the church, although efforts to establish state schools also gradually evolved here before the outbreak of the French Revolution. There was, of course, no question of any of these reforms in the Papal States – here the Church remained in control of the schools, in spite of the ban on the Jesuit order imposed throughout Europe in 1773. Nevertheless, regardless of who was teaching, the literacy rate in the Italian states remained shockingly low. This was especially the case in the south where only an estimated maximum of 20 per cent of the population could read and write. This figure was naturally higher in the cities than in the rural areas.

Fundamental reforms were carried out during the Napoleonic era, regardless of whether the Italian departments were ruled directly from Paris or belonged to the Kingdom of Italy or the Kingdom of Naples. Had the French ruled for longer, these would have had a considerably more positive effect, especially as a result of the expansion of basic education. In 1810 Murat introduced compulsory primary schooling for all. Education was divided into four sectors: elementary, lower and upper schools and universities. In the Kingdom of Italy, a comprehensive education plan was introduced in 1808 which provided for the establishment of a boys' grammar school in the capital of every department. Their equivalent in the south were the government colleges. Regulations for primary schools were published in Milan in 1812. The children were to learn reading, writing and arithmetic, as well as receive lessons in religion, patriotism and loyalty to the crown. Corporal punishment was abolished.

The Restoration brought a partial withdrawal of these French measures, leading to huge deficits, especially in primary education. Most of the Italian states took only a moderate interest in education. There was virtually no improvement in the literacy rate and by 1850 still only an estimated 20 to 25 per cent of the population could read and write. The first truly comprehensive and far-reaching school reform did not occur until 1859 with the *Legge Casati* in the Kingdom of Sardinia-Piedmont, named after its instigator Conte Gabrio Casati, the minister of education. These laws were then implemented in the conquered areas after the founding of the nation state in 1861 and remained in force until 1923. Primary school was set at a total of four years of which the first two were compulsory. There were two types of secondary schools: grammar schools or *lycées,* which offered a classical education and prepared students for further studies, and technical colleges. There were grammar schools in every provincial capital, named after local celebrities. Teachers were also trained in specialised institutions, the *scuole normali.* A striking factor of this reform was that it provided free compulsory education for both sexes in their early years.

These essentially progressive reforms caused heated debates amongst the political elite. While some saw a civic duty in education, conservative and Catholic forces were afraid it would direct the rural population to socialism. The argument of Pasquale Villari, an education politician and historian from Naples, was that the improvement of living conditions should take precedence over education. Even the democratically minded Giuseppe Merzario, writer and educator, was against compulsory education. He argued that the state had no right to impose education because the population did not understand its value. Moderate conservatives also expressed concern about the freedom of families and control by the state. They argued in vain – the state intervened with further laws punishing disregard for compulsory education.

At the same time there was urgent need for reform in the universities. Italy was the birthplace of universities and was proud of having the oldest university in Europe, the University of Bologna, which dates back to 1088. It was followed by

Modena, founded in 1175, Padova in 1222 and Naples two years later. However, as the cities diminished in significance during the Renaissance period, so these oldest and most prestigious universities in Europe lost their splendour. By the early modern period they were rarely attractive beyond the borders of their respective Italian states and only trained civil servants, lawyers, theologians and doctors for their own regions. While in its heyday the University of Bologna had attracted several thousand students, by the eighteenth century it had only three hundred. This did not change in the first half of the nineteenth century and in 1859, at the fall of the Papal States, twenty professors taught only four hundred students. The Papal States showed little interest in investing in university education.

Before 1800 it was no longer the cities but the ruling families who were the driving force in the education sector. They founded and supported academies, which enjoyed greater academic freedom than the traditional universities, which only concentrated on teaching. Then, during the Napoleonic period, fundamental reforms were considered, with the German education system as a model. Giovanni Scopoli, who had been appointed Director General of Public Education in the Kingdom of Italy in 1809, travelled to the German states in the spring and summer of 1812 specifically to discover the advantages and disadvantages of their institutions. After a four-month-long trip, he compiled a detailed report on German education for Viceroy Eugène Beauharnais. Scopoli first reported on the elementary schools and lycées, then in detail on universities. He gave a very positive assessment of the University of Göttingen, which at that time enjoyed the reputation of a modern, enlightened educational institution, and emphasised its scientific standards and administrative autonomy in particular. For personal reasons he was unable to visit the recently founded Friedrich Wilhelms University in Berlin. The collapse of the Napoleonic empire, however, prevented this report from having any practical impact on university reform.

During the Restoration, various reforms gave rise to model universities such as Padova and Pavia in Lombardy-Venetia, which were among the best in the Habsburg empire. The quality of Italian universities, however, varied considerably. Some were large, offering quality in all subjects but others in the provincial periphery were tiny. Significant improvements, not only to schools but also the university system, were brought about by the above-mentioned *Legge Casati* passed in Turin in 1859 and after 1861 implemented throughout the newly formed nation state. The law stipulated that, according to the centralist French system, a total of twenty-one Italian universities were all to work to the same nation-wide standards. These were the universities in Turin, Genoa, Cagliari and Sassari in the Kingdom of Sardinia-Piedmont, Siena, Pisa and Florence in the Duchy of Tuscany, Naples, Messina, Palermo and Catania in the Kingdom of the Two Sicilies and Bologna, Ferrara, Urbino, Perugia, Macerata and Camerino in the Papal States. In the case of smaller cities, closures were considered in favour of the larger universities.

University reform was hotly debated in parliament. Numerous publications also discussed the status quo of the universities at the beginning of the 1860s, thus providing valuable insights into the conditions of the day. They focussed on the question of how Italian universities so in need of reform could effectively educate a national leadership elite which would contribute towards building the nation state. The politicians concerned were particularly critical of the discrepancies in academic performance, staffing, examination standards, course structure and student admission requirements. Their discussions concentrated on Casati's comprehensive centralist reform of higher education. This was because it applied to the whole of the new nation state without any allowance for the situation and conditions at the numerous universities which had not originally been under its legislation This process was regarded as an expression of cultural hegemony on the part of Piedmont. One of the most controversial questions was how to restructure the smaller universities in line with the new law and in general how to achieve more consistency in the areas of academic appointments, student admissions and the university syllabus. When it came to defending the old systems and traditions, the provincial universities were supported by the local authorities, since it was of great importance to them that they could continue to educate their own ruling class locally. In the end, therefore, the highly complex debate on higher education policy reflected the conflict between the centre and the periphery, a conflict that caused many reform proposals to run aground.

Whereas Italian universities in the nineteenth century were primarily teaching institutions, research was still carried out at the numerous academies, of which there were several in every town and dozens in the larger cities. The larger and more important royal academies strove to be seen as scientific and academic, since they considered themselves primarily as research institutes in contrast to the universities, whose main task was teaching. The academies had libraries, published their members' research findings, organised lectures for an exclusive circle and offered prize money for solving research questions. Their academic staff were frequently uncomplimentary about the universities and some leading members of the academy movement refused to teach at universities. By the nineteenth century, however the academies were gradually passing their peak. In the Enlightenment period they had been seen as the nations' scientific flagship, but their influence diminished and they became ossified, stuck in their traditional ideas and structures. It was, however, still a privilege to be appointed a member of one of the famous academies. In the eyes of conservative aristocrats, the academies still offered the nineteenth-century nobility a splendid framework within which to orchestrate the poetic detachment they as dilettantes wished to retain from bourgeois academia and science and its prosaic reality. The social significance of the academies should not, therefore, be underrated. Admission to an academy required the appropriate networks. Candidates first needed someone, preferably an influential member, to assess whether their application had any chance of success and nominate them, and then further members to support the application. Applications that were rejected caused great bitterness. Carlo Negroni, for example, professor of law in Novara and later senator, had asked Ercole Ricotti, whom he had apparently known since his studies, to obtain his admission to the Turin Academy as a corresponding member. Ricotti was a full member of the Academy but was unsuccessful. Negroni then wrote him an angry letter in which he discredited the academicians and their work, berating them as 'nitpickers'.[18]

Belonging to as many well-respected academies as possible raised social and cultural capital significantly. It was the norm to belong to several different city academies and dense networks ensued. One example is the Marquess Gino Capponi, who played an important role not only in the leading humanities academies in Florence. Since academy membership was treated in the city as family property, Capponi's father, Pier Roberto, was able to push through his acceptance as a member of the *Accademia Colombaria* at the early age of eighteen, whereupon he was immediately elected president. These leadership positions were passed down through the generations in Florentine families. From 1827–1829 Capponi was treasurer of the *Accademia dei Georgofili* and in the 1860s president of the long-standing *Accademia della Crusca*. As from 1821 he jointly edited the journal *Antologia* with his friend the publisher Gian Pietro Vieusseux, originally from Switzerland, until it fell foul of the censors in 1832. He also started the *Giornale agrario toscano* in 1827 to promote liberal economic policies and from 1842, again with Vieusseux, the *Archivio Storico Italiano,* one of the first Italian historical journals claiming to publish source editions and research on the history of the whole of Italy. In 1862 it was managed by the newly founded historical society, whose president was again Gino Capponi. The publication of this journal and the foundation of the historical society independently of the academies are proof that their academic and scientific scope was considered out of date. New scientific associations which were initially quite distinct from the academies also emerged in other Italian cities. In many cases, the academies were now regarded as 'fusty' and were accused of being frozen in their ceremonial pomp.

## 5.6 Religion, denominations and lived piety

Towards the end of the eighteenth-century Italy, like France, Spain and Portugal, was an almost entirely Catholic country. Although some Jewish communities, the oldest being in Rome, could look back on a history uninterrupted since antiquity, in the nineteenth century the number of Jews in relation to the total population was only 0.1 per cent. This figure had been significantly higher in the middle of the early modern period, at 0.7 to 0.9 per cent in all Italian states. Since the late fifteenth century there had been systematic expulsions and amendment to laws which discriminated against Jews and imposed severe restrictions on their lives. In 1492, Sicily still had fifty-two flourishing Jewish communities with around 30,000 members making up as much as two to three per cent of the total population. Spanish rule wiped them out for ever. These Jews suffered the same fate as those in Spain, Portugal a little later and in the Provence – they were all expelled. Many fled initially from Sicily to the southern Italian mainland, from where they were also expelled some fifty years later. They then made their way to northern and central Italy, although many of them went on to Poland and Lithuania. Since the Dukes of Tuscany proved to be decidedly tolerant, a Jewish community began to grow in both Pisa and the coastal city of Livorno. In other Italian cities, however, they suffered recurrent expulsion or restrictions. Genoa expelled its Jews in 1555. Jewish residents in Bologna were under threat and migrated to the nearby Duchy of Ferrara, which pursued a similarly liberal settlement policy to Tuscany, since the Jews always contributed significantly to tax revenues and brought with them outstanding physicians and experienced merchants and bankers.

The first Italian city to forcibly confine its Jewish inhabitants in a ghetto, following the German model, was Venice in 1516; the ghetto in Rome was established by Pius V in 1555. All Jews were expelled from the Papal States except for those in Rome and Ancona. Subsequent popes sometimes tightened and sometimes relaxed anti-Jewish measures. It was not until the end of the eighteenth century that Emperor Joseph II introduced his *Patent of Tolerance*, granting the Jews in Lombardy greater freedom of worship, and total Jewish emancipation did not occur until the Napoleonic period. Italian Jews then enjoyed equality before the law and freedom of trade and settlement, but this lasted only until the fall of Napoleon. During the Restoration, pogrom-like riots and looting resurfaced. Pius VII, who had returned to Rome, again banished the Jews to the ghetto, thus subjecting them once more to degrading living conditions. These were powerfully described by the German writer and historian Ferdinand Gregorovius in 1853:

> What frightens the observer of the ghetto most is how cramped and dirty these winding streets and alleys are, with their houses towering high and narrow. The Jewish families sit piled on top of the other, as in a Roman columbarium. This compression of human dwellings is striking here in Rome, a city which is spread out over a wide plain and is characterised by immense spaces, by great and sublime dimensions in its architecture, and by palaces, one of which would perhaps suffice to house easily half the Jewish ghetto city.[19]

A few years later one of the greatest scandals created by the intransigent papal policies of the nineteenth century occurred in the Papal States and caused ripples throughout Europe. Shortly before the birth of their son Edgardo in 1851, a Jewish merchant couple called Martara had moved from Reggio Emilia to Bologna, where there was only a very small Jewish community of two hundred members. Their Christian maid, Anna Morisi, baptised the sickly infant Edgardo. Six years later a Dominican priest and inquisitor of the Church learned of this emergency baptism and had the papal police kidnap the boy from the family home because Christian children were not allowed to be raised by Jews. Despite his parents' fierce protests, Edgardo was brought up in a monastery and entered the order of Italian Augustinian Canons Regular as an adult. Kidnapping a secretly baptised Jewish child like this was not an isolated case, but within the charged political atmosphere of the *Kulturkampf* and wars of unification it attracted unusual media publicity. In spite of the intervention of the French, British and Austrian governments, Pius IX refused to relent and the child remained in the monastery.

In the liberal Kingdom of Sardinia-Piedmont, on the other hand, the new constitution of 1848 had already granted equal status to Jews – and Protestants – ten years earlier. In 1861, after the founding of the Italian nation-state, these new rights were transferred to the whole of what was then Italy. In the Papal States, the Jews had to wait until after the Porta Pia Breach in 1870 for such reforms to be introduced. In the second half of the century, once legal equality had been enforced, the Jews easily succeeded in integrating into mainstream society throughout Europe. Isaaco Artom, for example, served for a long time as private secretary to the prime minister, Camillo Benso Conte di Cavour, on whose early death he continued his career as a diplomat and senator. Officers of Jewish origin were included in the closest military entourage of the first king of the new nation-state, Victor Emmanuel. There were also Jews in the rank of general and a Jewish minister of war and it was generally possible for them to hold high offices in the judiciary, administration and the army. This would have been unthinkable in the German Reich, where in the Prussian section of the German army, Jews were barred from holding the rank of officer until World War I. In Italy, on the other hand, Jewish men and women had access to cultural, political and military leadership positions.

Protestants were even less common than Jews on the Apennine peninsula. Here in the homeland of the Catholic Church, attempts at reformation had no lasting effect and any reform endeavours were soon stifled by the Inquisition. The only Protestants who did live in Italy were those merchants mentioned in the previous chapter who had migrated from Switzerland and the German states to the major commercial centres, and some Anglicans from Britain. Protestant church services were only allowed to be held in the extraterritorial foreign missions in the capitals of the Italian states or in the Prussian embassy in Rome.

The Duchy of Savoy, which became the Kingdom of Sardinia-Piedmont in the eighteenth century, was the only place where a Protestant minority, the *Waldensians*, managed to survive, despite repeated expulsions. This religious community was founded in the Middle Ages in south-eastern France and is considered a forerunner of the Reformation and one of the most important groups of dissident Christians. Its members were constantly persecuted by the Inquisition because they preached apostolic poverty and rejected the official church. Only a small minority of them managed to survive in a secluded area in the western Alps of Piedmont. With the enactment of the constitution in 1848, they were able to practise their faith freely in the Kingdom of Sardinia-Piedmont, and after the founding of the nation state they were able to establish churches and schools throughout Italy.

The Jews, and to an even greater extent the Protestants, were religious minorities in a country that was completely dominated by Roman Catholicism as its state religion. The unique status of the Catholic Church in Italy was largely due to the fact that the popes had resided in Rome since late antiquity and not only acted as the spiritual leaders of the Catholics but also as the rulers of the Papal States, stretching from Bologna to Gaeta in the south. The Vatican in Rome was also the centre of Roman Catholicism worldwide. Throughout Europe the Catholic Church came under considerable pressure as a result of the Reformation and the religious wars at the beginning of the early modern period. From the Council of Trent in the mid-sixteenth century until the French Revolution, the Vatican's response to the challenge of Protestant reforms was to impose its own aggressive religious policies. The popes strengthened and centralised administrative structures and attempted to standardise religious beliefs and practices. They were assisted in this by the Roman Inquisition, which prosecuted religious deviance within the Catholic community, and by the Sacred Congregation of the Index. This acted as a central censorship body that placed all unorthodox, immoral and subversive writings on the index of forbidden books *(Index Librorum Prohibitorum)*, thus seeking to prevent their further printing or dissemination. Its purpose was to control everything Catholics read, believed and said. After the Council of Trent and the subsequent reforms, the Catholic Church also sought to prepare the clergy better for their task of persuading laypeople to dutifully follow the religious practices demanded by the ecclesiastical hierarchy. To this purpose, new religious orders, the catechism and priests' sermons were all controlled by the Vatican.

The key role played by the Catholic Church can be easily illustrated by looking at the layout of Italian cities. Most of the smaller towns were built around the church, which was situated on the central square near the town hall. Churches also dominated the major cities, vying with each other by building magnificent cathedrals such as the huge cathedral in Milan. In Rome, the gigantic St Peter's Basilica and its preceding church, the Basilica St John Lateran, whose dimensions were equally ambitious, are listed together with no less than five other magnificent church buildings as the seven main churches a pilgrim should visit in one day. Apart from cathedrals, numerous parish churches and abbeys were erected in all the larger cities. In Naples, for example, they amounted to more than two hundred.

Fig. 11 Francesco Paolo Michetti, The Vow, 1883.

These churches and their surrounding squares did not only provide opportunities for worship but also for other forms of everyday social interaction. *Piazzas* were and still are public arenas and places of social control.

By means of ceremonies, religious feast days and festivals to mark the agricultural year, Catholicism lent structure to the lives of urban and rural dwellers from baptism to funeral. The Roman Catholic Church also monopolised every stratum of society. The wealthy aristocracy of central Italy was integrated into the Vatican hierarchy in the role of bishops, cardinals, abbots, and secretaries, demonstrated by the fact that in the early modern period the popes always came from the most influential noble families, but the church also recruited numerous ordinary priests from the 'reserve of talent' in the peasant population. The clergy were omnipresent in society. So, for example, in late eighteenth-century Naples, of its four million inhabitants, ninety thousand were priests. This strong presence was by no means limited to the south of Italy. Even outside the Papal States the church as an institution had autonomous legal powers over marriages and the punishment of crimes. Before the French Revolution, the church shared its vision of a society organised along traditional hierarchical lines with the monarchy and the aristocratic elites, and together they acted as a stronghold of the old order. Both men and women from the upper classes were involved in a wide variety of Catholic institutions, religious orders and Congregations. They acted as intermediaries between the Church and a mostly illiterate population of the faithful and cared for marginalised groups such as the sick and the poor, orphans, prostitutes and prisoners. In this way the Catholic Church permeated all social strata and wielded a strong influence as a moral authority.

At first glance, the Catholic Church seemed to be synonymous with the papacy and the Vatican, which dominated life in Italy. However, efforts to control and standardise religious faith and practices proved to be less of a case of imposition from above and more of a protracted process of negotiation, meaning that well into the nineteenth century many rural areas had still not become fully Catholic. The gap between the official teachings of the Church and actual religious practices persisted. The clergy attested to the continuing vitality of a popular Catholicism rooted in oral tradition. Religion was blended with magic, superstition and belief in the supernatural. As a result, especially in the countryside, people continued to believe in witchcraft, black magic, night-time spiritual journeys and supernatural powers, finding expression for this belief in miracles, the popular cult of saints, the worship of martyrs' relics and the use of magic spells. The Vatican's attempts, therefore, to imbue a largely illiterate rural population with the fundamental doctrines and demands of the official Church achieved little success.

These religious practices were, however, by no means limited to rural areas. In Genoa, for example, the putative bones of St John the Baptist were publicly displayed whenever there was unusually severe weather at sea, since they were credited with the power to calm storms. To honour the role the saint played in the port of Genoa, a large number of new-born babies were baptised Giovanni Battista. Similarly, a striking number of children in Naples were given the name of its patron saint, San Gennaro. The cult of this powerful protector of the city, still practised today, is testimony to the survival of popular religious traditions at the local level. In general, almost all the towns and cities in Italy cultivated their own patron saints as an important symbol of local identity and unity. Precious shrines, sculptures and paintings were donated to them by the faithful and, in the urban context, they were revered by guilds, fraternities and neighbourhoods. Families even worshipped their own patron saints at home, believing that they would help and protect them in times of need. However, the role of religious rites was not only spiritual – they also provided opportunities to affirm personal status and prestige publicly on the occasion of baptisms, weddings and funerals.

Catholic rites had a more practical function in the countryside since they combined agricultural traditions with religious doctrine. The main purpose of religion here was to protect livestock, the family and the village. Uneducated peasants in the villages were largely superstitious and ignorant of the Church's teachings, since their contact to the outside world was mediated by rural priests often serving in the region from which they themselves originated. Generally speaking, popular religiosity reflected the wide diversity and fragmentation of the religious world in Italy. Hidden behind the monolithic façade of the official church there were many different types of Catholicism, mirroring political, social and cultural divisions. Religious organisations and practices, and the training of priests varied from region to region and between rural and urban areas. In the south the extremely high number of often very small dioceses contrasted with a striking low number of parishes, whereas in the north the opposite was true.

While stubborn popular religiosity was a thorn in its flesh, the Church had come under mounting criticism from liberal and democratic writers and politicians since the Enlightenment period. The French Revolution and its secularisation measures proved a critical turning point. After 1789 a deep rift had opened up between the Catholic Church and the politicians, journalists and philosophers who declared religion a private matter and wanted to banish the Church from public life. During the *Ancien Régime* the monarchs and aristocratic elites had used the Church for their own public representation and legitimisation, but in the course of the nineteenth century the alliance between crown and altar became increasingly fragile. In spite of this, the Church clung determinedly to its ideology and its notion of religious-ecclesiastical traditions and the preservation of conservative power, resisting the 'unreasonable demands' of modernity with all its might. From its point of view, any attempt by governments and societies to extricate themselves from the influence of church leaders was the work of Satan, intending to destroy the Catholic church. It considered 1789 the first victory of an anti-Christian sect and saw Freemasons and supporters of the Enlightenment but also, increasingly as the nineteenth century progressed, liberal politicians, democrats and socialists, as out to destroy the monarchy and the church. The Pope and especially the Jesuit order, understood any attempt to question official Christian society in which the church claimed to be the supreme leader of humanity as an attack on Catholicism. Most notably the Jesuits' combatant paper *Civiltà cattolica*, founded in Naples in 1850, polemicised eloquently against its opponents, that is against liberal Catholics who sought to reconcile Catholicism with modern society, 'forgetting' that the Church is queen, not servant; legislator, not subject; teacher, not student of the world.[20] Liberal Catholic theologians such as Antonio Rosmini or Vincenzo Gioberti who advocated fundamental reforms remained the exception.

During the course of the nineteenth century, however, anti-Catholicism grew as a transnational European phenomenon and the influence of the Catholic church receded. In 1846 there was brief hope that something might change at the Vatican, when on June 16 Conte Giovanni Maria Mastai-Ferretti, a native of the Marche, was elected pope, taking the name Pius IX. Immediately after his election, he issued a political amnesty, as was the custom, planned administrative reforms and approved a municipal constitution for the city of Rome. These and other measures were seen all too readily by liberals and democrats throughout Italy as the long-awaited signal that a progressive pope had come to power and that it would be possible to overcome the antagonism between the Catholic church and the modern social culture that had been developing since the eighteenth century. In all Italian cities large and small, there were constant torchlight processions, prayers and thanksgiving services, songs and poems in honour of this reforming pope. Two years later, when the Revolution broke out in Rome as well, the neo-Guelfs believed that now the hour had come for Pius IX to allow himself to be elected as the head of a federal Italian nation state. But the revolution, fought with particular ferocity in Rome, forced the Pope to flee into exile to the Kingdom of the Two Sicilies where he became ultraconservative and, on his return, battled uncompromisingly for both his secular government and his claim to spiritual leadership. His measures further fuelled the culture war *(Kulturkampf)* that had been simmering beneath the surface for some time and made Italy's path to becoming a nation state even more complicated.

## Notes

1 Franco della Peruta, Società e classi populari nell'Italia dell'800, Milan 2005, p. 51.
2 G. Casagrande, Manuale di carità e di pubbliche istruzione ai poveri famelici opportuno sempre, ma specialmente nelle circostanze di carestia, Verona 1816.
3 Le cagioni dell'accattoneria in Genova e il modo d'estirparnela, Ragionamento di Felice Isnardi, Genova 1838.
4 Saverio Scrofani, La mendicità a Napoli, in: Archivio storico per la Sicilia orientale, 1967, p. 146.
5 Marino Turchi, Sulle igiene pubblica della città di Napoli, Napoli 1861.
6 Paolo Macry, Borghesie, città e stato. Appunti e impressioni su Napoli, 1860–1880, in Quaderni storici 19 (1984), pp. 339–383, here p. 342.
7 Arno J. Mayer, Adelsmacht und Bürgertum. Die Krise der europäischen Gesellschaft 1848–1914, Munich 1984.
8 Stendhal, Voyages en Italie. Textes établis, présentés et annotés par Victor Del Litto, Paris 1973, p. 721f.
9 Thomas Kroll, Die Revolte des Patriziats. Der toskanische Adelsliberalismus im Risorgimento, Tübingen 1999, p. 149.
10 Anne-Louise-Germaine von Staël-Holstein, Sulla maniera e l'utilità delle traduzioni, in: E. Bellorini (ed.), Discussioni e polemiche sul Romanticismo (1816–1826), Bari 1943, p. 8.
11 Stendhal, Voyages en Italie. Textes établis, présentés et annotés par Victor Del Litto, Paris 1973, p. 16.
12 For more detail see: Axel Körner, Oper, Politik und nationale Bewegung. Mythen um das Werk Giuseppe Verdis, in: Thomas Höpel, Hannes Siegrist (ed.), Kunst, Politik und Gesellschaft in Europa seit dem 19. Jahrhundert, Stuttgart 2017, p. 101–110.
13 Giuseppe Mazzini, Pittura italiana moderna, 1841.
14 Antonio Canova, Scritti, H. Honour, P. Mariuz (ed.), Rome 2007, p. 434.
15 Johann Wolfgang von Goethe, Italienische Reise. Auch ich in Arkadien!, in: Goethes Werke, Hamburger Ausgabe in 14 vols., Erich Trunz (ed.), Munich 1981, vol. 11, p. 385.
16 Massimo d'Azeglio, I miei ricordi, S. Spellanzon (ed.), Milan 1956, p. 148f.

17 Francesco Hayez, Le mie memorie dettate da Francesco Hayez, Milan 1911, p. 60.
18 Biblioteca Civica Berio, Genova, Archivio Ercole Ricotti, Letter from Carlo Negroni, Novara, 6.1.1845.
19 Ferdinand Gregorovius, Der Ghetto und die Juden in Rom, in Jeschurun. Ein Monatsblatt zur Förderung Jüdischen Geistes 12 (1856), pp. 664–672.
20 M. Liberatore, Gli amatori del mondo e la Chiesa, in: Civiltà cattolica 28 (1877), pp. 15–23, here p. 3.

# 6. The Revolutions of 1847 and 1849

In 1848 large parts of Europe were hit by a wave of revolutions. As with the revolutions of 1789 and 1830 there had been a major crisis in agriculture in the preceding years and an additional crisis in the trading and banking sector in 1847. It is generally agreed that the movement began with the February revolution in Paris and that European liberals and democrats followed this example, mounting the barricades and seizing parliaments. However, a fact frequently overlooked is that the revolutionary process began in all the Italian states as early as the autumn of 1847.

In Italy and the German Confederation, in contrast to France, the revolutionaries were faced with a twofold challenge. At the same time as forming a united nation state they needed to introduce domestic reforms. Many of those who wished for a liberal state and a constitutional government, however, could imagine this without a united Italy. Most people identified first and foremost with their local region – Venetia, Piedmont, Sicily, Emilia Romagna and Lombardy, to name but a few. One of the most important liberal democratic thinkers of northern Italy, Carlo Cattaneo, even proposed the completely unrealistic idea of an autonomous Lombardy within a federal Habsburg empire. Other activists only operated in their own kingdom or duchy and would have been perfectly content with a loose confederation of Italian states. This was the view put forward by Giuseppe Ferrari in his pamphlet *Revolution and Reforms in Italy*, written in exile in Paris in January 1848, in which he proposed a confederation of republics. For the neo-Guelphs the ideal solution was a confederation of constitutional monarchies headed by the Pope. Mazzini's position was, however, completely different. His goal was a nation state of Italy and to this end he was even prepared to make a temporary pact with the king of Piedmont. Whatever their aims, however, the activists were all faced with one and the same massive problem – Austrian power politics. At the beginning of the 1820s and 30s, Habsburg troops had used armed force to quell any early signs of revolutionary uprisings and prevent them spreading. The question now was whether it would be possible to withstand Vienna and pressure the emperor to agree to fundamental reforms or even a federal structure.

As in the previous chapters, it is not possible here to tell just one story of these politically turbulent years for the whole of Italy. Again, we have to analyse the revolutions in each individual state and explain their differences and similarities. It helps to structure events by dividing the revolution into phases. In the first phase from autumn 1847 to spring 1848 liberal demands were resolutely enforced. The second phase, from March 1848 to summer 1849, was marked by the First Italian

War of Independence and, parallel to this, beginning at the end of 1848, a third phase was one of a shift towards more radical left-wing liberal and democratic stances in Florence, Rome and Venice.

## 6.1 The Constitutional Revolutions of 1847–1848

Contemporaries were amazed to find that two years before the European revolutions, the ultra-conservative Papal States appeared to be entering a liberal era. Pius IX introduced liberal reforms as soon as he took office in 1846 and was celebrated throughout the country as a symbol of a more open government. Only twelve months previously a swiftly supressed uprising in Rimini had provoked a lively international response. From his exile Carlo Farini published his reaction to this insurrection in 1845 in the *Proclama di Rimini (Proclamation of Rimini).* It was directed against the then Pope, Gregory XVI, and was sent to all the European governments, demanding more political freedom for the inhabitants of Romagna. After the Rimini uprising Massimo d'Azeglio published his travelogue *On the recent events in Romagna in 1846,* which was read all over Italy. In it he described the economic, political and social backwardness of the Papal States.

A cautious process of liberalisation began not only in the Papal States but also in Sardinia-Piedmont under Charles Albert. Both during the 1820–1821 revolution and after his accession in 1831 liberals had pinned their hopes on him in vain, but after the mid-1840s his rule was indeed less conservative. He made concessions to the press and permitted the publication of the journal *Messaggero torinese.* In December 1847, the newspaper *Il Risorgimento* appeared for the first time, edited by Cesare Balbo and Camillo Benso di Cavour. Cavour used it to promote his own convictions, which were influenced by British constitutionalism. This paper was to give its name to the cross-party nation state movement and later the entire epoch was to be called *Risorgimento.* Other reforms were introduced such as in the universities and particularly in the economic sphere where Charles Albert turned away from his previous strict protectionist policy and lowered customs duties at his borders. These first measures were followed in autumn 1847 by further, more radical reforms in the judiciary and health systems, and were greeted with public enthusiasm on the streets. Similar measures were introduced in Tuscany where in June 1847, Leopold II permitted the publication of political periodicals, relaxed censorship and appointed a liberal minister of the interior, Cosimo Ridolfi.

For Italy as a whole it should be noted that politically active Italians were already occupying public space in the cities in the autumn of 1847. Genoa was the most rebellious city in the Kingdom of Sardinia-Piedmont. Invoking its republican and mercantile traditions, its inhabitants protested against the constraints of administrative absolutism. The largest demonstrations took place in December 1847, led by Nino Bixio and Goffredo Mameli, who was Garibaldi's aide-de-camp and was killed during the defence of the Roman Republic in July 1849. A republican protest song composed by Mameli, *Fratelli d'Italia (Brothers of Italy)*, has been the Italian national anthem since the abolition of the monarchy in 1946.

Agitation against Austrian dominance was growing at the time. King Charles Albert exploited every opportunity to effectively promote his position to the public, particularly his trade policy. The main points of conflict with Austria were over the lucrative salt deliveries to Ticino (Tessin) in Switzerland and which railway lines should run through the Alps. After repeated harassment by the Austrian customs, Charles Albert openly threatened to support calls for the independence of Lombardy. His official position in 1847, however, remained moderate. Although he allowed Massimo d'Azeglio to organize military demonstrations with anti-Austrian slogans, he did not support them with his presence. The only hint at the Savoy dynasty's possible future path was Charles Albert's dismissal of his ultra-conservative foreign minister, Conte Clemente Solaro della Margarita, a fervent advocate of a pro-Austrian policy.

Meanwhile a violent intervention by the Austrians in Ferrara in July 1847 accelerated events. Metternich viewed the public expressions of sympathy for the new Pope in 1846–1847 with great suspicion. As a warning to Pius IX and all Italian liberals, he decided to make use of a garrison right granted to Vienna in 1815 in Ferrara, in the north of the Papal States near the border with Venetia. On 17 July 1847, an infantry battalion escorted by cavalry marched into the city to signal a military threat. The Pope officially protested against this intimidation by a member of the Holy Alliance. Although no combat ensued, the political and diplomatic consequences of the Austrian manoeuvre were far-reaching. The King of Sardinia-Piedmont immediately offered the Pope an alliance against the Austrians, which Pius IX rejected, being unwilling to wage war against a Catholic king. The events in Ferrara certainly lent new impetus to plans for a north Italian customs union, an idea developed in Rome in the 1840s based on the German model, which envisaged trade agreements between Tuscany, Modena, Sardinia-Piedmont and the Papal States. In autumn 1847 these treaties were understood by Charles Albert as a first explicit step towards an eventual political and miliary defence alliance. The only obstacle to the realisation of this project at the time was its rejection by the Duke of Modena, Francis V, who came from a branch of the Habsburgs and naturally opposed any action against Austria.

Diplomatic statements by liberal European powers, especially France and Britain, were strongly supportive of the interests of the Kingdom of Sardinia-Piedmont and the Papal States. The French prime minister, François Guizot, declared his sympathy for the Piedmontese patriots and assured the Pope of France's moral support. Britain adopted an even more resolutely anti-Austrian stance, remaining true to the policy it had pursued since the Congress of Vienna. Foreign Secretary

Viscount Henry Palmerston did not hesitate to state publicly that the occupation of Ferrara was the prelude to an Italian national revolution. He confirmed this opinion in a personal letter to Metternich in February 1848, warning him against fuelling a war of principles that would begin in Italy but spread throughout Europe and weaken the Habsburg empire. In autumn 1847 Lord William Minto had already been sent on an official mission to Rome, Florence and Turin to assure liberals and moderates of Britain's support for potential reform governments. His mission was interpreted by anti-Habsburg patriots as a blank cheque encouraging revolution, although its true purpose was to discourage radical movements. Metternich heeded the warnings from Turin and London and withdrew his troops from Ferrara.

The autumn of 1847 was distinguished by political protests throughout Italy. The most violent clashes took place in the Kingdom of the Two Sicilies. On 1 September the insurgents took the citadel of Messina in eastern Sicily, after which the rebellion spread into the hinterland. At the same time, uprisings of the same kind broke out just a few kilometres away from Messina on the mainland in Reggio Calabria. The unrest was fuelled by anti-Bourbon propaganda material, such as the *Protesta del popolo delle Due Sicilie*, published in summer 1847 by a Neapolitan follower of Mazzini, Luigi Settembrini, before he fled to Malta. However, Ferdinand II's Bourbon troops intervened swiftly and forcefully in southern Italy. Similar popular demonstrations took place in Lucca and Livorno in autumn 1847, as well as in Turin and Rome. The slogans chanted during all these rebellions were 'Long live Pius IX! Long live Italy! Long live the Constitution!'. The Pope's portrait was decorated with green, white and red cockades, as if he were the divine protector of constitutional rebels, moderate patriots or even democrats. While the governments in Piedmont, Tuscany and the Papal States responded to these protests by promising liberal reforms, the opposite was the case in the Bourbon Kingdom of the Two Sicilies. Ferdinand II took harsh action against the rebels and had the cities of Messina and Reggio Calabria bombarded, a brutal response that earned him a new nickname, *Re bomba*. Liberal revolutionaries were sentenced to death in Reggio Calabria on 16 November 1847. But even Ferdinand was eventually forced to give in to pressure from the streets and it was in the Kingdom of the Two Sicilies that in spring 1848 an Italian ruler first introduced a constitution.

Meanwhile in January 1848 the conflicts escalated in Lombardy. The population provoked the Austrians with a smokers' strike, which meant people demonstratively stopped smoking in public in order to reduce tobacco tax revenues. Related local unrest in turn led to violent repression by Austria in Milan and Pavia. In neighbouring Venetia, the lawyer Daniele Manin and the writer Niccolò Tommaseo had submitted a petition demanding a constitution; they were subsequently arrested. At the same time, outright revolutions began in Livorno and in the Sicilian capital Palermo, where barricades were erected on 12 January and the insurgents dominated the city within a few days. King Ferdinand II then granted an amnesty to the political prisoners he had sentenced in 1847. At the end of January, he promised to establish a constitution whose text was in fact published on 11 February 1848. This had an immediate impact on the political situation in the other Italian states. Despite his opposition in principle to any form of constitution, King Charles Albert was persuaded of its necessity by his entourage and a constitution was duly announced on 8 February and published on 4 March. This was the only constitution to survive the revolution. It shaped Italy's fortunes until the fascist March on Rome in 1922, after which it still remained in force, at least formally. In 1861, after the Second Italian War of Independence, it was simply applied unaltered to the other Italian regions.

At the same time, there was a significant increase in social unrest and uprisings in Italy in February and March 1848. As elsewhere in Europe, the revolution took place on two different levels. There was the institutional level, at which new cabinets and constitutions emerged, and the fundamental level in the public sphere, the cities and the countryside. Protests were directed against grain prices and financial hardship. A chaotic confusion of old and new demands arose, including demonstrations against tariffs and duties charged on food, and protests at the markets both against price increases for basic foodstuffs and because of their scarcity. In the forests timber was felled and game hunted illegally. Workers and day labourers protested publicly, demanding secure jobs and higher wages. Occurrences of this kind of 'widespread social crime' varied in intensity in the different regions and states. Nevertheless, they forced the old order to retreat (for the time being) and helped the break-through of the institutional revolution.

In the meantime, on 17 February, the Grand Duke of Tuscany had also introduced a statute in his state, although he initially refused to call it a constitution. The Pope for his part convened an advisory commission on 14 March and issued his constitution for the Papal States a month later. For the Sicilians a liberal government was not sufficient, they also wanted autonomy. Sicilian independence was proclaimed on 13 April, on condition that a constitutional monarchy be established and consigned to an Italian prince. The only territories that waited in vain for a constitution were those directly dependent on Austria, namely Lombardy-Venetia and the smaller duchies of Parma and Modena. The disputes there became all the more heated when news of the success of the revolution arrived from Paris and Vienna.

When Metternich's flight from Vienna became known in Venice on 13 March 1848 and four days later in Milan, liberals and democrats immediately congregated in these two capitals of the Austrian viceroyalty. In Venice, Daniele Manin and Niccolò Tommaseo vociferously demanded secession from the Habsburg Empire. In order to stop the revolution, the emperor in Vienna finally made some liberal concessions such as abolishing censorship and convening assemblies. But it was too late. There were massive popular demonstrations in Lombardy, even anti-Austrian uprisings. The situation escalated above all in Milan. What took place here is considered one of the most important uprisings of the 1848 revolution in Italy: the famous *Cinque Giornate* (*Five Days*), known to every Italian schoolchild. This five-day revolt broke out in the Lombardy capital on the afternoon of 17 March 1848 when news of the revolutionary insurgency in Vienna and the flight of the conservative chancellor Metternich arrived. There was intense and ferocious fighting on the streets and on 18 March barricades were erected. The Austrian military governor General Radetzky threatened to set the city on fire. An influx of Piedmontese volunteers arrived to support the insurgents in Milan and Charles Albert's regular troops were also expected to arrive on the Lombardy border. On 20 March all official buildings were in the hands of the revolutionaries and a war council was proclaimed with the liberal-democratic journalist Carlo Cattaneo as its president. The following day the unexpected happened – the poorly equipped Milanese triumphed over the retreating troops of the hated General Radetzky in a completely unforeseen victory. While Radetzky withdrew with his troops to the Austrian Quadrilateral near Verona, liberals established a provisional government in Milan on 22 March. Its members were staunch supporters of unification with the Kingdom of Sardinia-Piedmont, although this position was by no means uncontroversial. However, there was agreement on one point: the end of Habsburg rule was proclaimed.

The *Cinque Giornate* was essentially a spontaneous, uncoordinated uprising of the lower classes. What researchers long overlooked was the extraordinary and impressive commitment of women to the struggle. Some helped by preparing ammunition and caring for the wounded while others took up arms themselves. Examples are Giuseppina Lazzaroni, whose shots hit several Austrians, and Luigia Sassi Battistotti, who is said by popular tradition to have led around a hundred men. The high number of female victims among the Milanese insurgents also bears eloquent witness to this. Of around three hundred dead, almost every third victim was female, a figure that can only be explained by their active participation in the battle.

Identical scenes took place at the same time in Venice where popular uprisings were started in the streets by workers at the large shipyard, the Arsenal. They were then attacked by the Habsburg troops in the same way as in Milan. A lawyer, Daniele Manin, led the angry crowd with shouts of *Viva la repubblica, viva San Marco!* The insurgents succeeded in making some symbolic military conquests and occupying the state buildings at the centre of power, from which they flew the Tricolore. A provisional government was subsequently set up with Manin as its prime minister, who then proclaimed the re-establishment of an independent Republic of Venice. Since the Italian soldiers fighting in the Habsburg troops defected, the Austrians quickly admitted defeat and withdrew. Meanwhile, in Udine, vigilantes were also fighting Austrian soldiers. On 24 March, Charles Albert declared that he was willing to use armed force to support the insurgents in Milan and Venice.

Fig. 12 Giuseppe Mazzola, Vincenzo Malinverno (lithographer), The Five Days of Milan, second half of the 19th century.

In the central Italian duchies, the rebels also defeated their conservative, authoritarian rulers. Francis V fled from Modena on 20 March and was replaced at first by a government council, superseded the following day by a provisional government. In Parma, Charles II found himself forced to promise a constitution. Milan was, however, still the centre of the movement. The suddenness of the uprising, its willingness to use violence, its efficiency against the Habsburg troops, as well as the high number of victims – over 300 civilians killed and 600 Austrian soldiers dead – all this meant that, in the eyes of contemporaries, the *Cinque Giornate* rebellion was much more than merely an echo of the major revolutionary events in Vienna and Paris.

Once the reactionary conservative rulers had fled or shown their willingness to make concessions, the task was to draw up constitutions to consolidate the revolutionary achievements and new political rights. In the states in which constitutions were enacted, the rules of political life changed and the balance of power shifted. As with the previous revolutions, the Spanish Constitution of Cádiz (1812), the French *Chartes constitutionelles* of 1814 and 1830 and the Belgian constitution of 1831 were used as models. Common to all the new constitutions was a bicameral system with an upper house to which the sovereign appointed the members for life. This was the Senate in Turin, the Chamber of Pairs in Naples and the High Council in Rome. The election of members of the lower house depended on them having a high level of wealth, which deliberately excluded the lower and middle classes. The liberals who drew up the constitutions regarded property and education as essential for political participation. Power was distributed unequally in favour of the sovereigns, who in all constitutions were declared 'sacred and inviolable' as individuals. While they shared legislative power with the two chambers, they claimed executive power solely for themselves. Following the reforms that had already been conceded at the end of the 1840s, several fundamental rights were incorporated into the constitutions, namely equal civil and political rights, (albeit with restrictions on voter eligibility), freedom of the press, the inviolability of private property and the home, the right of assembly (in the Kingdom of Sardinia-Piedmont) and economic freedom (in Tuscany). Apart from the Papal States, where civil rights were only granted to Catholics, the constitutions were tolerant of other religions but designated Catholicism as the official religion. This was the second time since the Napoleonic era that the Jews were granted emancipation.

Since only elected deputies were allowed to vote on the adoption of the proposed constitutions, the new political systems of representative government were reliant on elections. Voting regulations were announced very swiftly everywhere – in all cases, voters had to be men who were at least twenty-five years of age and prove that they paid a high tax contribution or owned capital. The deputies were elected and the chambers convened within just two months, so on 8 May in Turin and in Rome just under a month later on 5 June. The voting regulations in Piedmont were of great importance in the long term. Equal and direct male suffrage was introduced, constituency boundaries were drawn up and electoral colleges created. In future these electoral colleges were to dominate the local public sphere and act as intermediaries between Turin and the periphery.

After the proclamation of a legal constitution, the sovereigns were obliged to integrate moderates and liberals into the government. As elsewhere in Europe, this meant a change of administration. The aim of the new March governments was to be distinctly different from the old crown councils and to enable them, as the embodiment of a new liberal style of government, to take the wind out of the sails of pressure from broad sections of the population. On 16 March 1848, Conte Cesare Balbo was appointed the first prime minister of a constitutional government in Turin. In April Carlo Troya assumed this office in Naples and in Tuscany it was first Marquess Cosimo Ridolfi followed by Marquess Gino Capponi. They were all politicians who had been in favour of constitutional government for decades. The elected members of parliament also came from the liberal and moderate camps. One example was Vincenzo Gioberti who had returned from exile after many years and was elected the first president of the Piedmontese parliament. In Milan, the provisional government was made up of moderate liberal aristocrats and was headed by Conte Gabrio Casati, who had steered the fortunes of Milan as mayor *(podestà)* since 1837. The only member of the democratic faction was the secretary of the provisional government, Cesare Correnti.

Since the war with Austria was not yet over, politicians were aware of the fragility of the situation and made several attempts to promote their cause both in Paris and in Frankfurt/Main, using long-established contacts with German academics and diplomats. So, for example, Gino Capponi wrote to Karl Mittermaier, a delegate to the Frankfurt National Assembly and a liberal lawyer and politician from Baden, whom he knew from his travels in Italy and who was considered a friend and expert on Italy. Capponi's letter emphasized the parallels between the 1848 revolutions in the German Confederation and in Italy and expressed the hope that Mittermaier would champion the Italian cause in the German parliament. It was to no avail. In his reply, Mittermaier insisted that he had to support the German cause and that there should be no interference in Trieste and Tyrol. Capponi's friend, Gian Pietro Vieusseux, was also similarly unsuccessful with his overtures to Alfred von Reumont, asking him to campaign in favour of the new political order. Reumont had lived in Florence since the early 1830s and worked for a long time as German correspondent for the *Archivio Storico Italiano* published by Vieusseux and Capponi. His comment on the political situation in Tuscany was that 'it is a mean thing to want to cause grief to the true father of Tuscany [Leopold II]'.[1] Solidarity was also sought in vain by Milan in the Frankfurt National Assembly. At the beginning of April, the provisional Milanese government sent a message to the German 'brother nation' in the hope that the members of the Assembly in Frankfurt would return their greeting and approve or even support the fight for freedom against Austria. There was no reply. A delegation from Milan fared no better in May when it travelled to Frankfurt with the express purpose of changing the National Assembly's mind. Even Conte Alessandro Porro from Milan and Giovanni Morelli from Verona achieved nothing. Although the President of the National Assembly, Heinrich von Gagern, assured them that the majority of Germans felt genuine sympathy towards the Italian nation, that was as far as it went. This was because, unlike in Italy, the revolution in Germany had stopped at the foot of the throne and at the time the National Assembly still recognised the Habsburgs as the highest authority in the nascent German Empire.

The only debate in the German parliament on the Italian cause in August 1848 turned into a complete disaster for the revolutionaries. A vote was to be taken on a motion to release the districts of Trento and Rovereto from the German Confederation. Only a few democrats were in favour of this proposal, the vast majority had no intention of ceding even an inch of territory. Furthermore, the German daily newspaper with the highest circulation, the *Augsburger Allgemeine Zeitung*, clearly sided with Austrian troops in the First Italian War of Independence.

Vienna's claims to northern Italy were recognised as legitimate under international law. The paper also frequently warned against French influence. In the issue of 12 May, for example, it stated:

> It is therefore easy to foresee what fate awaits the unfortunate land of Italy: for the time being it will bear the hardships of general upheaval and war and where it is no longer protected by the arm of Austria's justice, it will become prey to France or to internal anarchy.[2]

All but one of the constitutions in the Italian states were abolished after the victory of the counter-revolution in 1849. Due to this short lifespan, they were unable to pave the way to a liberal modernity. In spite of its political limits and restrictions, the only surviving constitution, that of Charles Albert in Piedmont, known as the *Statuto Albertino* or *Statuto* is, therefore, of particular importance. It emerged as the pioneering text of Italian parliamentary liberalism. In the long term, it enabled the development from a system of constitutional government to a parliamentary government. This was because it did not exclude ministerial responsibility and the compatibility of ministerial office and parliamentary mandate. The king, however, remained in a strong position because of his right to appoint and dismiss ministers. Twenty-two of the first twenty-three articles (from a total of eighty-four) concerned the king, three the ministers. Furthermore, the king could dissolve parliament at any time, continue to rule in its absence and dismiss existing cabinets and ministers. Charles Albert's successor, his eldest son, Victor Emmanuel II, was to make extensive use of all these rights.

The *Statuto,* in commemoration of whose proclamation a national festival was created, the *Festa dello Statuto,* remained the only constitutional basis of liberal Italy until well into the twentieth century. The work of the parliamentarians was very well received. Their speeches were published and an interested public was able to follow their debates. As in Frankfurt's National Assembly, a women's gallery was even set up, which was extremely popular. Whereas in Frankfurt it was mainly occupied by bourgeois women, generally the wives and daughters of members of parliament, in the capital of the Kingdom of Sardinia-Piedmont it was primarily noblewomen who were present. For them, being a spectator in the Piedmontese parliament did not mean sitting on the benches and passively following parliamentary proceedings. In their letters, they showed a profound knowledge of the dynamics of the political game. The interactions between individual parliamentarians, the government and the press did not escape their notice. They recognised and criticised the fact that the pressure exerted by both public opinion and the press influenced political decision-making processes and was even capable of shifting priorities. At the same time, women themselves entered this dynamic process of interaction as soon as they moved into institutionalised spaces. Attending parliamentary sessions with friends and relatives, the ensuing discussions and the visits to places where royal power was on display contributed to their political education and allowed them to take a stance within the political camps.

As significant as the *Statuto* was for the Kingdom of Sardinia-Piedmont, its eminently important role only emerged in the wake of the military conquest of the entire country by the Piedmontese.

## 6.2 The First Italian War of Independence and the Revolutions of 1849

The war waged by Charles Albert from March 1848 to March 1849 to liberate Lombardy-Venetia from Austria can be divided into two phases or even two separate wars. Italian historians tend to see it as one war with two phases, namely a longer period in 1848 and a shorter one in 1849. The course of events, intricate enough in itself, was complicated even further by the concurrent second radical wave of revolutions in Venice, Florence and Rome and by the military intervention of France.

On 23 March 1848 the future prime minister Camillo Cavour wrote in his newspaper *Il Risorgimento:* 'The hour has come for the Sardinian crown. [...] In view of the events in Lombardy, there is no room for hesitation or doubt. [...] The only option open to the nation, the government and the king is war!'.[3] The following day, King Charles Albert declared war on Vienna, describing his decision as an act of nationalism. He had not, however, previously reached any agreements with other Italian rulers, no doubt fearing that he would then have had to offer territorial compensation to allies such as Tuscany or the smaller duchies of Parma and Modena. Britain was anxious to avoid a new European war and did not support Charles Albert, who, for his part, rejected a half-hearted offer of help from Lamartine, the acting foreign minister of the French Republic. The king feared that the intervention of troops from revolutionary France might strengthen democratic and republican forces in Italy. He adopted a slogan already used by Gioberti and Mazzini in their writings, which became the well-known motto of the Risorgimento: '*L'Italia farà da sé*', meaning 'Italy will do it alone', that is, without allies. Initial support for the Kingdom of Sardinia-Piedmont came from some of the newly constitutional Italian monarchs. The Pope sent official volunteer contingents northwards, Ferdinand II in Naples also reluctantly sent troops to support Charles Albert, as did the Duke of Parma, who placed himself under the protection of Charles Albert. Together the other Italian sovereigns sent a total of just over 35,000 men. However, after just a few weeks they ordered their troops to return and in April, Pius IX also withdrew from the nationalist movement, arguing that he was the father of all peoples and could not therefore support a war against Catholic Austria. This shattered the neo-

Guelphs' dream of a federal Italy led by the Pope. After the retreat of Pius IX, Ferdinand II also saw his position vindicated and, with his generals, chose to concentrate on enforcing the counter-revolution. The immediate cause for this decision was rioting in Naples and Sicily, which was suppressed.

This meant that, in effect, Charles Albert fought against the Austrians under their leader Radetzky with only 95,000 men but supported by volunteers. Two phases of military operations can be distinguished one in March and one in July 1848. At first the Piedmontese were winning but in May they were driven back by the Austrians. The king and his generals were generally lacking in both determination and good fortune. Instead of vigorously pursuing the Austrians, still in shock after their defeat in Milan, they allowed Radetzky to retreat to the Austrian Quadrilateral *(Quadrilatero)* between the Mincio and Adige rivers, bounded by the fortresses of Verona, Peschiera, Mantua and Legnano. There he was able to regroup his troops from Lombardy and Venetia. Although the Piedmontese won minor battles and succeeded in conquering the fortress of Peschiera, they proved ill-prepared and their generals insufficiently trained. As a result, in spite of outnumbering the Austrians, they were unable to wage the war effectively. The volunteers showed more determination to fight after they had made their own way to the battlefields in Lombardy and Venetia and attacked the Austrians. This was the case, for example, with a body of soldiers led by the patriot Luciano Manara, who drove the Austrians back from the shores of Lake Garda in April and also with a group of volunteers from Tuscany, most of whom were students at the University of Pisa, who in May mounted heroic resistance to the Austrians at Curtatone and Montanara, not far from Mantua. Women also took an active part in the armed uprisings of the volunteer groups, in almost all cases supporting their husbands, brothers and sons. The fact that a woman like Cristina Trivulzio di Belgiojoso assembled her own troops in Naples, financed them and led them to Milan to fight against the Austrians was, however, the absolute exception. None of these groups was able to pose a serious threat to Radetzky. In the summer of 1848 (23–25 July) he crushed the Piedmontese army in the decisive Battle of Custoza. After this disastrous defeat, Charles Albert was prepared to negotiate. On 9 August 1848 the Armistice of Salasco was signed by the Piedmontese and Austrian generals. This was a catastrophe for the supporters of a nation state or an independent Lombard republic, who accused the king of treason.

Garibaldi was not prepared to accept this armistice but did not take part in any fighting until the end of July. Like many exiles, he had rushed back to his homeland after the outbreak of the revolution, but it took until June for him to reach Nice from South America with other volunteer fighters. He immediately offered to support the king with his small band of volunteers but his offer was rejected. He then placed himself at the service of the Lombard Republic. It was still governed by moderate liberals who, at the instigation of the Piedmontese prime minister, Cesare Balbo, had in the meantime organized a plebiscite on the incorporation of Lombardy into the Kingdom of Sardinia-Piedmont. Its outcome was in favour of Turin, as it was in neighbouring duchies. Mazzini, who had also travelled from London, founded a newspaper in Milan and was trying to gain political influence, protested against the plebiscite because only the urban bourgeois and aristocratic elites had been consulted.

In July, Garibaldi was commissioned by the provisional government to recruit volunteers in Bergamo. With these men, probably approximately 1,500 in total, he continued the war against the Austrians, even after the armistice had been negotiated. He organised the guerrillas on Lake Maggiore, both on land and on the water, and even though his men were poorly equipped, they managed to hold out for a fortnight against the vastly superior Austrian forces. However, Garibaldi failed to ignite a general uprising against the Austrians. The common people did not join forces with him; instead, many of his volunteers deserted, not having envisaged that the war would be so brutal and wretched. Moreover, the rural population in the mountain region, who were already poor but had to supply both the irregulars and the Austrians with food, were suffering and refused to support Garibaldi. At the end of August, he gave up the fight and fled to Switzerland. Nothing had been achieved on the military front and the Austrians had suffered no more than a few grazes. Nevertheless, Garibaldi was celebrated in Italy for his heroic courage, his will to fight and his determination not to give up against the Austrians. He is undoubtedly the most famous volunteer for the cause of the Italian nation state but was by no means an exception. Tens of thousands of volunteers took part in the war against the unpopular Austrians.

This concludes the first phase of the war. Two important conclusions can be drawn. First, that the other Italian rulers showed no solidarity with the nation state movement. The Pope's position was clear. By declaring neutrality at the end of April, he positioned himself against the nationalist cause, preferring to concentrate on the internal affairs of the Papal States. No solidarity was to be expected from Naples either, where the new liberal government was dissolved again in mid-May, the pretext being a popular uprising in Naples. King Ferdinand II refused to support General Guglielmo Pepe, who on 4 May had marched his troops to support the Piedmontese. Pepe had returned from exile in 1848 and is known as the man of three revolutions, adding 1848–1849 to the revolutions of 1799 when he was on the list of dangerous republicans and 1820–1821 when he fought for the liberal government in Naples against the Austrians.

Second, it is significant that, despite the defeat of the Piedmontese, events show that they dominated the whole of northern Italy. During the course of the campaign, a decision to become affiliated to the Kingdom of Piedmont had been taken in April by the Duke of Parma, in May by the provisional governments in Modena, Piacenza and Milan and in June by the Venetian assembly. Events also confirm the distrust of democrats, republicans and left-wing liberals felt towards sovereigns such as Ferdinand II and Charles Albert. The latter was accused, with good reason, of only supporting the nationalist war in order to profit from it by expanding his kingdom. None of this helped to increase the prestige of the crowned rulers in Italy, particularly as a second revolutionary wave was developing.

In Tuscany, the liberals increasingly lost prestige and influence because the prime minister Gino Capponi was unable to quell the unrest in Livorno. He resigned on 12 October. Under pressure, Leopold II appointed a new liberal democratic government led by the lawyer Francesco Domenico Guerrazzi from Livorno and Professor Giuseppe Montanelli from Pisa as foreign minister. A short time later, events in Rome escalated. On 15 November 1848, Prime Minister Pellegrino Rossiwas murdered in broad daylight as he entered the *Cancelleria,* his official residence not far from the Campo de' Fiori. The crime was modelled on the tyrannicide of Julius Caesar. He was stabbed to death by several young men dressed in the uniforms of the papal army that had been involved in the battles in Lombardy. The problem was that Rossi was by no means a tyrant but a moderate constitutionalist. The following day, demonstrators demanded the formation of a liberal government under the leadership of Terenzio Mamiani, an exiled activist of the 1831 revolution who had returned home in the more liberal climate of 1847. The Pope was now faced with the choice of taking drastic action or fleeing. He chose the latter option and travelled to Gaeta, near the southern border of the Papal States, in the carriage of the Bavarian envoy and under the protection of the King of Naples. In February, Leopold II followed him from Tuscany. Pius IX remained in exile for seventeen months. This situation had a profound effect on his pontificate, which lasted another thirty years. Whereas he had appeared to act with liberal convictions at the start two years previously, he now reverted to the arch-conservative policies of his predecessors. Rather than recognising the inconsistency of his behaviour, he complained of the ingratitude of his subjects. From then on, Pius IX believed that only an absolutist regime could prevent the downfall of the Papal States.

Meanwhile, 150 kilometres further north of where the Pope was residing, an experiment was attracting freedom fighters from all over Italy and even some international volunteers. This was the establishment of the Roman Republic. The revolutionary movement became increasingly radicalised, the Chamber of Deputies called for a constituent assembly and Mamiani's government was forced to resign. At the end of the year, a decision was taken to elect a new assembly of 200 deputies by universal male suffrage. On 5 February the first assembly convened. It was made up of revolutionaries, patriots and republicans such as Garibaldi, who since October had been assembling a small new army of volunteers in Tuscany and had immediately hurried to Rome. Mazzini also travelled from Switzerland, where he had fled after the Austrian victory in Lombardy. On 9 February the Roman Republic was proclaimed, and a month later the unification of the territories of the former Papal States with those of Tuscany, now also under a democratic government. For the first time since the outbreak of the revolution, two democratically governed territories were to be united. At the end of March 1849, Mazzini formed a triumvirate together with Aurelio Saffi from Rome and Carlo Armellini from Romagna, in which decisions were supposed to be reached collectively. Mazzini, however, took all the important decisions himself and turned the Roman Republic into a laboratory for his ideas, publicising them from April to June in his new newspaper *L'Italia del Popolo*. An ambitious reform programme was drawn up focussing on education, freedom of the press, the abolition of ecclesiastical privileges, and land reform. However, since the republic only existed for a few weeks, it was not possible to implement any reforms effectively apart from a few significant symbolic measures such as the introduction of universal male suffrage and the abolition of the papal emblems. The democratic constitution proclaimed on 1 July 1849 was never enacted.

The Roman Republic was attacked from two sides in the summer: from the south by Neapolitan troops and in the city's harbours by a French expeditionary force. Whereas in the spring of 1848 the Italian revolutionaries had still vainly hoped for support from the French revolutionary government, Napoleon III's French troops now helped the counter-revolution to victory. In December 1848 Napoleon had won a landslide victory in the democratic presidential elections in Paris. Since he owed this victory above all to the rural Catholic population and the traditional elites, he wanted to impress them with his military campaign on the side of Pius IX. Meanwhile, Mazzini and Garibaldi were wrangling over competences and questions of power. Mazzini, as the head of the triumvirate, prevented Garibaldi from being given supreme command because he considered him too high-handed. Disputes over the defence of Rome caused the final split between them. Some 20,000 volunteers fought doggedly for the Roman Republic, especially on the Janiculum Hill, but on 3 July they were forced to submit to the superiority of the French and Neapolitan troops. Garibaldi once again demonstrated his extraordinary courage and skill as a military leader. After the defeat, many revolutionaries managed to flee northwards, while Garibaldi and his irregulars left for Venice, where Manin was defending the last remaining Italian republic. Garibaldi's heavily pregnant wife, Anita, died on the run near Magnavacca, now Porto Garibaldi, north of Ravenna. This tragic loss helped enhance the popular myth of Garibaldi as a hero, since he appeared to have sacrificed everything for the nation, even his wife and child. He himself was able to escape from the Austrians. At the beginning of September, he was taken into privileged custody with the Piedmontese general La Marmora but was then once again forced into exile.

There was no need for the counter-revolutionaries to resort to armed force to defeat the republican government in Tuscany since internal contradictions and factional disputes caused it to fail of its own accord. During the winter, the liberal democrat government under Giuseppe Montanelli and Francesco Guerrazzi had persuaded the Chamber to draw up a new constitution. When the Grand Duke fled in February further turmoil ensued. The Palazzo Vecchio in Florence was occupied and a new provisional government was set up as a triumvirate, again led by Guerrazzi and Montanelli, now joined by Giuseppe Mazzoni, a patriot from Prato. Although this new government supported radical and revolutionary ideas, it was divided over the question of the form of government and clashed with revolutionaries who had moved from Livorno to Florence and who proclaimed a republic on 18 February, against the will of the triumvirate.

The following day, the revolutionary governor of Livorno, Carlo Pigli, proclaimed a republic there, but by the end of March the new government in Florence had declared that any republic in Tuscany was to be abolished. The democratic and revolutionary governments generally achieved very little; they introduced very few measures and were paralysed by internal tensions that prevented political decisions being taken. In April 1849, the moderates, actively supported by the rural population, demanded the return of the Grand Duke of Tuscany. Leopold II returned with his Commissioner Extraordinary, Luigi Serristori, in May just as the last republican resistance flared up in Florence and Livorno. Meanwhile, Austrian troops arrived in Pisa to restore the old order.

The longest to hold out was the Republic of San Marco in Venice. Considerable resistance was also mounted against the Austrians by the city of Brescia at the end of March. For ten days, its inhabitants fought heroically against the overwhelmingly superior Austrian troops. This extraordinary commitment earned the city the honourable title of 'Lion of Italy'. The fighting in Venice was even more spectacular, both in terms of its duration and the level of violence. In spite of the fact that the democratic prime minister, Daniele Manin, displayed remarkable organisational talent, on 23 August 1849, after two months of bombardment by Radetzky and weakened by an outbreak of cholera, the city was forced to surrender. Manin and his fellow campaigner Niccolò Tommaseo fled into exile.

A major reason why the Venetian Republic was able to survive for so long was that in March 1849 the Austrians were once again at war with the Kingdom of Sardinia-Piedmont. In Turin Charles Albert had allowed himself to be urged by liberal and democratic politicians to resume hostilities against Austria. The prime minister, Vincenzo Gioberti, who had been appointed the previous December, was the prime advocate and able to win the King's support. Gioberti was deeply disappointed by his moderate liberal ministers and even more so by Pope Pius IX, whose conservative turn made a federal nation state with the Pope as its head, long favoured by Gioberti, impossible to achieve. He therefore turned to the democrats and Mazzini. It was, however, probably not Gioberti's energetic advocacy alone that prompted Charles Albert to break the truce, as he started the war on 14 March, just when Vienna and Naples were concentrating their forces on fighting the republics in Venice, Florence and Rome. Nevertheless, the Piedmontese completely misjudged the military balance of power, having assumed that Austria would be weakened. Only nine days after their army was deployed, it suffered a decisive defeat at Novara and a further truce was concluded. Charles Albert immediately abdicated in consequence and died four months later in exile in Portugal. His eldest son, the 28-year-old Victor Emmanuel II, then took over government affairs and conducted the peace negotiations. His father's previous commitment to the liberal democratic Gioberti was for him an unwelcome political direction. Many revolutionaries had rightly suspected his father of being an expansionist conservative wolf disguised in nationalist sheep's clothing, but this assessment was even more true of the heir to the throne. In a letter in 1847 to the Duke of Modena, the future King Victor Emmanuel II had already declared his political stance towards the emerging opposition and this did not change throughout his subsequent thirty-year reign. He campaigned for a conservative league of Italian princes to oppose liberalism, which he utterly rejected, believing it would only weaken and ruin Italy.[4]

As Duke of Savoy, Victor Emmanuel had not read any romantic literature in his youth that could have aroused nationalist ideas in him. He was a reluctant pupil, only interested in military education and hunting. As king it was not the nation but the almost thousand-year-old dynasty that was of paramount importance to him and he saw his role as a monarch side by side with his peers, the other European monarchs. Over the next few decades, however, he skilfully instrumentalised the nation state movement in order to hugely expand the territory of his small kingdom. This appropriation of the liberals began as early as the time of the peace negotiations with Radetzky, who had incidentally been a guest at his wedding. Victor Emmanuel II later claimed that during negotiations over the constitution he had fought for the article calling for its abolition to be removed from the treaty. This was an outright lie since it had at no time been demanded by Austria. The liberal cabinet was dismissed and in August the king charged the moderate Massimo d'Azeglio with the formation of a government. Seventeen months after the start of the First Italian War of Independence, the peace treaty signed on 6 August restored the borders drawn at the Congress of Vienna in 1815. King Victor Emmanuel of Sardinia-Piedmont was compelled to pay a war debt of seventy-five million lira to Austria and the Duchies of Parma and Modena, whose rulers had once again allied themselves closely with Vienna. He was also forced to allow Austrian troops to be stationed in Piedmont. The conclusion of the war and the peace treaty was vehemently criticised by democrats and republicans throughout Italy, who refused to give up the fight. In Genoa, they even went so far as to form a provisional Ligurian government. However, Victor Emmanuel sent his general La Marmora and on 5 April the rebellion was summarily crushed.

Fig. 13 Antonio Dugoni, Portrait of Victor Emmanuel II, 1866.

As in the majority of European countries, by the summer of 1849, conservative governments were firmly back in control in Italy. The revolutionaries were persecuted and forced once again to flee into exile. In most European countries, the pre-revolutionary order was restored, the only exception being Piedmont, which retained its constitution. The revolution in Italy had failed on three fronts. First, attempts to drive Austria out of northern Italy by force using Piedmontese troops and irregulars had failed. Their own forces had been inadequate and *l'Italia farà da sé* remained an illusion. Second, it had become evident that the neo-Guelphist model was unrealistic. There was no chance of their plans being realised with Pius IX, who had fled into exile after the radical revolts in Rome and become an ultraconservative. The third reason for failure was not least that the democrats and liberals were so divided amongst themselves. The various different spheres of revolutionary action had been too fragmented with too little unity. The result was that they all had to surrender to the repression of the Restoration. Even today, the Italian phrase *Fare un quarantotto* (literally 'to make a 48') means 'to cause chaos'.

Mazzini's ideal of a brotherhood of nations remained a pipe dream. This was demonstrated by the attitude of the National Assembly in Frankfurt, if by nothing else. It continued to insist on its claims to Trieste and the Trentino. All that was left to the Italians, who bemoaned parallel developments in the German and Italian states and revolutions, was a deep sense of disillusionment. In a letter to Niccolò Tommaseo, Gian Pietro Vieusseux vented his disenchantment with the Prussian embassy counsellor Reumont as follows: 'One must not overlook the fact that although this friend of ours loves Italy very much, he treats it as if it were his own property. He belongs to the historical school that believes in the supposed rights of the Ottonian and Hohenstaufen dynasties'.[5]

And yet nothing was the same again. Rome and Venice became long-lasting symbols of the national revolution. Throughout Europe the conservative victory in Milan and Naples was tainted with the stigma of repressive 'foreign rule'. The revolution had unleashed an unexpectedly powerful force with such a broad impact that it became increasingly unlikely that it would be permanently suppressed. The revolutionary events also demonstrated the important role played by exiles, thousands of whom rushed back to their homeland from all over Europe, the Mediterranean and America to fight for their political ideals. They retreated into exile again in 1849. Giuseppe Mazzini also had to flee abroad once more, but his international prestige as a political visionary had risen further among his supporters. Mazzini's commitment elevated Rome to the long wished-for capital of the nation state movement. His renewed exile took him back to Switzerland, Paris and finally London.

Furthermore, as in other parts of Europe, a process of social and political emancipation had been started. Debating societies were founded by democrats in Rome, Venice and Florence, also emerging in smaller towns such as Faenza and Cesena.

Between 1847 and 1849, seventy-seven new newspapers were published. National Guards also existed in Rome, Venetia and Lombardy. Both the political clubs and the vigilante organisations were open to everyone in principle, but they were dominated by the local notables. They used them not only to counter conservative forces, but also to maintain public order and suppress lower-class riots. As in France, the majority of the rural population played no part in the revolution and frequently sided with their sovereign. It is worth remembering the enthusiastic reception with which Leopold II was greeted on his return to Tuscany. The focus of the protests by the lower classes was primarily on improving their precarious living conditions.

Decades of culturally and religiously charged nationalism were followed by disillusionment and political resignation after 1849. Liberal Catholicism had failed and the time had come for realpolitik. It was the beginning of a period of secular nationalism, whose most prominent representative was undoubtedly Conte Camillo Benso di Cavour. Like Bismarck in Germany, he is regarded as the inspired architect of the 'delayed' foundation of the nation state. In 1848 the Italians and Italian politics were still viewed disparagingly, particularly by the Germans and Austrians, in keeping with the motto: 'You can change masters, but you can't do without them'. In the words of Metternich, Italy was no more than a 'geographical concept' and a paradise for enthusiasts of antiquity. Twelve years later, however, this image had changed fundamentally. It was the chronically underestimated Italians who were to be the pioneers in nation-state building.

## Notes

1 Alfred von Reumont, Aus König Friedrich Wilhelms IV. gesunden und kranken Tagen, Leipzig 1885, p. 313.

2 Augsburger Allgemeine Zeitung, No. 133, p. 2123, 12.5.1848, „Die italienische Bewegung und ihre Bedeutung für Deutschland".

3 Camillo Cavour, L' ora suprema della monarchia. Il Risorgimento, 23.03.1848, in: Giovanni Gentile (ed.), Camillo Cavour. Scritti politici, Rome 1925, p. 106.

4 Le lettere di Vittorio Emanuelle II, raccolta da F. Cognasso, Turin 1922, vol. 1, pp. 142–143.

5 Raffaele Ciampini, Gian Pietro Vieusseux. I suoi viaggi, i suoi giornali, i suoi amici, Turin 1953, p. 431.

# 7. The Path to the Nation State

## 7.1 The reactionary states and the liberal Kingdom of Sardinia-Piedmont

After the reactionary rulers had succeeded in defeating the constitutional movement, the radical revolutions and the socially motivated uprisings of 1847–1849, they began to implement widespread measures to restore the status quo ante. Liberal improvements were reversed particularly swiftly in the Kingdom of the Two Sicilies, where Ferdinand II, nicknamed *Re bomba*, reverted to a hard-line absolutist regime. Liberal politicians were put on trial and convicted for actions that had been within the law during the constitutional phase. Now, after the revolution, the police were given the authority to implement considerably tougher and more effective measures. They had been accused of failure during the revolution, of not having exercised systematic control. From now on the focus of their patriarchal and political strategy was to be on the comprehensive surveillance of society. Lists were immediately drawn up of people who were suspected of having sympathised with the idea of a nation state and those who were considered liberal. The systematic collection of data on suspects was intensified. The first to be targeted were those civil servants who were considered unreliable, which led to waves of purges in the administration. Officers such as Carlo Filangieri, Prince of Satriano, who had reconquered Sicily for Ferdinand in 1849, were recalled as soon as they expressed any criticism.

Public opinion was now closely monitored, particularly in Naples. As in Milan before 1848, there were petty reports about people deliberately refraining from smoking cigarettes and cigars, since this was a popular form of political protest that led to a fall in state revenues from tobacco tax. Spies were deployed in public squares and cafés, and theatres were regularly observed by the police. The work of the police also became increasingly transnational since it was not only the subjects living in the kingdom who were under systematic surveillance after the failed revolution, but also the countless southern Italian exiles in the Kingdom of Sardinia-Piedmont, Switzerland, France and Britain and especially Greece and the Ottoman Empire. The Mediterranean came under particular scrutiny as an area where political refugees were active. A veritable web of spies was set up to observe them, their mail was checked and consuls and ambassadors were even required to keep a close eye on every single person in the exile communities. These diplomats were able to provide precise information on the whereabouts of the liberals and democrats who had fled, thanks to the passports they were required to issue to them. They were also generous in supplying the local police with information. Travellers to Naples were subjected to particularly stringent checks. Territorial control and transnational surveillance were closely linked, and in some cases diplomats exerted so much pressure on the governments of the host countries that the exiles were forced to leave the country. This was common practice in Europe.

The Bourbon regime had to rely on its immediate court entourage as well as a dwindling group of notables, the military and the police. Corruption and denunciation were the order of the day and the wiser members of the southern Italian elite simply withdrew and bided their time. The conservative political system was nowhere in such disrepute as in Naples. A growing body of criticism came from abroad, led by William Gladstone in London. A member of parliament, originally for the Conservatives, then the Liberals, and several times minister, he was a staunch supporter of an Italian nation state and criticised the harsh persecution and summary justice suffered by politicians and journalists. Francis II, on his succession to the throne in 1859, would have been quite willing to initiate change. He was, however, torn between conservative advice from Vienna and constitutionalist advice from London and failed to achieve anything of note during his short reign.

The political situation was similar in the neighbouring Papal States. Pius IX and his Cardinal Secretary of State, Giacomo Antonelli, pursued an arch-reactionary course in which they fought resolutely against any ideological and political liberalism. Antonelli mercilessly persecuted political opponents and restructured the police force. Their chief weapon against any outside influence was strict censorship which kept almost everything out. The precarity of the state-controlled publishing industry is further evidence of the cultural isolation of the Papal States. Support for the Pope was provided by a conservative Catholic movement active throughout Europe which was on his side. Thousands of young men came to Rome to serve the Pope as irregulars. They helped to reinforce the French troops that had been stationed in the Papal States by Napoleon III as a protective shield.

Leopold II, who had returned to Tuscany, adopted a policy of reluctant reform, as he had before the revolution. However, it was only possible to return to the old system to a very limited extent. On the one hand, because of their conduct in 1848, the Grand Duke now distrusted the aristocratic moderates he had previously cooperated with. On the other hand, the moderates, including Baron Bettino Ricasoli, knew that it would not be possible to introduce major reforms in their relatively small state without outside support. Having initially resigned themselves to the situation, they then increasingly set their hopes on affiliation with the Kingdom of Sardinia-Piedmont, the only constitutional state on the peninsula. In Lombardy-Venetia, where the aged Radetzky ruled with a heavy hand, the moderate liberals adapted in similar ways. Until 1856, the population was burdened with high reparation payments, mainly paid by the notables. Trials for treason and death sentences were not exclusive to the revolution period. Another uprising organised by Giuseppe Mazzini, which was attempted as early as 1853, resulted in bloody repression and the confiscation of the property of the Lombard elites. Many of them fled to Piedmont and agitated from there against the Habsburg monarchy.

The situation changed after the end of the Crimean War in 1856. Austria remained neutral, much to the annoyance of the Russian tsar, and became increasingly isolated in terms of its foreign policy. Vienna was anxious not to further alienate the European superpower Britain, which was ruled by Italophile liberals, and so felt compelled to ease the situation in Italy. Emperor Franz Joseph visited northern Italy with his young wife Elisabeth in 1857 and stayed in the royal palaces of Venice and Milan for four months. Although he attempted to make a public display of his power by means of magnificent court festivities and military parades, the local nobility boycotted the imperial receptions and, at a festive performance at the Opera house *La Fenice* in Venice, the emperor's boxes remained unoccupied. His reception in other northern Italian cities was similarly frosty. The Milanese authorities had to pay the peasants money to line the streets on the arrival of the imperial couple and on the occasion of a festive performance in *La Scala* for the emperor, the boxes of the Lombard nobility were occupied by their servants. This was an outrageous political provocation. In spite of this, Franz Joseph was prepared to oblige the northern Italians with numerous pardons, economic improvements, and the expansion of local government. The now ninety-year-old Radetzky was dismissed and Franz Joseph's younger brother, Archduke Maximilian, later emperor of Mexico, was appointed civil governor with the task of further de-escalating the situation. In the hope of persuading political refugees to return, Maximilian returned their confiscated assets, but still the majority of them opted to stay in Piedmont. Many of these exiles were to play an important role in the establishment of the nation state a few years later. Victor Emmanuel II bestowed them with honours in reward for their loyalty, thus tying them even more closely to his dynasty. The concessions from Austria had come too late. Furthermore, the Habsburg troops that had been stationed in the neighbouring duchies and the northern territory of the Papal States as a means of safeguarding Austria's power were not withdrawn.

The only place the constitution remained in force was the Kingdom of Sardinia-Piedmont, even though in the summer and autumn of 1849 the situation there was still unclear and uncertain. The liberal democratic majority in parliament refused to approve the peace treaty with Austria, while the conservatives insisted on the suspension of the constitution. The rebellious republican city of Genoa was still in a state of siege, the military defeats needed to be faced and a large war debt honoured. Given this situation, the young King Victor Emmanuel II even entertained the idea of restoring absolute power with the help of Austria. In fact, he appointed Massimo d'Azeglio, a moderate, as head of the cabinet and called an election. In the Proclamation of Moncalieri, named after his hunting lodge to the south of Turin, the king addressed the voters, threatening them outright by telling them that the government needed support for its policies and that they should elect a government that would sign the peace treaty with Austria. He assured them that in future he would follow the constitutional path but that if the country and the people withheld their consent, he would be compelled to take over responsibility for the future of the country once again in order to avoid chaos.[1] This proclamation, amongst others, was drafted by Massimo d'Azeglio. Unveiled threats are considered a key element of Victor Emmanuel II's style of government and of the constitutional history of the Kingdom of Sardinia-Piedmont and the later Kingdom of Italy. They raise the question of the true distribution of power during the *cinquantennio liberale (liberal fifty years)*. In effect Victor Emmanuel accepted neither the sovereignty of parliament nor that of the electorate. What emerged in the Kingdom of Sardinia-Piedmont was a 'pseudo-parliamentary system'.[2] If the cabinet and parliament managed to govern in accordance with the king's wishes, he accepted them, but if they did not the king would intervene in a crisis at any time, as he did in November 1849.

After the elections in December 1849, the newly elected parliament was made up of a majority of moderates, but included numerous conservatives committed to supporting the clerical milieu. Its members ratified the peace treaty with Austria as desired. Prime Minister d'Azeglio and his cabinet then embarked on a path of moderate modernisation. They began by reforming the outdated reactionary ecclesiastical legislation, a move which was bound to cause conflict with the conservative right wing in parliament. Within the government, there were signs of a shift in the balance of power towards the moderate centre. The Minister of Justice, Conte Giuseppe Siccardi, held lengthy but inconclusive preliminary negotiations with the Curia, and then submitted the first, highly controversial bills in February 1850. They proposed the abolition of ecclesiastical asylum and jurisdiction, meaning the clergy would be placed on an equal legal footing with every other citizen. Non-observance of religious festivals was no longer to be penalised. In an attempt to prevent abuses of inheritance law through last-minute wills and testaments, ecclesiastical corporations would only be permitted to acquire land and accept donations with state authorisation. Not only the church, but also Victor Emmanuel's mother and his wife, both pious Habsburgs, exerted huge pressure on him to prevent these laws. Since the king had himself been brought up a strict Catholic, he was troubled by any conflict with the Pope.

The parliamentary debates on Siccardi's bill marked the first decisive break between the moderate liberals and the ultra-conservative right. One of the most ardent advocates of the bill was Conte Camillo Benso di Cavour, whose eloquent speeches attracted attention in parliament. His response to the conservative critics who accused him of supporting revolutionary laws was that they were merely in keeping with the times. The conservative wing voted against the bill as expected and it was ultimately only passed with the support of left-wing liberals. It was also accepted by the Senate, after which Catholic conservative circles, with the support of Rome and the encouragement of the Piedmontese right, launched a vigorous campaign against the secularisation measures, labelling them anti-Catholic. When the Minister for Trade and Agriculture, Pietro di Santa Rosa, died in August 1850, he was denied the last rites, which in turn led to public outrage and uproar. The Archbishop of Turin called on his diocesan clergy to join the opposition regardless. His arrest and imprisonment in Sassari in Sardinia marked the provisional climax of this culture war.

Cavour's powerful contributions to the debate in parliament in favour of these laws were the foundation for his political rise. In 1848 he had already spoken out in favour of religious freedom in his newspaper *Il Risorgimento* and shown himself to be a staunch advocate of the separation of church and state. D'Azeglio was anxious to have Cavour in his cabinet, initially as minister of agriculture and then of finance. The king agreed but with the warning '[...] be aware, he will soon relieve you of all your portfolios'.[3] He was proved right. In November 1852, Victor Emmanuel II appointed Cavour as Prime Minister. Apart from a brief interruption in 1859, he remained in charge of Piedmontese politics until his untimely death in June 1861.

In his years as minister of trade and then minister of finance, the first goal on Cavour's agenda was to raise the Kingdom of Sardinia-Piedmont to the economic and political level of the major European powers. Like all large landowners in northern Italy, Cavour was an ardent supporter of free trade policies. He rejected any form of protectionism, which he felt would give the state too much power and constrain the individual. It was his belief that liberalism alone would lead to the spread of prosperity, from which everyone would ultimately benefit. A series of trade agreements were designed to prove that, after the defeats of 1848–1849, the state was capable of partnership and willing to reform. Cavour concluded the first of these with France in November 1850. He used both economic and political arguments in parliament to gain support for his policy, which he saw as representing the 'desirable unity that should prevail among the free peoples of Western Europe'.[4] Further trade agreements with Belgium, Britain, Switzerland, the German Customs Union, the Netherlands and eventually even Austria followed. Railway construction was also vigorously promoted during this period. A first railway line now connected Turin and Genoa, which developed into an international port with overseas shipping companies. Progress was also achieved in the banking sector and with the establishment of a stock exchange.

Fig. 14 Carlo Bossoli, King Victor Emmanuel II, Cavour, the ministers and the court descend the grand staircase of Palazzo Madama after the opening of the fifth subalpine legislature, 1853.

Fig. 15 Michele Gordigiani, Portrait of Camillo Benso di Cavour (1810–1861), 1862.

Cavour stood for a policy of what is known as '*connubio*', a word that can be understood in its direct, literal sense as a marriage and in its more political, figurative sense as an alliance of unequal partners. This *connubio* was put forward by its advocates as a response to the threats posed by a possible authoritarian restoration. Cavour distanced himself from both the arch-conservatives and the democrats. The coalition he created between the broad-minded right and the moderate left worked not least for two reasons. First, the bourgeoisie valued aristocratic ways of life and, second, the aristocrats kept themselves less strictly apart from the bourgeoisie than their peers north of the Alps. In practice *connubio* was implemented by means of an alliance between Conte Camillo Benso di Cavour and the bourgeois lawyer Urbano Rattazzi, an influential representative of the left-wing liberal parliamentarians. Cavour took the place of the ailing and ineffective Prime Minister Massimo d'Azeglio on 3 November 1852 and proceeded to appoint experienced and competent ministers to work with him. His cabinet was chosen according to his guiding principle of '*franchement libéral, nullement révolutionnaire*' *(genuinely liberal, in no way revolutionary).*[5] Rattazzi acted as the president of parliament with the important task of mediating between the chambers, the cabinet and the king. In order to secure Rattazzi's active support, Cavour made him minister of justice in 1853 and minister of the interior in 1855, risking alienating himself still further from the conservatives. This marriage of convenience between the moderates and the left-wing liberals ensured a comfortable parliamentary majority until the elections in 1857.

Cavour took his programme of domestic political modernisation in two main directions: legal and administrative rationalisation, and secularisation. A series of reforms was designed to restructure the Piedmontese army, the post office and the administrative bodies and in 1854 a new civil code was introduced. These measures met with no significant opposition in parliament. This lack of resistance may have been the reason why Cavour supported one of Rattazzi's bills on ecclesiastical policy. It proposed the abolition of all religious communities that were not dedicated to pastoral care, teaching or nursing, as well as the confiscation of the assets of contemplative orders. The money was not to be collected by the state but was to be channelled into a '*cassa ecclesiastica*' and used under state supervision for pensions, care of the poor and to supplement the meagre salaries of ordinary parish priests. It was approved by the Chamber of Deputies but only passed by the conservative senate after the king had expressed his support. The architects and executors of the law were immediately excommunicated by the Pope, but this had absolutely no effect.

Cavour was a master of balance and led the 'Grand Ministry' skilfully, concentrating initially on domestic policy but never losing sight of foreign affairs. This was where he was to enjoy his greatest success. In the summer of 1852, whilst still minister of trade, he accompanied the king to Paris and London. Victor Emmanuel II proved to be unsuited to diplomacy because of his blustering manner and

Napoleon III preferred to negotiate with Cavour. Nothing concrete was achieved on this trip, but at least Italy's problem, namely Austrian rule in its northern territories, was discussed at a European level. Austria was and remained the principal enemy, above all because in 1848–1849 it was able to assert itself throughout the Habsburg Empire. After the revolution, its officers adopted the slogan: '*Hätten wir Italien nicht erobert…!' (If we hadn't conquered Italy…!)* and many of them had this proud word *W I R* (*we*) engraved on the blades of their sabres. It had become a catchword demonstrating not only the inner unity of the officer corps, but also its determination to counter any further attempt to use armed force to weaken the unity of the Habsburg Empire. It was highly symbolic that it was composed of the initials of the names of those who were seen as the fathers of victory in the previous battles in Prague, Vienna and Milan, the generals Windisch-Grätz, Jelacic and Radetzky. This was the origin of the acronym W I R.

The attempts at insurrection on the part of the left did not cease, in spite of the military strength of the Habsburgs, and helped to provide Austria with a pretext for repression. In the autumn of 1852 Mazzini founded a *Comitato Italiano* and from Ticino he orchestrated another uprising in February 1853 in Milan, but this was easily crushed by the Habsburgs. The fact that the property of Lombards who had acquired Piedmontese citizenship while in political exile was confiscated as a punitive measure gave Cavour a welcome opportunity to protest loudly at an international level. Diplomatic relations with Vienna were broken off. In addition, Cavour accused Austria of permanently violating the provisions of the 1815 Treaty of Vienna by stationing troops in the duchies and the Papal States.

As prime minister of Piedmont, Cavour used every opportunity to attract international attention to the Italian question. The next opportunity was the Crimean War in 1853. In July, the Tsarist empire occupied the Danube principalities of Moldavia and Wallachia, which belonged to the Ottoman Empire. Britain, however, did not participate in a further 'partitioning' of Turkey, as had been hoped, but instead shielded Constantinople with its fleet. Russia then destroyed the Turkish fleet at Sinope, a port on the Black Sea, so that Constantinople was now completely dependent on the support of the Western powers. In the spring of 1854, the fighting developed into the first war between major European powers since the Congress of Vienna. Napoleon III sided with Britain, while the tsar relied on forming an alliance with Vienna, in return for having provided troops to help put down the revolution in Hungary in 1848. However, Austria not only remained neutral but joined the Western powers to force Russia to withdraw from the Danube principalities. The consequences of this decision in Vienna were severe. The decades of co-operation between the Habsburg emperor and the tsar came to an end and developed into hostility on the Balkan peninsula. It also considerably restricted Vienna's scope for future action in foreign policy.

The initiative now lay with Britain and France. A fierce naval war, but with no battles at sea, shifted from Turkey to the Crimean Peninsula and its naval base Sebastopol and continued to drag on, causing the Western powers considerable problems in providing supplies by sea. The Crimean War developed into the first modern trench war and also the first war in which steamships were used. It was also new to have reporters on the ground, whose articles informed the global readership of the catastrophic situation in the medical care system. The journalists reported on the events in the Crimea by telegraph without any major time delay. A series of articles in *The Times* triggered large-scale fundraising campaigns in Britian, and Florence Nightingale, a pioneering nurse, rushed to Constantinople to set up a hospital for wounded British soldiers.

Since the reactionary Ferdinand II, King of the Two Sicilies, sympathised with the autocratic tsar and made it difficult for the fleets of the Western powers to use his ports in southern Italy, the port of Genoa became particularly important for delivering supplies during the Crimean War. Cavour was faced with serious political problems at home and therefore delayed Piedmont's entry into the war. As late as January 1854, he wrote: 'We are fighting against inflation, new customs duties, the priests and the reactionaries, and if there is a war besides, we will be in real trouble.'[6] There were more articles in the Piedmontese press about the development of grain prices and the rampant cholera than about the Crimean War. Cavour's attitude did not change until, as a result of an agreement to restore peace against the tsar, Austria allied itself with Britain and France at the end of 1854 and the Western powers urged Piedmont to provide troops. Victor Emmanuel was in favour of the war in any case and it was only parliament that saw it as a pointless waste of resources. Britain then offered loans to equip the Piedmontese troops and at the end of January 1855, the king signed a military convention agreeing to provide 15,000 Piedmontese soldiers to reinforce the British and French troops. Cavour gave one of his impressive speeches in parliament, maintaining that Italy would improve its international standing if it supported liberalism in the fight against the dominance of reaction in Europe. At the beginning of February both chambers finally voted in favour of the military operation.

By the time the Piedmontese troops arrived at the scene of war in the summer, 10 per cent of their soldiers had died of cholera. The rest took part in the last decisive battles with minimal losses. The Russian troops were forced to evacuate the fortress of Sebastopol. In the meantime, Tsar Nicholas I had died and his more liberal son Alexander II put an end to the pointless fighting. Piedmont's international reputation was enhanced as a result of this successful military engagement. At the international peace congress which began in Paris in February 1856, Cavour was present as his country's representative alongside those of the major European powers. Although he did not achieve anything concrete for Italy's 'cause', he used his presence there as a skilful networker, establishing and deepening relationships and regularly meeting the French emperor, his family and diplomats. Cavour's great moment came during a night session on 8 April. Various topics were on the agenda, including the Italian question. The British Foreign Secretary, George William Earl of Clarendon, accused the Pope and the King of Naples of mismanagement. Cavour in turn criticised the military presence of Habsburg troops in the Papal States and the duchies. The Austrian prime minister, Karl Ferdinand Count von Buol-Schauenstein, who was also present, refused to concede that the committee had any authority to negotiate over Italy. Nevertheless, the final congress resolution mentioned the Italian issue as an international problem.

Italy remained a controversial topic in European politics. Turin's claim to the political leadership of Italy was increasingly recognised in Western Europe, with the liberal press in particular seeing Cavour and the Kingdom of Sardinia-Piedmont as the representatives of the entire peninsula. Meanwhile, in 1856–1857, Mazzini and his followers made further heroic but futile attempts at insurrection in the Duchy of Modena, in Sicily and in Calabria. The worst defeat came after Carlo Pisacane landed in Sapri, Campania. He was a Neapolitan aristocrat and a socialist who had fought as a volunteer against the Austrians in 1848 and defended the Roman Republic with Garibaldi. Now Pisacane and a small group of supporters freed three hundred prisoners on the island of Ponza, of whom only a few were political prisoners, and took them to the mainland near Sapri. Once again, however, it was not possible to persuade the masses to revolt and Pisacane and his companions were surrounded by Bourbon troops and killed.

Exiles gradually began to realise that these attempts at insurrection would lead nowhere and that it would only be possible to create a nation state under the leadership of Victor Emmanuel II and Cavour. From then on national unification would take precedence over demands for democracy. The traditional centres of political exile in London and Paris were replaced by Genoa and Turin, the home of the *Società Nazionale Italiana*, which developed into one of the most important propaganda instruments supporting a constitutional nation state. The foundation of such a society had been suggested by Cavour in his correspondence with the Venetian Daniele Manin, who was living in exile in London. Manin launched the society in August 1857 but died shortly afterwards and Conte Giorgio Pallavicino-Trivulzio, who could also look back on a remarkable 'career' in the struggle against Austria, now became president. He belonged to the group of Lombard aristocrats who had planned an uprising in Milan in 1820, at a cost of fifteen years imprisonment in the Špilberk fortress. He was a member of the 1848 provisional revolutionary government in Milan and was one of the exiles whose estates were sequestered after the uprising of 1853. In the 1850s, he was a member of the Turin parliament. The secretary of the *Società Nazionale Italiana* was journalist Giuseppe La Farina, one of the leading democrats of the 1848 revolution in Sicily. Every morning, he secretly passed on information about the activities of the society to Prime Minister

Cavour, who did not declare his support for it officially, but used it to further his aims. La Farina also managed to win Giuseppe Garibaldi over to the *Società*, a significant boost to its prestige. Garibaldi, who had recently returned from exile in America and was living as a landowner on his own small island of Caprera, near Sardinia, was elected its Honorary Vice President. From Piedmont, the society quickly spread, driven by the involvement of the liberal aristocracy in the duchies of Parma, Modena, Tuscany, Lombardy and Romagna. Their motto was VERDI, an acronym for *Vittorio Emanuele, Re d'Italia (Victor Emmanuel, King of Italy)*. Thus, the name of the most famous contemporary composer became a code word for the nationalist movement. Daubed on the walls of buildings, it was a further means of provoking the occupying forces, who were easily enraged by the loud humming of Verdi's most famous arias. In 1859, the *Deutscher Nationalverein (German National Association)* was founded in Frankfurt/Main, modelled on its Italian counterpart. Whereas the Italian society was dominated by liberal aristocrats, north of the Alps it was led by liberal bourgeois dignitaries.

An assassination attempt, which took place in Paris on 14 January 1858 again drew global attention to the Italian question. It was a bomb attack on Napoleon III. The emperor was unharmed, but ten people were left dead and hundreds injured. The conspirators were arrested that same evening; all those involved were Italian. The group was led by Conte Felice Orsini, who came from an old aristocratic family in Rome and had been living in exile for decades, fighting for the Italian cause. In 1857, he published his political memoirs in London, recounting his experiences and failures. At his execution on 13 March 1858, he shouted: *'Viva l'Italia'*. His speech for the defence, read out by a lawyer at his trial, was printed in the French newspaper *Moniteur universel.* Before his death, he wrote a letter to Napoleon III, not asking him for pardon, but calling on him to give Rome back the freedom that its children had lost because of the French in 1849. He wrote a second letter to Cavour, published in the *Gazzetta Piemontese,* in which he justified his action. Contrary to Cavour's fears, the assassination attempt did not play into Austria's hands. Napoleon III gradually became convinced that the only way to end the revolutionary uprisings and assassinations was to find a solution to the Italian question.

In July of the same year, Cavour accepted an unofficial invitation from the emperor Napoleon III to the summer resort of Plombières, a thermal spa in the Vosges. There they held several hours of private talks in the *Pavillon des Princes.* Two topics took priority. The first was a French Piedmontese alliance that would enable a war to be waged against Austria in northern Italy and the second, the marriage of fifteen-year-old Clothilde, daughter of Victor Emmanuel II, to Prince Napoleon, son of Jérôme Bonaparte, the former King of Westphalia and a cousin of the emperor. Napoleon pledged to support the Kingdom of Sardinia-Piedmont in its struggle against Austria. The aim was to liberate the whole of northern Italy as far as the Adriatic. Lombardy, Venetia, the two duchies of Parma and Modena and the northern regions of the Papal States were to fall to Victor Emmanuel and the House of Savoy. This would create a large northern Italian state with eleven million inhabitants. Rome and its surroundings would remain under papal rule, while the remaining parts of the Papal States and Tuscany would form a kingdom of central Italy, which would be ruled by Jérôme Bonaparte. If the Kingdom of the Two Sicilies remained neutral, it was to continue to exist, in deference to Russia. The ultimate objective was a confederation of states based on the German model with the Pope as honorary president. The only task remaining was to draw Austria into a war.

The next step was taken by Victor Emmanuel II himself single-handedly, without consulting Cavour, who was utterly appalled by his reckless approach. On 10 January 1859, the king used his traditional speech at the opening of parliament to publicly provoke Vienna. Despite his respect for the treaties, he said, he could not remain unemotional in the face of the cries of pain (*grido di dolore*) that were reaching him from so many parts of Italy. This now famous phrase, *grido di dolore*, sent shockwaves through international diplomatic correspondence. The perception both in Italy and internationally was that this small, militarised, liberal kingdom in the north-west was prepared to lead the nation-state movement. Clothilde's wedding to Prince Napoleon took place in January as agreed. It was sneered at by the Piedmontese aristocracy since in their eyes the Bonapartes were petty upstarts, but it was celebrated by the ordinary people, who understood its political implications. Also in January, a military alliance was concluded in which the emperor pledged to support Piedmont in the case of an unprovoked attack by Austria. In return, Victor Emmanuel II promised that in the event of an alliance, Savoy, the ancestral home of the royal dynasty, and Nice, the birthplace of Garibaldi, would be relinquished to France. Nation-state principles were disregarded in the case of these two French territorial gains. If there were a war, France would provide 200,000 soldiers, Piedmont 100,000, Napoleon III would assume supreme command and Piedmont was to bear the cost. Possible motives for this alliance on the part of Napoleon are generally considered to be to weaken Austria, to achieve French hegemony, to create Italian states dependent on France and to demoralise social and revolutionary movements.

Meanwhile, in Piedmont Cavour was carrying out a massive rearmament programme and was at the same time fearful that the desired war might not break out after all, since in March Britain was attempting to defuse the tense situation by convening an international congress. He did everything in his power to prevent this from happening. He provoked Garibaldi into staging uprisings in the duchies, threatened France with the publication of the secret treaties and prophesied an imminent victory for Mazzini and his revolutionaries. At this point, the Austrians made a serious diplomatic error. In a Crown Council session on 19 April, they decided to issue an ultimatum to Turin on 23 April demanding an agreement to reduce the size of the Piedmontese army within three days. Neither London nor Paris had been informed of this step. Cavour rejected the ultimatum on 26 April. Two days later, Austrian troops crossed the Ticino, thus fulfilling the conditions required to trigger the Franco-Piedmontese alliance.

Map 4 Italy 1861.

## 7.2 The Second Italian War of Independence and the proclamation of the Kingdom of Italy (1860–1861)

Right from the start of the war, the fact that rail transport made it possible for France to organise swift movements of troops proved a decisive advantage. The Franco-Piedmontese troops were led by their monarchs. Franz Joseph initially entrusted the supreme command of the Austrian army to Count Franz von Gyulai, whose plan was to march straight to Turin. However, he reacted too slowly and lost valuable time so that Garibaldi, who was appointed Piedmontese general and was fighting with his Alpine troops from Biella, was able to conquer Varese and defeat the Austrians at San Fermo. The first major victory for the French was won by the French general Count Patrice de Mac Mahon on 4 June 1859 at Magenta, causing the Austrians to retreat across the river Mincio. It was, however, the second French victory on 24 June at Solferino and San Martino, not far from the Austrian Quadrilateral, that was decisive. It was the most ferocious battle of the Wars of Independence and one which left its mark on the monarchs. Five thousand soldiers lost their lives and there was inadequate medical treatment for the twenty-five thousand wounded. Henri Dunant, a young Genevan merchant who happened to be travelling by, was so horrified by the gruesome scenes he witnessed that a few years later he founded the International Red Cross, so that in future independent aid workers would be able to provide better medical treatment to the war wounded.

Meanwhile, Prussia mobilised its troops and Wilhelm, the Prince Regent, also asked the German Confederation to partially mobilise their armed forces. Russia and England offered to act as mediators for Wilhelm. Further fighting in the Quadrilateral was inconclusive since the French troops were weakened and the Austrians firmly entrenched inside their massive fortifications. As a result, Napoleon III was prepared to make peace. He wanted to avoid a war with the German states at all costs as, above all, he feared that Prussia might attack France on the Rhine border. On 8 July 1859, the two emperors, Napoleon III and Franz Joseph, signed an armistice in Villafranca, north of Mantua. Italy was from then on to be a federation. Austria ceded Lombardy to Napoleon III, who passed it on to the Kingdom of Sardinia-Piedmont. Venetia remained part of the Habsburg Empire but was also to be a member of the future Italian federation.

In central Italy, meanwhile, the liberal insurrectionary movement had created facts on the ground. The supporters of the *Società Nazionale Italiana* took advantage of Vienna's weakness and drove the dukes out of their palaces in Florence, Parma and Modena. Without the protection of Austrian troops, the governments in Bologna and other cities in the northern Papal States simply collapsed without a shot being fired. The papal officials withdrew from Emilia Romagna and the Marche. The only area where the papal troops managed to suppress the uprisings was in Umbria –

Fig. 16 Enrico Alessandro Fanfani, The morning of 27 April 1859, 1860.

with particular brutality in Perugia. The ensuing provisional governments were led by liberal politicians, Marco Minghetti in Bologna, Bettino Ricasoli in Florence and Luigi Carlo Farini in Modena and Parma, in close collaboration with Cavour, who supplied them with weapons. They then declared their annexation to Piedmont. However, the terms of the armistice in Villafranca determined that Parma, Modena and Tuscany be restored and an amnesty proclaimed. Reforms and an amnesty were also strongly recommended to the Pope. The original aim – a free Italy as far as the Adriatic – was thus no longer on the cards. No more than a fraction had been achieved. Victor Emmanuel II had already accepted this compromise in consultation with Napoleon III. Cavour was furious and gave the king an ultimatum to continue the war, but he was excluded from further negotiations. His last resort was to tender his resignation on 12 July 1859. He felt betrayed by the French emperor and cheated of his life's work. The Italian and European liberals also accused Napoleon III of betrayal and the name Villafranca became synonymous with betrayal. A recurring image used by the Lombard press was *sorella Venezia in catene (sister Venetia in chains).*

The peace negotiations took place in neutral Zurich. Austria would have preferred not to give Victor Emmanuel II or his representatives a place at the negotiating table at all. This was because Franz Joseph believed that the policy of the Piedmontese king supported the principle of the nation state, which the emperor considered revolutionary and a threat to the multinational Habsburg superpower. From his point of view, it was a fundamental attack on the existence of the Habsburg Empire. During the war, the allies had formed a legion of Hungarian exiles and defectors, and Cavour had received Lajos Kossuth, the leader of the Hungarian Revolution of 1848–1849 and a tireless campaigner for a separate Hungarian nation state. All this was a clear provocation for Vienna. During the negotiations in Zurich, Franz Joseph insisted categorically that the dukes were to be reinstated to their government posts. His top priority was to restore legitimate authority in these countries, if necessary by means of armed force. In November, the peace agreement was signed in Zurich, basically reaffirming the terms of Villafranca. However, facts on the ground were not so easily created.

Napoleon III used the print media to win the support of the public in just the same way as he had at the beginning of the war with the pamphlet *Napoléon III et l'Italie*. A pamphlet entitled *Le Pape et le Congrès* appeared shortly before Christmas 1859 and caused a sensation. Its main topic was the anachronism of papal rule. Its anonymous author described himself as a devout Catholic but it soon became clear that the pamphlet had been written by the publicist Viscount Arthur de la Guéronnière on behalf of the emperor. He argued that it was in the Pope's best interests to reduce the size of the Papal States, as it would allow him to concentrate on his immensely important spiritual duties. His point was that the Pope needed to be relieved of the secular burdens of government: *"Plus le territoire sera petit, plus le souverain sera grand" (The smaller the territory becomes, the greater the sovereign)* and therefore the focus of his secular rule should be on Rome and its surrounding area.[7]

In Turin, meanwhile, Victor Emmanuel II was ruling without parliament, whose members he had dismissed when they did not do as he wished. In the summer a government was formed under Prime Minister Alfonso La Marmora and the interior minister Urbano Rattazzi, but it proved unable to cope with the complex situation and, for want of an alternative, the king had to entrust Cavour with forming a government once again. Previously there had been constant friction between them and the king had been glad to be able to dismiss his uncomfortable prime minister in Villafranca. Cavour, in turn, was not always able to conceal his intellectual superiority over the king. On 23 January 1860 Cavour not only assumed the office of prime minister in the new government, but also that of foreign minister. He did not fill the portfolios exclusively with Piedmontese, which proved to be a skilful move. He chose General Manfredo Fanti from Modena as the minister of war and placed the Lombard Stefano Jacini in charge of public affairs, meaning he was responsible for setting up the administrative structure of the new kingdom.

The solution to the Italian problem was ultimately decided in an international framework, although not by the Concert of Europe. Austria refused to take part in a congress at which territorial changes to the Papal States would be negotiated and the planned European congress failed to materialise. Neither France nor Britain had any interest in implementing the provisions of the Treaty of Zurich, as this would have required considerable military force with no guarantee of the desired result. At the beginning of March, the provisional governments, secretly supplied with weapons by Cavour, held plebiscites in Tuscany, Emilia, Modena, Parma and what was formerly the northern part of the Papal States, Romagna. They were given the choice between unification *(unione)* of the territories with a constitutional monarchy under Victor Emmanuel II or the formation of a separate kingdom, although nothing was stipulated as to what this should look like. All men over the age of 21 who had citizenship had the right to vote. The outcome was overwhelmingly in favour of a union with Piedmont. A month later, a referendum on union with France was held in Savoy and Nice, whose official result was a unanimous victory for Napoleon III. This referendum was preceded by heated discussions in the Turin parliament. Garibaldi, who sat in the Chamber of Deputies as the unlikely representative of his home town Nice, never tired of publicly and emotionally castigating the national betrayal it represented. He resolutely resigned his seat and retired, embittered, to Caprera, soberly justifying this move as a political realist on the grounds of political necessity.

Policy should now have been focussing on consolidating what had been achieved. Victor Emmanuel II ruled a large kingdom in northern and central Italy. However, it did not include Venetia, large parts of the Papal States and the Kingdom of the Two Sicilies and it was precisely from there that further advancement towards a united Italy was fuelled, albeit unintentionally. Sicily, where autonomy had been repeatedly fought for by its political elites, often supported by the wider masses, rose up once again. Their enemy was the resident of the royal palace of Naples, the 23-year-old Francis II, the last ruling Bourbon, who surrounded himself with arch-conservative counsellors. His minister of war was the ninety-year-old General Francesco Antonio Winspeare and his commanding generals were only slightly younger. On 4 April 1860, there was another uprising of artisans in Palermo, led by Francesco Riso, which quickly spread from the capital to other cities and the countryside. A four-week guerrilla war raged, which the overwhelmingly superior Bourbon troops were barely able to contain. The peasant population was motivated to join the uprising by their heavy tax burden, the unfair distribution of land, and problems with irrigation systems. The global public was not oblivious to this hardship. Karl Marx, who was earning his living in exile in London as a correspondent for the *New York Daily Tribune*, reported on 17 May 1860:

> At present political, administrative and fiscal pressure weighs on all classes of the people, and these grievances are in the foreground. But almost all the land is still in the hands of relatively few large landowners and barons.[8]

Although this seemed to be just another call to break away from Naples, this time it was very different. Since the network of the *Società Nazionale Italiana* enabled them to get help from the mainland, the Sicilians were no longer acting in isolation.

Two of their representatives, Francesco Crispi and Nino Bixio, travelled to Genoa, where they approached Garibaldi, requesting his support. These two nation-state promoters had also been fighting for their political goals for years. Crispi had been involved on the side of the left-wing liberals in Palermo in 1848. He then lived in Marseille and Turin until he was expelled, after which he joined Mazzini in exile in London. In the late 1880s and 1890s, he was to frequently steer Italy's politics as minister of the interior and prime minister. Bixio, on the other hand, had taken part in the revolutions in Milan and Rome in 1848 and become one of Garibaldi's most important generals in the Second Italian War of Independence. It was therefore only logical that they turned to him for help as one of the few from whom they could expect successful armed intervention in Sicily. Garibaldi hesitated initially because he suspected the *Società Nazionale Italiana* and its representatives of merely spreading propaganda and not fighting actively. In any case he was planning to 'liberate' Nice again. However, he was swayed by these two Sicilian patriots, Crispi and Bixio, and negotiated with the king for weapons and money. Since the king saw Garibaldi as a counterweight to a strong Cavour, he was supportive of him and would have been quite prepared to meet Garibaldi's demands, but Cavour prevented him. It has long been assumed that Cavour was the mastermind behind Garibaldi's expedition to Sicily. This theory is, however, untenable. Cavour even tried unsuccessfully to have Garibaldi arrested in the harbour of Cagliari on the journey to Sicily, calling it a mad venture. He feared that the European powers would intervene. When they failed to do so and Garibaldi achieved his first successes, Cavour felt compelled to back him publicly, for fear of otherwise suffering a considerable loss of prestige.

Garibaldi's supporters gathered in Genoa. Legend has it that two steamships, the *Piemonte* and the *Lombardo*, were captured, but in fact they had been made available in advance. Around one thousand volunteers boarded, many of them under the age of twenty, many of them students from Pisa, but most of them experienced fighters from the 1848 revolution who had risked their lives for independence in Milan, Rome and Venice. Among this famous *mille (thousand)* were Giorgio, the son of the recently deceased Daniele Manin, and Menotti, one of Garibaldi's own sons. Five days later, on 11 May 1860, Garibaldi reached Marsala on Sicily with these poorly armed men. He had chosen the less secure west coast for the landing, not least because this was where the insurgents were strongest. Garibaldi was always in close communication with the writers and journalists among his troops and they constantly informed the world press of his activities. The British press in particular offered its readers romanticised accounts of his adventures, which increased his support still further. In theory Garibaldi and his thousand men had no chance against the Bourbon troops, who had 20,000 men protecting the city of Palermo alone. But tactical skill, the will to fight and the influx of additional volunteers, but whose total number in Sicily never exceeded 3,000, made the seemingly impossible possible, namely to defeat the Bourbons.

Three days after landing, Garibaldi somewhat presumptuously proclaimed himself dictator of Sicily and from then on issued decrees. The first violent clash took place at Calatafimi where, on the march from Marsala to Palermo, 1,400 Garibaldines plunged fearlessly into chaotic hand to hand combat with 1,800 better-armed Bourbon soldiers and were victorious. Although this battle was meaningless in military terms, it had a huge psychological effect on the fighting morale of the volunteers, which was already very high. On 27 May, they conquered Palermo in a fierce street battle. The Bourbons retreated to the fortified hill of the royal palace and bombarded the city from there, killing around 600 civilians. Their commander general, Francesco Lanza, completely overestimated Garibaldi's forces and negotiated for a truce, even though he still commanded 18,000 men. Shortly afterwards the Bourbon troops left the island without further fighting.

The next task now was to establish a functioning provisional government and administration. Garibaldi was quite simply out of his depth when it came to the task of acting as dictator of Sicily and governing in the name of Victor Emmanuel. He had an outstanding talent for recruiting irregulars, giving patriotic speeches and motivating soldiers, but he was not a politician and had no idea of government policies or how to implement them. He appointed Francesco Crispi as his First Secretary of State and then reinstated the municipal councils, national guards and mayors who had governed the island briefly in 1848. He was unfamiliar with the social and political problems in Sicily and the only Sicilians he knew were exiles who came from the same social circles as he did. His interest in the administration was limited and he relied on the old elites to manage it for him. His top priority and primary goal, to which all else was rigorously subordinated, was liberation from foreign rule by military force.

Garibaldi dreamed of an army of the south, and one of his first decrees was aimed at a *levée en masse (mass mobilisation)*. However, the legendary revolt that had broken out during the revolution in France in 1792 did not materialise in Sicily. There had never been compulsory military service on the island and the absence of strong young men to carry out farm labour inflicted an enormous burden on the countless poor peasant families whose livelihoods were already threatened by harsh living conditions. At the beginning of the uprisings, the peasants had supported Garibaldi with isolated violent attacks against the Bourbon army and the police. But to leave home and become a soldier was a different matter and in case of doubt they quickly returned to their fields. Garibaldi announced that common land and plots of land that large landowners had taken possession of unlawfully would be redistributed to those who fought against the Bourbons. Some onerous direct taxes were also abolished. These measures did not, however, have the desired effect. The Sicilians insisted on the validity of the previous legislation and dodged compulsory military service. When local riots broke out, they were ruthlessly suppressed by the National Guards. One of the worst excesses in this context occurred in Bronte on Mount Etna where Nino Bixio inflicted harsh punishments on the rebellious deserters to set an example. Five leaders were summarily executed and thirty-seven were subsequently sentenced to life imprisonment by a court. Garibaldi approved of Bixio's brutal behaviour since the peasants and their social hardship were of secondary importance to him. They in turn had no interest in fighting for a national unification that was completely beyond their imagination. For the rural population, Garibaldi was no longer a celebrated liberator, but at best a new conqueror.

Meanwhile, Cavour followed Garibaldi's successes with deep suspicion. Since he was afraid of Sicily becoming a republic, he pushed for its rapid annexation to Piedmont. He sent weapons, ammunition and 15,000 men to Sicily as well as several liberal representatives of the *Società Nazionale Italiana* to control Garibaldi, including La Farina. Garibaldi, however, expelled him from the island for his attempts at political interference. He, Garibaldi, was adamant that Sicily should be independent, since he feared, not without reason, that Napoleon III and Cavour would instrumentalise his conquests for their own political purpose. After conquering the entire island, he crossed over to the mainland to complete his task. Here the same scenes evolved as in Palermo and no serious resistance was put up by the poorly motivated Bourbon army. First, Garibaldi easily conquered Reggio Calabria und thus obtained much-needed weapons, ammunition and provisions. Then, on the way to Naples, one fortress after another surrendered. In Calabria, the Garibaldines were in fact joined by large numbers of volunteers. At Soveria Mannelli 10,000 men abandoned the fortress between Catanzaro and Cosenza without resisting, demonstrating once again how demoralised the royal troops were. Garibaldi could

Fig. 17 Gerolamo Induno, Garibaldi in Marsala (11 May 1860), 1861.

now afford to leave his troops and rush to Naples, first by coach, then even by train. In Naples he was given a triumphant reception, possibly the greatest of his life, and certainly his last.

His main opponent during these months was Cavour, who feared that the dictator Garibaldi was too self-reliant and would realise his democratic ideas in the south. However, the liberals, who stood united behind Cavour and occupied key posts in Sicily, won the trial of strength over the democrats because the supporters of Mazzini and Garibaldi were hopelessly divided. Garibaldi was, furthermore, steadfast in his loyalty to Victor Emmanuel II. On 3 August, he introduced the Piedmontese-Italian constitution in Sicily and instructed civil servants to swear allegiance to the king. Meanwhile in Naples, Francis II tried to save his kingdom at the last minute by following the advice of Napoleon III and approving a constitution. This did not prevent the Kingdom of the Two Sicilies from literally imploding. In mid-July, the Austrian envoy wrote to the foreign minister Count Rechberg in Vienna reporting 'confusion in the palace, the collapse of the administration and anarchy in the streets – that is the sad summary of the situation'.[9] On 5 September, just two days before Garibaldi's triumphant entry into Naples, the king left the capital and retreated to Gaeta, the same fortress town on the northern border of his state to which the Pope and the Grand Duke of Tuscany had fled in 1848. To forestall further successes by Garibaldi, Cavour sent troops to the Papal States and Abruzzo. Unrest had broken out again there and was once more brutally suppressed by the papal troops. This provided Cavour with the justification for an invasion, with the prior agreement of Napoleon III, since he was the only one who could deter the Habsburg monarchy from military intervention in an emergency. Europe's conservative governments gradually intensified their objections to the disempowerment of the King of Naples, but the neighbouring great powers went no further than recalling their envoys from Turin. Prussia did not even do that, limiting itself to a formal note of protest.

On the French side Napoleon III now pushed for the revolutionary movement to be curbed, but it had long since spiralled out of control. In the hope of restoring law and order, he, together with Cavour and Victor Emmanuel II, decided that plebiscites should be held in the Marche and Umbria, after which they would be united with the Kingdom of Italy. At the same time, the French emperor continued to stand behind the Pope because he needed the support of the Catholics in France. The plan proposed in the pamphlet *Le Pape et le Congrès* was implemented and the territory of the Papal States considerably reduced, now comprising only Rome, Latium and the Patrimony of St Peter. It was even out of the question for Napoleon to attack Garibaldi and his troops in Rome since this would have discredited him with the liberals once and for all. Cavour's policy, however, was supported not only by the French, but also by the British. They were particularly anxious for stable power relations in Italy since they hoped that this would strengthen stability in Europe. They did not want more territory to be ceded to France nor, under any circumstances, a fresh military conflict to be provoked with Austria.

Piedmontese troops under the war minister Fanti marched into the Papal States. In spite of numerous volunteers from all over Europe, the papal army, led by the French General Juchault de Lamoricière, lost the only significant battle at Castelfidardo in the province of Ancona. Provisional governments were now also set up in Umbria and the Marche. With the new target of Naples, Victor Emmanuel II formally assumed supreme command of his troops, although in fact they were led by Fanti, a vigorous opponent of Garibaldi. A revolutionary uprising had turned into a battle for a nation state fought by the regular royal army. The liberal press campaigned for the war, claiming that it was the only way to prevent a clash with France and further radical revolutions in Italy. Cavour was, meanwhile, preparing parliament for the territorial expansion of the kingdom. A law authorising the government to incorporate further territories into the Italian state without making any changes to the systems of the state or the constitution was passed with a substantial majority. This time, the decision was taken by parliament before holding the plebiscites, whose function was merely to endorse it.

In late summer the conflict between Garibaldi and Cavour reached a new climax. Both publicly and in a letter to the king, Garibaldi demanded Cavour's dismissal. However, Victor Emmanuel II refused to let Cavour go. In the meantime, the democrats Giuseppe Mazzini, Giuseppe Ferrari and Carlo Cattaneo had arrived in Naples and were pressurising Garibaldi to set up a constituent assembly, while he in turn was trying to persuade the provisional governments in Palermo and Naples to accept the democrats' plans. There were demonstrations both for and against the establishment of a constituent assembly. All this added to the liberals' existing fear of civil war and further revolutionary activity. Their distrust of Garibaldi grew and it was seen as essential to disempower him. At the end of October, the royal army marched into southern Italy and on 21 October, plebiscites on unification with the Kingdom of Italy were held in Sicily and on the mainland. The vote was overwhelmingly in favour, but these ballots were not secret and were subject to considerable public pressure. This result sealed Garibaldi's political failure. On 26 October 1860, he met the king in Teano, around twenty kilometres north-east of Capua, a meeting that became the subject of countless emotional depictions of a warm greeting of equals. The reproduction on the cover of this book of a painting by Carlo Ademollo is a particularly good example. Legend has it that after they had shaken hands Garibaldi and Victor Emmanuel rode away together. It was the subject of countless illustrations in paintings, prints and even large-format frescoes in the town hall of Siena, as well as stories in school text books and history books. In actual fact this encounter and subsequent negotiations with the king led to nothing but disappointment for Garibaldi. He had hoped that as a reward for their commitment, all of the now 20,000 soldiers in his volunteer army would be admitted into the royal army, but only a few select individuals were accepted, one of them being his lieutenant general Nino Bixio. The king also turned down his request to be appointed governor of Naples. Garibaldi proudly rejected the king's generous offer of money and in his frustration withdrew to his country estate in Caprera once more, having failed to achieve his key aim of liberating Rome and Venice.

In Turin in February 1861, Victor Emmanuel II opened the first parliamentary session with deputies from almost all parts of Italy. They elected him king. Although he was the first monarch of the nation state, he kept to the tradition of numbering from the House of Savoy and, in accordance with the rule of succession, called himself the Second. In such cases he always decided in favour of the dynasty and not the nation. His title 'King of Italy' and not 'King of the Italians' is another demonstration of his conservative stance. The entire formula 'by the grace of God and the will of the people' contains only a half-hearted concession to the principle of popular sovereignty. On 17 March 1861 Victor Emmanuel was proclaimed king, officially founding the Kingdom of Italy.

Just a few days later, following rousing speeches by Cavour on 23 and 27 March, Parliament passed another important resolution with an overwhelming majority. It stated:

> Having heard the explanations of the Ministry, and trusting that the dignity, honour and independence of the Pontiff and the complete freedom of the church are safeguarded, this chamber resolves that, in accordance with France, the principle of non-intervention shall apply, and that Rome, as the capital acclaimed by the opinion of the nation, shall be annexed to Italy.[10]

This settled the future political direction of Italy. Rome alone could be its capital, but only in agreement with French diplomacy and with recognition of the spiritual power of the Pope.

Cavour died suddenly of a malaria attack on 6 June 1861 at the age of just fifty. There would not be another prime minister of his calibre for decades to come. The future of the Papal States seems to have preoccupied him even in his final hours. According to Cavour's niece, Marchioness Alfieri, he told Luigi Carlo Farini: 'I want the people of Turin to know that I am departing this life as a good Christian'. His final words to Father Giacomo during the administration of the last rites were apparently: 'frate, frate, libera Chiesa in libero Stato'.[11] This principle of a 'free church in a free state' was one he adhered to until the very end, hoping in vain for a peaceful understanding between church and state.

In Italy, France and Britain, Cavour's death was greeted with widespread dismay, but it met with a much more muted response in the German states. No meaningful entries on Cavour can be found in Otto von Bismarck's works. Many Prussian conservatives regarded him in any case as a creature of Napoleon III. Four years passed after his death before it occurred to the renowned national liberal Heinrich von Treitschke that Cavour's method could serve as a model for the foundation of the German nation state. In a letter he mused:

> The most useful thing I could write now would undoubtedly be an essay on Cavour, not too long, but knowledgeable and effective. We have nothing in German of merit about this great man […]. An account of him could demonstrate the nature of true inspirational realpolitik to our public much more effectively than any general discussion.[12]

The essay was published in 1869 and is much more than merely a depiction of Cavour. It provides a history of Italy since the Congress of Vienna and describes Cavour's political actions as a model for the Prussian path to a unified state. Victor

Emmanuel II is largely ignored, Mazzini is portrayed as an enigmatic demagogue and Garibaldi as a courageous fighter but politically incompetent.[13] Treitschke is also unsparing in his treatment of all those who opposed Cavour's great project. The Bourbons and Habsburgs are depicted as lawbreakers who tortured and humiliated the Italians and used all available means to maintain their rule by force; members of the court in Naples are compared to rats; the Pope's counsellors are described as homeless country squires and clumsy zealots; and religious superiors as behaving with plebeian crudeness. In contrast to this bleak picture, Cavour's luminous figure shines all the brighter. Treitschke sees him as both a power politician with an exceptionally keen mind and a master of acute political calculation. 'How much patience, how much devotion this quiet work demanded of the clever man who unseen and single-handedly directed the course of the unification movement!', wrote Treitschke. For him Cavour's early death left a gaping hole.[14]

Cavour's death did indeed mean the loss of a state leader who had acted with far-sighted consistency and exerted a substantial influence on the king. Although there were subsequent frequent changes of government, all the future prime ministers had worked with Cavour before and basically continued his policies. The moderate liberals, later described as the *Destra Storica (Historical Right)* remained in government until 1876 when the left-wing liberals took over power. Victor Emmanuel had allowed himself to be directed by Cavour but none of his successors managed to gain such a strong hold over the king. The influence of the military and courtiers on political decision-making processes also began to increase. They held an average of 30 to 40 per cent of all ministerial posts during the reign of Victor Emmanuel II, mainly though not exclusively in the foreign, war and naval ministries. The king selected a general such as La Marmora, who had fought the wars of independence with him, to be prime minister three times. One of his personal aides, Conte Luigi Federico Menabrea, was also appointed to the office of prime minister three times. Conte Luigi Guglielmo Cambray-Digny, his Master of Household and therefore one of his chief courtiers, was made minister of finance, agriculture, and trade and industry several times and his Master of the Hunt was made minister of war in the same cabinet. Similarly, foreign ministers such as Giacomo Durando had previously served as aides-de-camp to the king at court and had a close and trusting relationship with the king. Over the years the number of positions in the royal household occupied by the *Casa militare,* the military cabinet, increased noticeably. More recent studies on the monarchy have also found that a 'court party' was able to exert considerable pressure on the king and bring down prime ministers by means of their intrigues but that they, in turn, were manipulated by Victor Emmanuel II for his own political purposes.[15]

The next task on the agenda was to complete the unification of the nation state by incorporating the Papal States and Venetia. As in previous years, events unfolded on two different levels. The democrats, republicans and left-wing liberals used publications, protests and weapons to try and achieve their goal, while the king and his ministers acted through diplomatic channels and waged war. Much depended on Napoleon III's stance and he was in no way prepared to champion the Italian cause again. The supporters of Garibaldi and Mazzini continued to agitate incessantly. Associations of war veterans were formed after 1861 from the troops of those Garibaldines whom Victor Emmanuel II had refused to integrate into the regular army. In most cases they were republicans. Garibaldi also campaigned for rifle clubs to be established to give Italians the opportunity to carry out military exercises and learn how to use rifles. Almost two hundred of these societies were founded between 1862 and 1865 under the patronage of the *Tiro a segno nazionale (National rifle shooting)* committee and the joint leadership of Garibaldi and Crown Prince Umberto. Large national shooting competitions were held in Turin, Milan and Florence, among other places, and all the competitions, even the local ones, offered the chance to demonstrate patriotic support for the occupied provinces. Garibaldi was able to draw on this reservoir of willing fighters when required. In 1862, he, the hero and freedom fighter, was invited by the government on a tour of northern Italy and officially received by the king and the prime minister, Urbano Rattazzi. A tour of Lombardy immediately followed and Garibaldi was received by mayors and prefects in many places. He gave speeches in front of emotionally charged audiences, who repeatedly chanted the slogan '*Roma e Venezia*' and took part in paramilitary exercises with his veterans' associations. All this was done in apparent agreement with the monarch. However, when the irregulars set off towards Venetia they were arrested and Garibaldi, who 'happened' to be staying at a nearby spa, was taken into custody. During demonstrations for the release of the prisoners, riots broke out and the military fired into the crowd, killing four people and injuring many more. Garibaldi's activities were thus halted for the time being, but his headstrong behaviour was not officially condemned – he enjoyed far too much popularity with large sections of the population for that. Prime Minister Rattazzi and the king were attempting to continue Cavour's tactics in 1862. The aim was first for the revolutionaries to conquer territory, and then for these territorial gains to be sanctioned by diplomacy once the deed had been done. This time, however, this strategy of double dealing failed.

However, Garibaldi was not discouraged and stubbornly persevered with his mission. On his release in June 1862, he proceeded to travel around Sicily, once again collecting weapons and volunteers. The slogan *O Roma o morte (Rome or death),* which he shouted to the crowd on an appearance in Marsala, became the rallying cry for his troops from then on. Victor Emmanuel II, meanwhile, announced that any further possible steps towards a nation state would be decided by him and him alone and anyone acting contrary to this would be committing high treason. Garibaldi, however, was convinced that he was still acting in the king's interests and that this official announcement was only addressed to Napoleon III as a form of appeasement. He succeeded in recruiting an estimated 3,000 irregulars, his so-called 'Roman Legion', crossed with them to the mainland without any intervention by official troops and began marching towards the papal city of Rome. Unlike two years earlier, however, the Red Shirts were not joined by any other volunteers in Calabria; the garrison of the fortress of Reggio Calabria remained loyal and kept its gates closed. Napoleon III, meanwhile, threatened massive military intervention, triggering the government's decision that, since General Enrico Cialdini was already at war with the brigands in the south, they would deploy him against the irregulars. The peasants kept both themselves and their livestock hidden, which meant that Garibaldi's troops suffered from a shortage of supplies and their ranks dwindled. Those that remained retreated into the Aspromonte mountains where on 29 August 1862 the overwhelmingly superior royal troops attacked the Garibaldines. The battle lasted only a quarter of an hour, there were twelve casualties and Garibaldi was shot in the leg, resulting in an extremely painful and protracted injury. He and his fellow irregulars were arrested and imprisoned in the fortress of La Spezia.

The international press and the Italian public were outraged at Garibaldi's injury. They disputed the official version of events, which reported that the Garibaldines had put up fierce resistance that could only be broken by force of arms. The democratic press repeatedly condemned Garibaldi's undignified prison conditions and the great pain caused him, and this in turn led to protests in La Spezia and other cities. These public demonstrations denounced a government apparently willing to protect the Pope but to shoot at its own veterans. This reinforced the image of two contradictory Risorgimentos, one for which the people were prepared to make sacrifices and the other embodied by the king and politicians. The Rattazzi government was forced to resign and, instead of the treason trials against the prisoners that had been scheduled in accordance with the king's announcement, an amnesty was granted. In December 1862 Garibaldi returned to his island of Caprera.

After a brief interlude of a cabinet under Farini, Marco Minghetti, who was prime minister from March 1863 to September 1864, once again attempted to move forward on the question of Rome by diplomatic means. He negotiated a convention with Napoleon III and his foreign minister Édouard Drouyn de Lhuys, which was signed in September 1864. Under its terms, France undertook to withdraw its troops from the Papal States within two years and, for its part, the Italian government promised to be responsible for the protection of the Papal States and to defend them from any attacks. Italy would also tolerate the formation of a papal army, for which the Pope was permitted to recruit international volunteers. It also stipulated that the seat of government should be moved from Piedmont, on the periphery, to Florence in the centre of the country. This September Convention was not greeted with any great enthusiasm in France or in Italy – quite the contrary. In France Catholics accused Napoleon III of abandoning Pius IX. In Italy both left-wing supporters of the idea of the nation state and conservative supporters of the Savoy dynasty declared it a betrayal. They were shocked by the decision to move the capital to Florence, since what they wanted was a strong Piedmontese state that would extend over large parts of Italy and be governed from its capital Turin, the ancestral seat of the monarchy. In protest, the traditional Piedmontese elites boycotted the royal theatre on the following New Year's Day. Many people expected Florence's status as the capital to be no more than provisional.

The September convention sparked riots in the streets and squares of Turin once again. They vented both the frustration of the Piedmontese over the loss of their capital and their indignation at having to abandon Cavour's vision of Rome as the capital *(Roma capitale),* which parliament had voted for in 1861. The demonstrations continued for several days and their suppression claimed more than thirty lives. In parliament, the more moderate left, which had grown into a strong opposition force, remained incensed by the decision for weeks. Minghetti suffered the same fate as Rattazzi after Aspromonte: the king dropped him and he was forced to resign as prime minister.

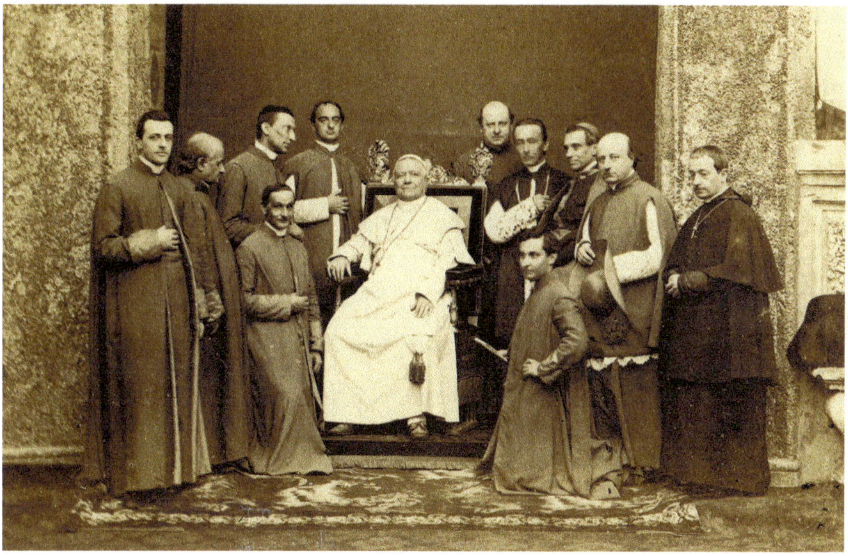

Fig. 18 Giovanni Maria Mastaï Ferretti, Pope Pius IX (1792–1878), Italian pope from 1846 to 1878 and his entourage in the Vatican, c. 1865.

In December of the same year, the Pope fomented the already heated debate, and the ideological battle between Liberalism and Ultramontanism came to a head. Pius IX published the encyclical *Quanta Cura (With What Concern),* in which he decried religious freedom and the separation of church and state. Its eighty-point appendix, the *Syllabus Errorum (Syllabus of Errors),* listed and condemned the errors of modernity: pantheism, rationalism, socialism, communism, liberal demands for state sovereignty over schools, equal rights for non-Catholic denominations and many more. When Napoleon III, who had repeatedly exhorted the Pope to introduce reforms, learnt of the encyclical he was furious and forbade its dissemination in French churches. Many of the wiser Catholics in Italy gradually began to realise that losing the Papal States would not necessarily harm the Church.

Once the young Kingdom of Italy was proclaimed, both Prime Minister Cavour and Marquess Alfonso Ferrero La Marmora, who succeeded Minghetti in September 1864, judged it prudent to seek a rapprochement with Prussia and Bismarck in order to be able to act against Austria. For this they needed Napoleon's consent. The focus of La Marmora's government after the September Convention was on winning Venice. There were two ways of doing this: either Italy could reach an agreement with Vienna by negotiation or it could attempt to profit from shifts and conflicts in the European power system. In autumn 1864, Vienna rejected the proposal of compensation for a peaceful handover of Venetia, in other words of selling it to Italy. Instead, the Austrians redoubled their efforts to secure control over the territory, particularly by insisting on increasingly Germanising the administration and the judicial system, a development that the Venetians found more and more difficult to tolerate. They organised a campaign of internal resistance, working with the nationalist movement in the Kingdom of Italy. The notables mounted passive resistance by refusing to elect their representatives to Austrian committees. Small insurrectionary movements also led pockets of active resistance in the northern mountains. The public mood became increasingly rebellious and anti-Austrian – less so in the countryside but particularly in the cities.

## 7.3 The Third Italian War of Independence and the conquest of Venetia and Rome (1866 and 1870)

The Italian prime minister, La Marmora, watched the tensions in the German Confederation carefully. After the 1848 revolution, the battle between Prussia and Austria for its undisputed leadership had soon reignited, even though the two powers had fought together against Denmark over Schleswig-Holstein in 1864. In January 1865 La Marmora offered military assistance to Prussia in the event of war with the Habsburg monarchy. This move had been agreed with Napoleon III, who expected to play the role of arbitrator in the event of a conflict and hoped it would gain him territory in Belgium and on the Rhine. The Prussian prime minister, Otto von Bismarck, who had been in office since 1862, had already allowed for the Kingdom of Italy as an ally in his calculations, but initially favoured peaceful solutions and attached more weight to diplomatic relations with Austria than with Italy. The first rapprochement between Prussia and Italy had come in 1864 with the signing of a trade treaty and the approval of a project to build a tunnel for the Gotthard railway in order to shorten the route between the German states and Italy. By the summer of 1865, Bismarck seemed prepared for an imminent war. Unexpectedly for Italy, however, in August the two principal powers of the German Confederation reached an agreement in Bad Gastein over their joint rule of the 'Elbe Duchies' of Schleswig, Holstein and Lauenburg. La Marmora was deeply frustrated by this Gastein Convention. From then on diplomatic negotiations between Italy and Prussia were overshadowed by distrust. Prussia was in any case convinced that Italy was dependent on France, while in Florence the government suspected that Bismarck's only use for Italy was as a threat if there was a conflict. In autumn 1865 La Marmora once again proposed that the Austrians sell Venetia to Italy, but they trusted the Gastein Convention to protect them from further Prussian aggression and refused. This was their final missed opportunity to cede Venetia peacefully and avoid a potential war on two fronts.

At the beginning of 1866 Bismarck decided to wage war against Austria, a conflict that was carefully prepared by Field Marshal Helmuth von Moltke. Italy now returned to the stage as an ally and at the end of March General Giuseppe Govone was sent to Berlin to negotiate a secret treaty between Italy and Prussia. It determined that in the event of an armed conflict between Prussia and Austria, Italy would declare war on Austria and, if there was an allied victory, Venetia would be ceded to the young Kingdom of Italy. Bismarck, however, refused to agree to Trentino being annexed by Italy as desired, as it was part of the German Confederation. Prussia assumed command of the alliance. Italy hoped not only that it would win Venetia, but also that being at the side of a militarily strong Prussia when it won the expected victories would increase its prestige. Govone was mistaken when he wrote to Victor Emmanuel from Berlin that Prussia was still a long way from starting a war.[16] Bismarck was merely seeking for a reason to attack. Once again London proposed an international congress to decide the fate of Venetia. Prussia, meanwhile, was making demands on the Austrian government for ever more far-reaching federal reforms, which, if they had been introduced, would in principle have meant no less than Prussian supremacy. When the Austrians refused to comply, Bismarck accused them of breaking the federal treaties and on 17 June 1866 declared war on Austria.

Three days later Italy followed suit. It mobilised 200,000 infantry troops and Garibaldi was given an official mission to participate in the war, this time with 35,000 volunteers. Austria, on the other hand, was only able to send 75,000 soldiers to the southern front, as the majority of its troops were deployed against Prussia. The Italian fleet was mobilised in the Adriatic. It was technically well-equipped and at least a match for the Austrian fleet if not superior to it. Overall, conditions seemed very favourable for Italy at the start of the war. Victor Emmanuel II once again assumed supreme command. On 24 June, however, the southern Austrian army under the command of Archduke Albrecht won a remarkable victory at Custoza, the place where – to add insult to injury – Radetzky had destroyed the Italians in the summer of 1848. The numerically superior Italian troops were poorly prepared and their generals Alfonso Ferrero La Marmora and Enrico Cialdini made serious tactical errors. At this stage not even a deployment plan had been drawn up. After this unexpected defeat, the Italian government was divided and paralysed, completely at a loss as to how to continue the war. The victories they had hoped for in the naval war also failed to materialise. A month later, on 20 July, a crucial battle finally took place not far from the Adriatic island of Lissa, and here Italy suffered the next sensational defeat against the Austrian fleet, caused by the incompetence of the commanding admiral Conte Carlo di Persano. The public reacted to these two ignominious defeats with vociferous demands for further military action. Once again it was Garibaldi who delivered. He advanced into Trentino with his volunteers and was victorious in a battle at Bezzecca on 21 July. All in all, however, the potency of his guerrilla tactics was wearing off. Now, the Austrians simply copied them and so avoided a decisive battle.

The war had in fact been long since decided by the Prussian victory at Königgrätz on 3 July 1866. This name came to be a symbol for a historic catastrophe, a defeat of immense proportions. The northern Austrian army was quite simply outclassed by the Prussian army. This was a disaster and neither the Austrian army nor the Habsburg monarchy ever fully recovered from its consequences until the end. The Austrian public was taken completely by surprise by this defeat. Their immediate reaction to the grim news from the Bohemian front ranged from consternation to rage. Despite the victory of the southern army in Italy, a retreat was inevitable. After Königgrätz, Emperor Franz Joseph turned to Napoleon III, asking him to act as mediator in negotiations. Vienna was now prepared to surrender Venetia. Cardinal Antonelli, Pius IX's right-hand man, is said to have proclaimed with pathos '*casca il mondo*' *(the world is falling apart)*, which may have been true, at least for the papal world of Rome. Without Vienna as a conservative regulatory power in future, the fall of the Papal States was inevitable.

Bismarck was keen to conclude peace quickly after Königgrätz in order to create a fait accompli within the German Confederation and pre-empt any territorial claims to the left bank of the Rhine by Napoleon. An armistice was signed as early as 25 July in Nikolsburg in southern Moravia. The surrender of Venetia was now sealed, but Austria was spared any further territorial losses. Prussia then put massive pressure on the Italian government also to negotiate a peace treaty with Austria. Most importantly, Garibaldi was to vacate the territories he had conquered in Trentino. In the peace treaty of 3 October 1866, Emperor Franz Joseph officially recognised the existence of the Kingdom of Italy and the Prussian representative agreed that Austria would surrender Venetia to France on condition that it was handed over to Italy. This meant that Italy only acquired Venetia as a result of Prussian victory. The Third Italian War of Independence, which had been greeted with such euphoria at the outset, was perceived in Italy as yet another disgrace. The fact that Venetia was handed over to Napoleon as a consequence of Prussian victory and that he then transferred it to Italy in the same way as he had Lombardy in 1860 was the source of further humiliation. Fierce debates in parliament and in the press about who was to blame for the defeats heightened these perceptions. Pasquale Villari, university professor and conservative politician, concluded in his remarkable volume *Who is to blame?*:

> The war is over and we have retained Venetia. The goal we had been preparing for six years has been achieved with fewer sacrifices than we were prepared to make. But nobody is satisfied. The image we had of ourselves can no longer be maintained.[17]

On 21 October, as in the other provinces, a plebiscite resulted in overwhelming support for the unification of Venetia with the Kingdom of Italy. A few weeks later, the citizens of the former Maritime Republic gave their new king an enthusiastic welcome. Now that Venetia belonged to the Kingdom of Italy, all that was lacking for Victor Emmanuel II to become the king of all Italians was Rome and Lazio (Latium). The problem here was that the people preferred to celebrate Garibaldi as their only victorious general and that he continued to campaign in public for the liberation of the Papal States and Trentino. Once again, the government had him arrested and imprisoned, this time in the Piedmontese fortress of Alessandria, together with several hundred volunteers. And again, demonstrations were organised, demanding the liberation of both Garibaldi and of the Papal States. The government allowed Garibaldi to retreat to Caprera but from then on, all his contacts and activities were under stricter state surveillance.

Rome still remained as the only outstanding obstacle of national unification. Pope Pius IX had no intention of renouncing his secular power and the public protests continued unabated. 1867 was another year marked by new waves of political agitation both inside and outside the Papal States. In Rome supporters of the Italian nation state prepared an uprising against the government and the papal army, but their attempt to storm the Capitol and the Serristori barracks in October failed. Garibaldi was still determined to complete his life's work. In September 1867 he escaped from his guards, fled to Sardinia and crossed from there over to the mainland. Once again, the government did not initially intervene and stood by while in the capital, Florence, his speeches fomented support for a march on Rome and he was cheered by the crowds. Garibaldi marched with his volunteers towards the Papal States once more but, since the masses could not be mobilised and the rural population was loyal to the Pope, he had too few supporters and was no longer able to build up a truly dangerous military force as he had done in 1860. He was arrested not far from the border of the Papal States in the province of Siena and released only because of massive public pressure. He immediately went back into battle to support the Romans who were trying to set up military bases outside the city gates. The Garibaldines won an initial minor victory against the papal troops at Monterotondo, 28 kilometres north of Rome, but were defeated on 3 November by French troops under General Pierre de Failly at Mentana on the Via Nomentana. The two French battalions were armed with a new weapon called the Chassepot rifle, which was a repeating rifle capable of firing twelve bullets per minute. This new system superseded the method of fighting with bayonets in one-to-one combat, which the volunteers had employed so successfully. The advancing volunteers were effortlessly mown down by the French rifle volleys. Although the survivors were able to retreat from the Papal States, they were arrested again, and Garibaldi was taken to the fortress near La Spezia once more. This time there were hardly any demonstrations in support of his release. He received the same punishment of house arrest on Caprera. There he felt abandoned and betrayed by his supporters, became embittered and unable to come to a rational analysis of his failure.

Napoleon III had disembarked French troops in the harbour of Civitavecchia to support the papal troops. This intervention had serious consequences. The renewed presence of French troops in Italy to protect the Pope amounted to a breach of the September Convention, which led to huge waves of indignation and unprecedented anti-French sentiment. Mazzini published an appeal urging the Italians to liberate Rome from the French and papal troops. After the events at Mentana, he said, nothing could be expected from their own monarchy but 'damage, dishonour and malice'. That was not all. He also wrote a letter to Bismarck asking him to provide financial support and a few thousand rifles to prevent a potential Italian-French alliance against Prussia. Bismarck was astonished by this letter.[18]

In the final event it was not the republicans who brought about the downfall of the Papal States, but a further military victory for the unpopular Prussians. With the aim of completing the formation of the German nation state, Bismarck provoked Napoleon III into fighting a war, which he, in turn, was only too happy to do, in the hope of gaining political prestige at home in France. He wished to divert attention from the socio-political disputes, protests and acts of rebellion that had been increasing in France since the mid-1860s. Bismarck tried to win over Italy as an ally once again, but the government in Florence rejected his advances, considering its natural ally to be France, who had done much to assist in Italy's state-building process to date. When the war began in July 1870, Napoleon III had to withdraw his troops protecting the Papal States. He requested urgent military support from Italy, but this was not granted. There were several reasons why Italy chose to remain neutral: the state was facing a serious financial crisis; the Italians were war-weary after the experiences of 1866; and democrats and left-wing liberals were threatening further protests if Italy entered the war. In addition to this came the fact that the fate of the French Empire was sealed by the Battle of Sedan on 2 September, when Napoleon III was forced to capitulate and was taken prisoner. The Third Republic proclaimed in Paris did not want to gamble away all its political capital from the outset by accepting the peace terms, above all the surrender of Alsace-Lorraine, and fought on desperately. The Pope could not have expected any help from the French republicans in any case. The Italian government, headed by its prime minister Giovanni Lanza, was determined to exploit the new constellation of European powers to resolve the question of Rome. Italian democrats and republicans were already preparing for further military action of their own and the government felt that putting an end to the Rome issue was the only way to prevent them.

Meanwhile, Pope Pius IX convened the First Vatican Council in Rome, beginning in December 1869. He intended it to continue the battle against liberalism, civil rights, the separation of powers, tolerance and the natural sciences, and the council allowed itself to be instrumentalised for this purpose. Seven hundred mostly Italian, French, German and Austrian prelates met in the Vatican. From the start the council was dominated by debate on papal infallibility. However, a liberal minority, consisting mainly of German and Austrian bishops, were excluded from the most important deliberations. One of their fiercest spokesmen, Ignaz von Döllinger from Munich, published a series of provocative articles in the *Augsburger Allgemeine Zeitung* in a vain attempt to prevent the measure being passed. Nevertheless, on 18 July 1870, a large majority in the council voted in favour of the dogma and on the same day, papal infallibility was solemnly proclaimed in St Peter's Basilica. This decision meant that the Catholic Church had finally manoeuvred itself onto the political sidelines, a danger that even many theologians had warned against. The '*Syllabus Errorum*' had already been regarded as an attack on the values of modern culture and politics, but the dogma of infallibility brought the antagonism between liberalism and ultramontanism to a peak and fuelled the constantly smouldering culture war. Even the Austrians disassociated themselves from Pius IX by pointedly suspending the Concordat of 1855. A day later Napoleon III declared war on Prussia, a step which immediately posed a threat to the existence of the Papal States.

The Italian government, always anxious to maintain a semblance of acting within the law, made a final attempt to reach an agreement with the Pope through diplomacy. He, however, refused to accept the occupation of the Papal States in return for guarantees of his spiritual independence and authority. Parallel to this, the Italian government informed the European governments of its intention to send troops to the Papal States to prevent revolutionary uprisings. There was no serious objection from any side. In mid-September royal troops under the command of General Raffaele Cadorna began to move into papal territory, but, although the Pope was only able to put up a token resistance, he was not prepared to give up without a fight. On 20 September, Italian troops advanced along the Via Nomentana and reached the city wall, which still completely surrounded Rome, and there shot the famous breach at Porta Pia. This was a purely symbolic act as there was no serious fighting, but it became the subject of countless photographs and historical paintings. The Pope turned down offers of asylum from Austria and remained in the Vatican, where he declared himself a prisoner and did everything in his power to disavow the young Italian nation state, also excommunicating all those who had taken part in the conquest of the Papal States.

Fig. 19 Rome, 20 September 1870: Porta Pia and the breach opened by the Italian artillery. Contemporary photograph.

In spite of this, the Italian government still attempted to negotiate a settlement with the Pope. The Law of Papal Guarantees passed in May 1871 offered him freedom of self-government and the status of an independent sovereign in the extraterritorial ecclesiastical state of the Vatican with diplomatic rights. He would be permitted to retain not only the Vatican, but also the Lateran and his summer residence on Lake Albano, a villa in Castel Gandolfo, as part of his extraterritorial possessions. He was also offered an endowment equal to his current income. The Pope refused everything. For him it was intolerable to accept his sovereignty and his income from the Italian nation state. Instead, he continued to be financed by donations from European Catholics, the so-called *Peter's Pence*, and to run the ecclesiastical government in the Vatican. When the king visited Rome, he stayed in the Quirinal, a city palace that had formerly belonged to the Pope. After some hesitation the Italian capital was relocated to Rome in the summer of 1871 and since its ministries needed space, they were partially accommodated in secularised monastery buildings.

Pius IX's aggressive rejection of the Kingdom of Italy caused a deep rift in the country. He remained true to his convictions and continued to fight against what he considered the 'rogue state'. His papal bull *'Non Expedit' (It is not Expedient)* in 1874 prohibited Catholics from participating actively and passively in elections and thus in practice from participating in political life. This meant that a politically influential Catholicism, such as that represented in the Centre Party in the German Reich, was not able to develop in Italy until after the World War II with the '*Democrazia Cristiana*', the Christian Democracy party. In fact, a reconciliation between the state and the Catholic Church was only achieved under the fascists, when Benito Mussolini and Pope Pius XI concluded the Lateran Treaties in 1929. They were in principle identical to the Law of Papal Guarantees of 1871. The Pope recognised the city of Rome as the seat of the Italian government, while the Italian state guaranteed the territorial and political sovereignty of the Vatican. The Holy See was also granted compensation totalling 1.75 billion lira.

The formation of the state was thus largely accomplished. Trentino did not become part of the Kingdom of Italy until after World War I, in return for its relatively unsuccessful military support for the Allied forces. While the southern part of the region is predominantly Italian, in the northern region of Alto Adige (South Tyrol,) the German-speaking population interpreted this as an annexation and some have not come to terms with it to this day.

The task now for the new Italian kingdom was to establish a functioning state. This is the topic of the following chapter, which takes us from the foundation of the Kingdom of Italy in 1861 to the breach at Porta Pia in 1871. In this decade, the most important foundations of the state were laid, but at the same time a terrible civil war began in the south of Italy, where the population fought against the impositions of the modern and efficient Piedmontese administrative state.

## Notes

1 Telesforo Sarti, I rappresentanti del Piemonte e d'Italia nelle tredici prime legislature del regno, Rome 1880, p. 16 ff.
2 Adriano Viarengo, Vittorio Emanuele II, Rome 2017, p. 126.
3 Maurice Paléologue, Cavour: Ein großer Realist, Berlin 1920, p. 60.
4 Cavour, Discorsi parlamentari, Vol. 2, pp. 408–434, speech of 21.1.1851.
5 Cavour, Epistolario, Vol, 9, p. 307.
6 Luigi Chiala (ed.), Camillo Cavours gedruckte und ungedruckte Briefe. Translation by M. Bernardi, 4 vols, Leipzig 1884–1886, Vol. 2. pp. 301–303.

7 Le Pape et le Congrès, Paris 1859, p. 11.

8 Karl Marx, Friedrich Engels, Werke, Vol. 15, Berlin 1961, p. 45.

9 Le relazione diplomatiche fra Austria e il regno delle due Sicilie, series III, Vol. 2, p. 181; Szechényi's report to the Foreign Minister Count Rechberg of 16 July 1860, source in French.

10 Armando Saitta (ed.), C. Benso di Cavour. Discorsi parlamentari, Vol. 15 (1859–1861), Florence 1973, p. 502.

11 Franx Xaver Kraus, Cavour, 1901, p. 79 f.

12 Heinrich von Treitschke in a letter to Salomon Hirzel on 28 November 1865, in: Heinrich von Treitschke, Briefe, ed. Max Cornicelius, Leipzig 1913, Vol. II, p. 437 f.

13 Heinrich von Treitschke, Cavour, in: Historische und Politische Aufsätze, Vol. 2, Die Einheitsbestrebungen zertheilter Völker, Leipzig [7]1913, pp. 243–402.

14 Ibid., pp. 354 and 400.

15 See especially Filippo Mazzonis for his innovative approach to the analysis of the monarchy and its significance in the political system of the new nation state; Filippo Mazzonis, La Monarchia e il Risorgimento, Bologna 2003.

16 Lettere di Vittorio Emanuele, Vol. I, p. 784.

17 Pasquale Villari, Di chi è la colpa, 1st edn., Milan 1866, pp. 385–422, here p. 385.

18 Jaspar Ridley, Garibaldi, Milan 1975, p. 672.

# 8. The Nation State: Consolidation and Resistance

## 8.1 Centralism or federalism?

The Kingdom of Italy was solemnly proclaimed on 17 March 1861. The new state was beset by legal, political and social problems from the very start. Cavour disappointed the expectations of the many supporters of the Risorgimento who had hoped for a constitutional assembly, by emphasising in his speeches the crucial role of the royal family in the formation of Italy. He declared that the king ruled by the grace of God and the will of the nation and that the previous ordinal numbering of the Savoy dynasty would be retained so that Victor Emmanuel would continue to be called 'the Second'. The numbering of legislative periods was also retained, making this the eighth parliament. The constitution to which the monarch had agreed in 1848 stipulated that responsibility for policy was to be shared between parliament and the executive. In practice, however, the only opportunity for communication between the king and parliament was at the opening of the parliamentary session at the beginning of the year when Victor Emmanuel delivered a speech written by his ministers to the two assembled chambers.

The question was what form the new kingdom should take. Would it be better to adapt the centralist model of neighbouring France or would a federalist system based on the Swiss or American model not be the more promising way to govern and gradually unite the extremely heterogeneous regions? The main supporters of the centralist model were Piedmontese politicians, whereas politicians from other regions tended towards federalism, in the hope that it would give them more autonomy and political scope.

One staunch opponent of centralised administration was Marco Minghetti. He was born in 1818 as the son of a large landowner in Emilia. After studying history and economics, he travelled frequently to Switzerland, Belgium, France and Britain, forming his liberal world view during these years of political apprenticeship. While still in the Papal States, he was a member of the *Società Nazionale Italiana* in his home town of Bologna. In the new kingdom, he held various ministerial posts in government and was even prime minister from 1863–1864. His proposal was to create new and larger administrative units in the form of more autonomous provinces, at least for a transition period. He also advocated delegating the responsibilities of individual ministries to local administrative officials and assigning tasks to elected local bodies. Minghetti believed that his plans to reconcile the demands of the state with demands for local diversity would be a way of creating a balance between French centralism and the administrative independence of very disparate regions, as practised in the USA and Switzerland. But it was to no avail. His plans met with such stiff resistance from the majority of the deputies and, above all, from Cavour, that they were not even put to a vote in parliament. Cavour thought that the demands of a modern society would meet with local opposition and was, therefore, afraid that there would be excessive reactions in politics locally, while the small group of those in government wanted to safeguard liberalism and their newly acquired national unity at all costs. On the one hand they feared the polarising, regressive forces that were influenced by the Bourbons and agitating from Rome. On the other, they were afraid of the no less dangerous democratic forces that were extremely dissatisfied with the outcome of the founding of the nation state and who were suspected of fuelling the discontent of the masses in order to reshape the institutional structure.

In the difficult months that followed unification, the centralised system already in place in Piedmont was finally adopted as the less costly and risky option. In October 1861, the administrative system introduced there two years previously was extended to the whole of Italy by the government under the first prime minister, Ricasoli. It was modelled on the pattern of state organisation developed by Napoleon I. As in France, executive power outside the urban areas, which had previously been exercised by governors or a general intendant, was now assumed by prefects. They were the heads of the provinces, the only territorial subdivision between the municipalities and the central state. On 23 October 1859 a law was passed by the Piedmontese government, the *Legge comunale e provinciale,* whose initial aim was to regulate the situation in the recently annexed region of Lombardy, but which was gradually extended to apply to the whole of the Italian peninsula. This law abrogated or suppressed any autonomy enjoyed by the provinces. It was argued that existing geographical and historical differences made it necessary to create a binding unification of all powers in order to pool economic and intellectual resources, this being the only way to create a modern state. The only region to retain its existing administrative structures was Tuscany, much to the annoyance of politicians in Lombardy and Emilia.

On 20 March 1865, however, the law was revised, with a view to ensuring uniform administration and governance throughout the new nation state. Various annexes confirmed or extended existing laws. They essentially endorsed the centralised and hierarchical structures of the state. Mayors continued to be appointed by the king and were responsible solely to the government. Local political life was controlled by the ministry of the interior through the prefects, whose task it was to communicate the government's political principles. As the central actors, they were responsible for the process of national unification down to the municipal level. The prefects also presided over the provincial deputation *(deputazione)*, the executive body of the provincial council, which was in charge of all municipal administration.

The public safety laws that had been in force since 1859 were upheld or even toughened, particularly in the area of social control. They made it possible, for example, for house arrest, warnings and fines to be imposed on those deemed 'lazy'. Other annexes related to infrastructure, the healthcare system and the formation of a privy council. A further significant annex abolished the special tribunals that had passed numerous death sentences during the fight against robber gangs in the south. This measure shows that the greatest problems with these brigands had been overcome, but it was also a step towards extending the rule of law.

In August 1862 a court of audit was established to oversee public finances. In January 1866, a civil code, a commercial code and a merchant navy code all came into force throughout the country. The civil code was clearly based on the Napoleonic *code civil* and established a legal system that focused on the protection of private property and of the family. This was a victory for the 'bourgeois revolution', whose goal had been to eliminate any traces of the feudalism of the *Ancien Régime* once and for all. Attempts to harmonise criminal law, however, failed. In Tuscany the resolution to abolish capital punishment passed in 1786 remained in place, whereas it was not until 1889 that it became law in the rest of the country. The government interfered in the careers of judges by imposing transfers or awarding promotions, preventing the judiciary from being truly independent.

The politicians in charge introduced far-reaching institutional changes up and down the country. They were staunch supporters of a liberal European culture and their faith in the institution of parliament was based on their trust in the persuasive power inherent in the principles of reason, personal freedom and equality. However, as soon as these moderate, liberal politicians were faced with a military or political crisis, they reacted in a manner that was far from liberal, as will be seen in the third section of this chapter. After unification, any kind of social disturbance was seen by liberals as a threat to the stability of public institutions. The creation of the Italian nation state was on the whole an important step in the development of moderate liberalism in Europe. It is clear, however, that considerable weight was still carried by traditional elements, first and foremost the dynastic policies of the House of Savoy, which provided considerable scope for authoritarianism.

## 8.2 The political class: winners and losers

Before 17 March 1861 an array of different factions – socialists, democrats, republicans, liberals, monarchists, supporters of a centralised state, federalists, secularists, Catholics, legitimists, conservatives and reactionaries – were all engaged in political agitation. However, their political positions either only partially overlapped or were totally incompatible. By no means all of them wanted an Italian nation state; many hoped that the individual states would become independent or more liberal. It is, therefore, not surprising that the ranks of the malcontents swelled swiftly after 1861. There was also a parallel Italy with many facets and dimensions, a country that was resentful. Those advocates of an Italy that was socialist, republican, localist, Catholic, reactionary or legitimist were left wanting.

Unification was and remained controversial due to the political and cultural attitude of the elites and the social barriers of the liberal political system. This was reflected not least in the electoral system and the extremely high level of taxable income required to be eligible to vote. Just under 2 per cent of the twenty-two million inhabitants were enfranchised and of those, only about half – some 240,000 – went to the polls in 1861. They elected 443 deputies, 300 of whom were loyal to Cavour. The number of senators was increased from 161 to 212 in order to include more representatives from the new territories. They were appointed for life by the king, had to be at least forty years old and belong to one of the categories defined in the *Statuto 1848*, namely bishops, ministers, diplomats, officers, prefects and presidents or vice-chancellors of universities. They were joined by the princes of the royal family.

The majority of elected deputies to the new parliament were large landowners and lawyers. The level of continuity during the parliament's first thirty years of existence is striking. After 1861, over 50 per cent of the deputies retained their mandate for three or four legislative periods, and a sizeable number (17 per cent) for five or six. It was not until 1882 that the income barrier was lowered, allowing 7 per cent of the population to vote. Universal male suffrage was introduced shortly before World War I. There were no political parties in 1861; members of parliament were elected on the basis of close network relationships or clientelism. The majority voting system meant that at the constituency level there was no need for party political frameworks as there was close contact between candidates and voters. The prominence of the candidates was crucial – those who held authority in society had a good chance of winning. Political weight and social prestige depended on personal networks and contacts with individuals and groups. There were close relations of patronage, whose aim was to mediate between political power and civil society and thus guarantee the necessary visibility for voters' concerns. They ranged from providing material aid and giving recommendations, to exerting pressure to secure support at the next election. This meant that prefects, judges and civil servants were appointed and promoted on the basis of their political achievements. They in turn did not fail to guarantee their firm support for the government's candidate.

An insight into this kind of network is provided by the correspondence of Silvio Spaventa. He was born in Chieti, a small town in Abruzzo, and paid for his opposition to the Bourbon regime after 1849 with ten years in prison. After 1861 he was member of the *Destra Storica* for Naples. In his correspondence there is a letter from a judge written in 1868 saying:

'I don't know how I can help you to be re-elected […]. Tell me what I can do. I could write to the attorney general of L' Aquila and the public prosecutor Re Troise, he is from Chieti and related by marriage to the Cocco family there.' Spaventa himself stated that on the whole

> […] elections are not political issues here, but are determined by financial means, connections and coercion. It is man-to-man combat. Augusto Vecchi from Florence has written [to support me] and is getting others to write. Today I am writing to my friends Salomone and Nicotera. The group around Avitabile [editor of the magazine *Il Dovere*] is supporting me, Serracapriola has been written to from here [Naples]. Even Caprara has written in my favour.[1]

This political system fostered the elitist character of the Risorgimento. It led not only to a low degree of legitimacy and a limited capacity for integration, but also to conflicts between the centralised state apparatus and the periphery that were difficult to overcome. These conflicts erupted with full force during and after the foundation of the nation state in a fierce gang war in the former Kingdom of the Two Sicilies.

## 8.3 *Il Grande Brigantaggio:* Civil war or gang crime?

Gangs of bandits and robbers are a European phenomenon with a long history reaching back to the Middle Ages, not only in the south of Italy. In the Napoleonic empire, serious, systematic attempts were made by the gendarmerie and the military to put a stop to them, but to no effect. The causes of gang crime were deep-rooted and the causal link between economic motives on the one hand and social, political, cultural and institutional motives on the other worked in both directions. Social and economic backwardness created a vicious circle, which makes it pointless to attempt to analyse what was the cause and what the consequence. Prior to 1861 violent and illegal practices were facilitated by the weak governments in the Kingdom of the Two Sicilies. Widespread poverty also contributed significantly to the fact that the lower classes were easily recruited into gangs, gangs that spread terror. A further problem in the south of Italy was the unequal distribution of land. The bulk of the land was divided into huge estates and the farmers' relationship with the estate owners was one of unequal dependency. Even more critical, however, was the behaviour of the estate managers towards the day labourers, on whom they inflicted social harm and humiliation. This was compounded by a traditionally high propensity for violence in the south. It was not uncommon for conflicts in the villages and feuds between notables to be resolved by violent means.

In September and October 1860, even before Garibaldi handed over his troops to King Victor Emmanuel, there were military operations by Bourbon soldiers in Abruzzo, backed by the rural population. In Ariano Irpino (Avellino province) in the region of Campania, they killed liberal supporters of the nation state, whose numbers were in any case significantly lower in the rural south than in northern or central Italy. Meanwhile, Francis II and his court, who were in exile in Rome, were intent on employing both words and weapons to stir up opposition to what they called 'the' Piedmontese. The Bourbon establishment hoped that the great powers would form an alliance with the Vatican and reactionary European powers and act in dynastic solidarity with Spain, therefore again intervening in the conflict in their favour. They backed the volunteer troops who were marching from the Papal States to Abruzzo and Campania and who were joined by local groups. Legitimist committees organised money, food and weapons on a local level for the armed units in the Basilicata and Apulia. As in all conflicts since the French Revolution, volunteers from all over Europe took part in the fight for the 'good' cause, in this case for the restoration of the Bourbon kingdom. Among them was a Prussian-born convert, Theodor Friedrich Klitsche de La Grange, a former papal officer and conservative religious writer. He was appointed brigadier general by Francis II, and, with the popular support of the rural population, heroically led the Bourbon uprising in Abruzzo as the 'Garibaldi of reaction'.

The gangs that already existed were reinforced by returning Bourbon soldiers and non-commissioned officers who had been dismissed, as well as by peasants and day labourers who rejected the new policy of universal conscription. Their operations used guerilla tactics and the liberals in Turin labelled them 'brigandage'. More precisely, they spoke of the *'Grande Brigantaggio' (the Great Brigandage)*, by which they meant the groups of several hundred people who carried out raids either on foot or on horseback and who were brazen enough to attack inhabited villages, aided by local Bourbon loyalists and peasants from the surrounding countryside. This fighting was at its fiercest between the autumn of 1860 and 1861.

At the beginning of July 1861, thousands of 'reactionaries' and peasants rose up in around thirty villages in Irpinia, a region of hills and mountains to the east of Avellino in Campania. Some Italian national guardsmen and infantry soldiers were killed. The military repression that followed was extremely harsh. The village of Montefalcione was set on fire and more than a hundred insurgents were executed by summary court martial. At the beginning of August, there were uprisings in the mountainous region of Matese, and in Ponteladolfo the legitimists proclaimed the restoration of Bourbon rule. An Italian army unit was overpowered, two soldiers fell in battle and a further forty who had been taken prisoner were massacred with volleys of bullets by the insurgents on the piazza in Casalduni. The Italian military again reacted with extreme brutality, their troops looting and burning the two villages to the ground. In Ponteladolfo, four hundred men, women and children were murdered indiscriminately. Both the brigands and the irregulars as well as the National Guards and the infantry inflicted relentless violence on their respective enemy.

Fig. 20 Band of Brigands from Basilicata, c. 1860.

The most famous leader of the brigands, Carmine Donatelli, known as Crocco, mounted his main operations in the Basilicata. After raiding several villages in April 1861, he eventually reached Melfi, where the local notables had proclaimed the restoration of the old regime. The Italian troops and the local national guards exerted so much pressure on Crocco that he retreated to the nearby mountains. There he was joined by a band of Spanish volunteers who had disembarked in Calabria but had failed to achieve anything there and so moved on to the Basilicata. They were led by José Borjes, a Spanish general, who tried in vain to transform the brigandage into a political uprising. In his diary, he claimed that his fight for the 'true cause' was motivated by ideological conviction not personal gain.[2] Borjes did not reflect on why his first foray into Calabria failed, why the bandits did not fight alongside him, why national guards formed in the villages to pursue him, or why the 'good' peasants he encountered did not join him but took his money and then reported him to the police. A power struggle soon broke out between the two leaders. Although Borjes had been put in official command by Francis II, he failed to seize control. Some villages also mounted stiff resistance to Crocco and in autumn 1861 he decided to disband his approximately two thousand strong 'army'.

The lower classes in southern Italy were not united in a wish to fight for the king and the church, nor for the nation state. The pamphlets circulating there when brigandage was at its height and which completely discredited Piedmontese rule were of little help. The citizens of Monopoli in the province of Bari signed a statement describing the situation and stating that His Majesty's loyal subjects were now weary of tyranny, shameless robbery, plunder and waste, unfair taxes, cruel state laws, scandals and corruption. They complained that a diabolical war was being waged against the religion of their ancestors, the Holy Catholic and Apostolic Church in Rome, against the great Pope Pius IX, the Vicar of Christ on earth, his cardinals, bishops and all good priests, who were being mercilessly imprisoned or exiled. Monasteries were also being plundered and the aristocracy expelled from the country. As if that were not enough, they reported, public safety was jeopardised, arbitrary arrests were being made based only on suspicion, and thousands of citizens were languishing in wretched conditions in prison without trial. They were all victims of the despicable revolution imported from the odious Piedmont, they wrote, and: 'Wherever we look, we see nothing but misery and suffering and the bloody traces of a bitter civil war'.[3] From the point of view of the supporters of the Bourbons, the new government, which they never referred to as Italian but always as Piedmontese, stood for revolution, tax burdens, war against religion, mass arrests and summary courts. Corresponding images were also spread on the international stage. The Bourbon government in exile appealed to the international public for support in the fight against the Italy of sects (an allusion to Freemasonry) and revolution, which it maintained was crushing the good Neapolitan people under the boots of its military. In 1863 Viscount Oscar de Poli, an ardent royalist, caused a furore by publishing a travelogue in Paris with an emotional and inflammatory description of the horrific atrocities committed by the Piedmontese in southern Italy.[4]

After the fall of the Kingdom of the Two Sicilies, one serious problem proved to be the fact that not only were frustrated Red Shirts from Garibaldi's troops roaming aimlessly through the country, but also a much larger number of dismissed Bourbon soldiers. Their officers, especially those who adhered to the traditions of the Murat period, tended towards the liberal nation-state movement whereas the non-commissioned officers and regular soldiers remained loyal to the old Bourbon dynasty. The most tangible outcome of the administrative reforms introduced by the Bourbons in the first half of the nineteenth century was a professional army which recruited its troops from the lowest social strata and enabled some of them to climb the social ladder. When the dynasty came to an end, the soldiers were dismissed and returned home with no financial resources. They were nostalgic for the good old days, ostentatiously wore their old uniforms in public, were despised by their liberal political opponents and pursued by the police. They were the ones who incited the peasants. Another group wanting to actively support the reactionary movement was made up of the chief municipal officers and the commanders of the Bourbon bourgeois militias. Many of them had acquired considerable status before 1860 but lost it again with the defeat of the Bourbons and therefore fought first as irregulars, then as bandits.

One example of thousands of such fates is the well-documented life of Pasquale Romano, the son of a shepherd from Gioia del Colle in Apulia. In the Bourbon army he reached the rank of a sergeant, learnt to read and write and served with dignity. After its defeat, he returned home, still wearing his uniform and puffed with pride, but found it impossible to revert to his former life. He joined a secret Bourbon committee formed in Gioia del Colle and became its military delegate. This was one of the many committees in which bourgeois citizens and men from the lower classes cooperated, for example in carrying out instructions from the Bourbon general Tommaso Clary. Clary had put down the uprising in Messina in 1847 and initially retreated into exile in Rome with Francis II. Now he returned by order of the king to be the commander of volunteers and brigands. The supporters of the committee swore to reinstate Francis II, '[...] King by the grace of God, defender of religion and beloved son of our Holy Father Pius IX' and to kill 'the devil incarnate, Victor Emmanuel, and his followers'.[5] Rumours proliferated and fake news was spread to keep the tension high. This included news of landings by Russian troops and of the return of the king at the head of an Austrian army. Cavour's death on 6 June 1861 was seen as a sign of divine providence and a positive omen for the reconquest. On 19 June, the governor had the members of Romano's secret committee arrested. Romano himself managed to escape and start an uprising in which he and his insurgents pursued ex-Garibaldians and liberals. The regular troops deployed against him responded with excessive violence. Again. the number of victims remains unclear – there may have been fifty, a hundred or a hundred and fifty – but what is clear is that there were many among them who had not taken part in the violence. Romano fled and became the leader of a new gang of bandits, who he made swear allegiance to the king and the church, at the same time assuring them that whenever possible his actions would be lawful. Although the number of his followers was gradually shrinking, Romano remained free and a dangerous threat for a long time. Here he fought courageously, there he plundered a farm and murdered its inhabitants. He was killed in battle in 1863 and was celebrated thereafter by the legitimists as a person willing to sacrifice their life rather than betray their native country and honour. Both his life and death provided rich material for chilling tales, legends and myths.

The irregulars and the brigands supported each other as long as they could, but after the late summer of 1861 they no longer attacked urban centres. The prospect of the king's return diminished, support from the court in exile failed to materialise, the presence of the Italian army increased and the Bourbon committees were arrested by the police: As a result, the irregulars turned to the tactics of traditional guerilla warfare. With renewed vigour, they began to carry out guerrilla raids in the countryside and especially in the mountains. 'They used to be called *Franceschini (supporters of Francis II),* now they are simply called brigands'.[6]

The next question is how the new rulers dealt with the problems of rampant crime, unrest, uprisings and deviance in the south. It can be assumed from the above that they frequently resorted to extreme force, which was not always justifiable. It was mainly experienced officials and military officers from the Savoy dynasty who were deployed to southern Italy to establish law and order. Unlike in the provinces of northern and central Italy, the administrators here in the south were not prefects but governors, who were able to revert to the tool of a state of emergency to enforce government authority. In the first two years of the 1860s, the government almost always revealed its less liberal side by frequently declaring a state of siege. This had a demoralising effect on the population, who repeatedly had to endure censorship and restrictions on freedom of assembly. In Naples, the role of governor was assumed by a military officer, General Enrico Cialdini. As head of the civil administration, he was the most important local politician appointed by the government. During the wars of independence, he had distinguished himself as a skilful officer in action against Austrian and papal troops. Now he launched a massive military operation against the brigands and insurgents in the south. At the height of the conflict, the Italian military presence amounted to 120,000 men. The number of brigands is estimated at 80,000 and the total number of victims at 15,000, of which 10,000 were brigands and civilians and 5,000 Italian troops.

In December 1862, a government commission was set up in Turin which spent six months investigating brigandage in southern Italy and the following August, parliament passed an emergency law based on the commission's report. It was named Pica's law *(Legge Pica)* after the Member of Parliament Giuseppe Pica from Abruzzo, who was an expert on conditions in the south and had played a key role in its drafting. It was intended to be an emergency and temporary instrument against banditry and constituted a violation of Articles 24 and 71 of the *Statuto Albertino,* which guaranteed every subject due process and equality before the law. Under the *Legge Pica*, the Italian parliament made brigandage a punishable offence whose suspects could be tried by summary court martial. It was also the first law of the unified state to clearly establish *camorrismo*, i. e. belonging to the Mafia, as a crime. The punishment for these offences ranged from several years' imprisonment, through life-long forced labour to summary execution. Anyone who gave themselves up to the police or was prepared to co-operate with them could hope for mitigating circumstances. The law was only in force for a short period and only applied to the provinces in the south that were branded 'infected'. At the end of December 1865, the parliamentary deputies in Turin refused to extend it again. By this time, brigandage had been successfully suppressed and an agreement reached with the Mafia.

It is clear from the debate surrounding the *Legge Pica* and from numerous letters and memoirs of officers and high-ranking officials who went from the north to reform the south that, amongst the hardliners at any rate, there was little understanding of the economic, social and political conditions in the Mezzogiorno. They were convinced of their superiority in terms of civilisation, and that this therefore justified their necessary mission to bring it to the area. The words of Luigi Carlo Farini, Cialdini's predecessor as governor in Naples, have become notorious. He appeared above as a revolutionary in Romagna (1831), an exile, and a close confidant of Cavour in the run-up to the founding of the nation state. Farini accompanied King Victor Emmanuel II on his way to Naples in October 1860. From Teano, after Garibaldi had handed over power to the king, he reported his impressions of the south to Cavour, who had never been there. 'But, my friend, what lands are these, Molise and Terra di Lavoro! What barbarism! This is not Italy! This is Africa: compared to these peasants the Bedouins are paragons of bourgeois virtue'.[7] This sentiment was echoed by Giuseppe Massari, a moderate politician and member of parliament, even though he had been familiar with conditions in the south since his childhood. He was born in Taranto and socialised as an exile after 1830 in the salons of Cristina Trivulzio di Belgiojoso and Costanza Trotti Bentivoglio Arconati in Paris. After 1848, he worked as a journalist in Turin and became friends with Cavour. Massari's background qualified him to become a member of the parliamentary commission enquiring into brigandage, which he interpreted in his report as a struggle between barbarism and civilisation. Robbery and murder, he claimed, would escalate into rebellion against society.[8]

In his book about brigandage on the borders of the Papal States, published in 1863, the Piedmontese general staff officer Conte Alessandro Bianco di Saint-Jorioz went even further. 'The brigands kill and plunder like beasts thirsting for blood and booty', he wrote. 'They are not creatures made in the image of God'.[9] The metaphor that was circulating was ethnocentric: the brigands were black, bestial, primitive, cunning and evil. These stereotypes, based on a kind of Manichean dualist thinking beyond rational explanation, positioned the brigands in a visually rich and emotionally charged realm of monsters. It may not have been particularly original to deny the enemy their claim to humanity and compare them to wild animals – there are numerous parallels in the centuries before and after 1900. Its purpose in 1860–1865, however, was to use this image publicly to sway opinion in favour of the extremely harsh measures taken against the brigands and, at the same time, to motivate the troops on the ground. They were conscripts from all over northern and central Italy sent to fight the illegal and criminal activities of the brigands, and were, like them, mostly uneducated peasants, more concerned with saving their own skins than with acting as standard-bearers of a superior civilising mission. The officers in charge of the troops were different: they believed that the military had a key role to play in building the nation state. Bianco di Saint-Jorioz, for example, was convinced that the only moralising agent in the southern provinces was the army.[10] General Francesco Lanza also declared that unity should be preserved 'with the army and in the army'.[11] In this way the Italian army became an instrument of state unity and a bulwark against rebellion and reaction. The elites supportive of the nation state also considered the army a symbol of an emerging nation and a means of creating loyal Italian citizens.

Both the supporters of the former Bourbon kingdom in the south and their opponents, the liberal representatives of the young Italian kingdom, spared no effort to denounce each other in the public arena, internationally and through the media, by portraying them as amoral, dangerous and illegitimate. Both sides were fighting for their own political system and their most cherished values. The colonial-style stereotypes circulated by the liberals justified their use of force as the only way of accomplishing their civilising mission in the south. The governing elites in the north had only a limited understanding of the mentality and living conditions of the southern Italians. In the mid-1860s, the government succeeded in more or less suppressing the activities of these criminal gangs. Brigandage violence had never gripped the whole of the south and was mainly rife in the poorest and most isolated regions in the interior of this former Bourbon kingdom. With a few exceptions, the cities and richer coastal regions with better infrastructure were not affected. The violence caused poverty and obstructed the markets but was also provoked by poverty and the remoteness of the markets.

This battle against the institutions of the new nation state that broke out soon after its foundation and was fought during the *Grande Brigantaggio* was, to a certain extent, a continuation of the traditionally widespread practice of illegality which has deep roots in the Italian south. Whether this was a civil war or criminal banditry was and still is a matter of opinion. Former and current Bourbon loyalists interpret the events as a heroic war of liberation. Liberal left-wing historians see it as an understandable reaction of the lower classes to an authoritarian, repressive state. The supporters of the liberal nation state at the time saw their role as a public duty and, in the long term, a successful civilising mission.

Massive military force made it possible for the young government to largely overcome brigandage in the south, but, in spite of their initial determination, they were ultimately forced to capitulate to the machinations of the Camorra and the Mafia. Although it was during the political upheavals of 1860 that the new rulers encountered these criminal organisations for the first time, rumours and unreliable information about them had been circulating before. The origins of the Camorra can be found by returning to the Bourbon Kingdom of the Two Sicilies of the 1850s. Here, criminal gangs were used by the Bourbons to impose law and order in the poor, overcrowded neighbourhoods of Naples and their activities were tolerated in the prisons. Their operations were carried out in connivance with the police and the prison guards and in fact the dividing line between these two groups and the *camorristi* was unclear. After the 1848 revolution several prominent liberal notables were held as political prisoners under miserable conditions in the dungeons of Naples and on the islands, which means there are valuable eyewitness accounts. This kind of ego-document must naturally always be interpreted with a certain degree of caution, but the basic features described here seem plausible.

A particularly impressive and detailed account of the situation in the Bourbon prisons was written by Sigismondo Castromediano, Prince of Morciano and Conte di Cavallino. He was born in 1811 and before the 1848 revolution lived in Lecce as a historian and private scholar with a moderate anti-Bourbon stance. At the end of June 1848, after Ferdinand II had imposed the constitution in February, he joined the patriotic circle in Lecce and became one of the four secretaries of the society. With the authoritarian turn in the early autumn, Castromediano was arrested and sentenced to thirty years imprisonment in chains for conspiracy. He served eight of these in various prisons before being pardoned and exiled in May 1858. In all the prisons he passed through, in Naples, on Procida, in Benevento and Avellino, the Camorra were in charge. In his book *Political Prisons and Dungeons*, he describes in minute detail how members of the Camorra, as prison inmates and guards, controlled, harassed and extorted their fellow inmates. First, every prisoner had to make a donation towards the candles on the altar of Our Lady in the prison, which were never lit. Then, in the overcrowded prisons, rent had to be paid for a small space in a cell, i. e. a place to sleep. This sum was called *pizzo* in prison jargon – a word that is still used in Italy today for protection money to be paid to the Mafia. The Camorra turned basic needs such as eating and sleeping into favours that prisoners had to pay for. A system of power emerged, controlling whether these favours were granted or withdrawn as punishment. If appropriate bribes were offered to the guards, the prisoners would be given safe, private cells, proper clothes instead of the humiliating prisoners' garb, better food, wine and books.

The Camorra was a strictly hierarchical organisation whose members swore allegiance to a code of values in which honour and secrecy were absolute. They were prepared to protect their members at any moment and at all costs, if necessary, by violent means. Stabbings were the order of the day and prisoners could be murdered at the behest of the Camorra.[12] The British conservative politician William Ewart Gladstone, who was in Naples in 1851, had also heard reports of the inhumane treatment of elite political opponents in the Bourbon prisons. He informed Lord Aberdeen of these conditions in two letters which were published in Britain in a ninety-page brochure that quickly went through several editions.[13] The court in Naples naturally dubbed this malicious propaganda. But a further pamphlet appeared in 1857, written by the Neapolitan economist Antonio Scialoja, in which he denounced the abuses and machinations of the Camorra from his position as an exile in Piedmont.[14]

The Camorra's influence was by no means limited to the prison system. The police in Naples, the *gendarmerie,* was riddled with criminals whose task it was to control the poorer neighbourhoods, where they exercised outright territorial control. On his return home from Naples, Marc Monnier, a Swiss hotelier, described a system of protection money that had to be paid by doormen, coachmen, grocers and butchers. In the harbour the Camorra also smuggled goods on a large scale.[15] In political crises, the Bourbons used the Camorra to mobilise the poor for their own purposes and showered agitators with money in return for inciting the people against their political opponents. This was precisely the danger that was threatening again in the turbulent summer of 1860. In the period before Garibaldi entered Naples, both the Bourbons and northern Italian politicians tried to bribe the Camorra over to their side. The Camorra sided with Garibaldi and when he arrived in Naples by train and entered the city, he was accompanied by high-ranking *camorristi*, adorned with cockades of the nation state. The people understood this symbol. Peace and order would be maintained.

The governors and officials who were appointed to the new government in 1861 tried to fight crime with all means at their disposal. The first in office were Governor Farini and his police minister Silvio Spaventa. Spaventa could be considered a qualified expert since, like Castromediano and numerous other liberal opposition figures, he had spent a decade in Bourbon jails after the 1848 revolution. Armed with high moral principles and a firm belief in the value of Piedmontese administration, he made it his declared aim to eliminate criminal banditry. As early as mid-November he ordered mass arrests and seized vast quantities of weapons and police uniforms which were being used to extort protection money. He succeeded in arresting Salvatore de Crescenzo, one of the Camorra bosses in charge of maritime smuggling. In the new year, Spaventa decided to purge the police force and fire many corrupt prison officers. He also prepared a detailed report for the government about the organisation of criminal gangs. It concluded that the Camorra originated in the prisons, that there was a separate section of the Camorra for each of the twelve districts of Naples and that its members behaved like a sect. Its hierarchy, according to Spaventa, was based on a unique system of exploitation and its main sources of income were extortion, smuggling and prostitution.

Spaventa's hard-handedness was not well received in Naples. He was increasingly criticised for acting like a Piedmontese even though he was in fact a southerner and, in January 1861, first demonstrations against him took place on the streets.

The backdrop to all this was an economic crisis which had a severe effect on the population. The removal of the Bourbon court led to the loss of thousands of jobs and sources of income and to a slump in consumption. Governor Farini, however, was not even prepared to acknowledge the reality of the loss of Naples' status as a capital city. In a letter to his political colleague Minghetti, he denigrated the former Bourbon capital, writing disparagingly: 'Naples is the capital of idleness and prostitution for all sexes and all classes.'[16] In April 1861, Camorra supporters stormed the police headquarters and broke into Spaventa's house to lynch him, but unsuccessfully. In June a further scandal occurred. One of the two Mata brothers protecting Spaventa as his bodyguards stabbed a high-ranking police officer in broad daylight. Rumours circulated that Spaventa was using the brothers and their gang to intimidate opponents of the regime. Whether true or not, Spaventa was compromised, resigned from his post and returned to Turin. What followed was the same dreary routine. The police struggled to overcome the Camorra by means of repression, mass arrests and public announcements, but it never took long for its bosses to recapture the lower city.

The Mafia posed a similar problem in Sicily. They did not control the prisons but exercised territorial rule in the countryside. There their main activity was to 'protect' the numerous large and small producers of lemons, a lucrative source of income in the nineteenth century. Besides the police, there were small private armies, gangs of bandits and armed family gangs. In the countryside brigandage was not the only major problem; there were also angry clashes with the local people who were intent on avoiding conscription. The liberal, moderate politicians in charge inevitably provoked hatred by imposing a state of emergency to enforce harsh rule. No high-ranking official in the new system of government went to the outskirts of cities without an armed escort.

The hinterland of Palermo with its cathedral city of Monreale was considered a stronghold of the Mafia. On 16 September 1866, disaffected troops gathered on the slopes of Monreale, which overlooked a wide bay with citrus and orange groves, and set out to storm the city of Palermo. Among them were men dressed in Garibaldi's famous red shirts, chanting *Viva la Repubblica*. What ensued was an outright, politically diffuse rebellion which the Mafia, led by bosses such as Turi Miceli, used as an opportunity to break into prisons, destroy criminal records and kill police officers and their informers. In the city the gangs from the surrounding area were joined mainly by artisans. Barricades were erected and official buildings and citizens robbed. It took the military seven and a half days to quell the uprising. No convincing interpretation of this last major uprising of our period has been given by historical research. The fact that the events that took place were so diffuse and the groups involved so heterogeneous means that the valid interpretations put forward by researchers are influenced by their political position. The dissidents who gathered in Palermo and other towns in the province in 1866 came from all factions.

The uprising was well-timed since the majority of Italian troops were in the north fighting against Austria in the Third Italian War of Liberation. In Palermo, liberal-minded men attempted to restore law and order. These included the mayor, Conte Antonio Starabba di Rudinì, himself a Sicilian, and the newly appointed prefect, Luigi Torelli from Lombardy. Torelli had fought at the barricades against the Austrians during the *Cinque Giornate* in 1848 but was now on the side of the government. Since taking office in April 1866, his official reports had repeatedly expressed concern about the security situation in Palermo. He drew attention both to the high level of crime rate and the fact that a further source of trouble stemmed from the establishment of a modern, secular state in opposition to the Catholic church. At the beginning of July, religious orders were abolished, suddenly putting 1,500 of the 5,000 monks and nuns dismissed out on the streets in Palermo alone. Massive economic problems were compounded by an extreme drought that threatened agriculture. On top of that, cholera was rampant in the city. All in all, Torelli's position was extremely precarious even before the outbreak of the revolt.

In addition to the Mafia, the participants of the mid-September Palermo uprising in 1866 included the people of the city, who were suffering from the economic crisis, and elite autonomists and socialists. The composition of the revolutionary committee alone speaks volumes. It was headed by Prince Bonanno Principe di Linguaglossa and included Baron Pignatelli, Baron Giovanni Riso del Castello di Colobria, the Prince of Ramacca and other influential noblemen. An avowed Mazzinian acted as secretary of the committee. There was a total lack of consensus as far as the political goals of the rebels were concerned. They included autonomists, conservatives, liberals, democrats and early socialists. The only bond uniting the lower classes was social protest. There was, therefore, no precise political thrust to the unrest. There was, however, unity in its opposition to the political maxims of the government in Florence, fuelled by an existential crisis. The revolt was directed against the expansion of the powers of the nation state and its administrative measures.

After the violent military suppression of this uprising, there were no more spectacular revolts. The political system gradually consolidated – only the Mafia remained. Neither the Bourbons, nor the politicians of the *Destra Storica*, nor the more left-liberal parliamentarians who replaced them were able to overcome the problems with the Mafia and the Camorra in the long term. Even Mussolini fought against this hydra in vain, in spite of his extremely harsh repression of organised crime and his boast that he had wiped out the Mafia. Notwithstanding increasing signs of resistance to their various gangs by the population in Italy in recent years, this system based on honour, robbery and revenge, which was established in the nineteenth century, continues to operate, the only change being in its weapons and goods.

## Notes

1 Luigi Musella, Individui, amici, clienti. Relazioni personali e circuiti politici in Italia meridionale tra Otto e Novecento, Bologna 1994, pp. 37 and 59–60.
2 His diary was published by Marc Monnier, Notizie storiche documentate sul brigantaggio nelle provincie napoletane dai tempi di Fra Diavolo sino ai giorni nostri, Naples 1862.
3 Marco Meriggi, Dopo l'Unità. Forme e ambivalenze del legittimismo borbonico, in: Passato e Presente 83 (2011), pp. 37–56, here p. 40.
4 Oscar de Poli, Voyage au royaume de Naples en 1862, Paris 1863.
5 Antonio Lucarelli, Il brigantaggio politico delle Puglie dopo l'Unità. Il Sergente Romano, Bari 1922, p. 59.
6 Andrea Sangiovanni, "Evviva Francesco morendo gridiam": aspetti politici del brigantaggio in Abruzzo, in: Trimestre 2, 2001, pp. 223–295, here p. 255.
7 Camillo Benso di Cavour, La liberazione del Mezzogiorno. Carteggi di Camillo Cavour, vol. 3: Ottobre–Novembre 1860, Bologna 1960, p. 208. Terra di Lavoro was a province of the Kingdom of Naples located with its capital, Caserta, north of Naples.
8 Giuseppe Massari, Relazione della commissione d'inchiesta del deputato Massari letta alla camera nella tornata segreta del 3 maggio 1863, in: Tommaso Pedìo, Inchiesta sul brigantaggio, Manduria 1983, pp. 105–229, here p. 208.
9 Alessandro Bianco di Saint Jorioz, Il brigantaggio alla frontiera pontificia, 1860–63, Milan 1864, p. 36.
10 Ibid., p. 27.
11 Francesco Molfese, Storia del brigantaggio dopo l'unità, Milan 1964, p. 190.
12 The duke only published his memoirs shortly before his death: Sigismondo Castromediano, Carceri e galere politiche, Lecce 1895.
13 William Ewart Gladstone, Two letters to the Earl of Aberdeen on the State Persecutions of the Neapolitan Government, London 1851.
14 Antonio Scialoja, I bilanci del Regno di Napoli e degli Stati Sardi con note e confronti, Turin 1857, pp. 106–111.
15 Marc Monnier, La camorra. Notizie storiche raccolte e documentate, Florence 1862.
16 Camillo Benso di Cavour, La liberazione del Mezzogiorno. Carteggi di Camillo Cavour, vol. 3: Ottobre–Novembre 1860, Bologna 1960, letter dated 14 November 1860, p. 329.

# Conclusion

This book presents a comprehensive survey of the history of Italy for the period from 1770 to 1870. There is a need for an overview of this kind, not only for university teaching, but also for comparative European research, as the works currently available are either out of date or focus almost exclusively on questions of the cultural history of politics. In the wake of a culturalist turn in the humanities, economic and social history have taken too much of a back seat in Italian historiography. For this reason, a more balanced approach has been attempted here. Although the majority of existing overviews begin in the Napoleonic period, much is lost by not starting before then. It would be helpful to carry out a careful analysis of the German historian Reinhart Koselleck's concept of the 'saddle period', *Sattelzeit* (1750–1850), which has hardly been received in Italy, to test the value of applying it in future to Italian historiography. The significance of the introduction of liberal French legislation, for example, can be better appreciated with a sound knowledge of the situation in the Italian states before 1789. Important impulses from the reform era also continued to have an effect even after the Congress of Vienna. This suggests that the idea of restoration with regard to the Italian states requires critical (re-)evaluation.

It has been the aim of this study to promote a shift of emphasis by using different angles and interpretations. First, it was necessary to rectify the previous overemphasis on the role of the bourgeoisie. Since the 1990s, Italian social historians have applied the Bielefeld School research paradigms of the bourgeoisie to Italy. The problem is, however, that the bourgeoisie in Italy was far smaller in number than in the German states. It was the aristocracy whose social, political and economic presence was evident in the many Italian cities, not least in the salons, lodges, associations and numerous academies. This suggests that the role of the Italian bourgeoisie could hardly have been as dominant as otherwise claimed. Research on the German states also needs urgent reconsideration in this respect. Despite the numerous historical studies that have appeared on both sides of the Alps on the subject of the bourgeoisie, its image remains remarkably blurred. Since it cannot be adequately defined either within the analytical category of class or as a legal category, research has turned its focus to culture. This has resulted in many analyses that assign a central role to the values, lifestyles and behaviour of the middle classes. Yet German and Italian studies have long overlooked the fact that politics, culture and the economy were shaped by the nobility and the bourgeoisie jointly. They rarely acted as opponents but as collaborators in a hybrid aristocratic-bourgeois culture. What most nineteenth century research reveals is not a bourgeois society, but a society of notables and dignitaries. The concept of notables has been used for a long time by French researchers to good effect. It is a term that comprises aristocratic and bourgeois groups who occupied leading political, social and economic positions by virtue of their property, education, career and family. It would also be a more appropriate term to use in Italian social history.

A further aim of this book has been to take a critical look at studies of the Risorgimento period with a cultural history approach. Countless publications in the last twenty-five years claim that it was literature, historiography, opera and historical painting that mobilised Italians *en masse* to fight for the establishment of a nation state, thus refuting older theories that the nation state was a project of the intellectual and ruling elites. Unfortunately, this argument suffers from being hermeneutically circular. Texts from 'highbrow literature' were analysed and their mobilising effect maintained, with no attempt to verify their reception. Paolo Macry has rightly warned against the assumption that there was mass mobilisation for the nation-state movement without a more rigorous examination of the sources.[1] The logic behind the actions of those willing to be recruited by Garibaldi in Sicily, for example, was different. Theirs was not so much a fight for a nation state of any kind as a rebellion against Bourbon rule from Naples. It was generally the case that neither the Italian nor the Prussian kingdom was keen on mass participation in the political or military sphere, at least not if it involved volunteer organisations acting outside the control of royal officers.

This analysis has also attempted to more fully integrate transnational discourses. After the revolutions and uprisings of 1821 and 1830, thousands of aristocratic and bourgeois officers and intellectuals, but also landowners and rentiers, lived for decades in exile. They could be found outside Italy elsewhere in Europe, in the East, and in South and North America. From there they did their best to influence politics in their home country. In 1848, they returned to engage in the revolution but when it failed, many had to flee again. It is relevant in this context that after the founding of the nation state, exiles also contributed their political experience to the development of the new Kingdom of Italy. It was, however, not only members of the opposition, but also economic liberals who undertook long journeys to Western Europe to collect ideas for modernising Italian society, its economy and politics. Naturally the rulers involved were also all part of European alliances and power constellations.

Finally, the book intends to provide scope for an international dimension to the wave of research on the foundation of the German Reich. *Italia docet (Italy teaches)* does not only apply to research on fascism. The diplomacy and wars masterminded by Bismarck, Napoleon III and Cavour led to a close relation between the foundation of the Italian and German nation states. It was chiefly the German historian Heinrich von Treitschke who canonised the interpretation of the creation of these two nation states as parallel developments following a shared historical logic. There is, however, good reason to suggest adopting a comparative perspective even in the period before this. Both countries were subjected to processes of fundamental modernisation and transformation during the French Revolution and as part of the Napoleonic Empire. After 1815, the dispute over this revolutionary legacy dominated the political scene both south and north of the Alps. Conservative forces made every effort to restore the pre-revolutionary status while their opponents fought for revolutionary principles. For a long time, Italy was looked upon with disdain – an attitude that was reinforced by pro-Austrian and Greater German perspectives. Nevertheless, it was this chronically underestimated Italy that pioneered nation state formation in 1861.

A further issue is the fact that authors of works applying the currently predominant discourse analysis approach tend to ignore the question of what was actually meant by a nation or a nation state. Should it really encompass the whole of the Italian peninsula or did the people of Sicily, Tuscany, Piedmont, Lombardy and Venetia dream of much smaller nation states? Ultimately, however, it was not the romantics with their enthusiasm for any or every kind of nation state who were responsible for driving the foundation of the Italian nation. On the contrary, it was the combined efforts of Cavour, the liberal elites, and Victor Emmanuel II with his desire to expand his kingdom, as well as the shift in the balance of power in Europe after the Congress of Vienna. Italy was helped to found its nation state both directly and indirectly by Britain and France when they turned away from the political principles of the Holy Alliance, as well as by Prussia's vision of becoming a great power. On its own, Italy would not have had sufficient military strength. The formation of the Italian nation state also signified a further important step in the global development of liberalism. It was accompanied by a large wave of support from progressive Europeans, which swayed their respective governments.[2]

By the end of the nineteenth century a great deal of progress had either been made or was well under way in Italy, such as in industrialisation and literacy, and the masses were also gradually becoming accustomed to being part of a nation state. The population was growing, as were the cities, and prosperity was increasing. These developments were, needless to say, also embedded in European and global contexts.

## Notes

1 Paolo Macry, Masse, rivoluzione e Risorgimento. Appunti critici su alcune tendenze storiografiche, in: Contemporanea. Rivista di storia dell'800 e del'900, XVII, 4 (2014), pp. 673–691.

2 Marco Meriggi, Die Konstruktion von Staat und Nation. Der Fall Italien, in: Gabriele B. Clemens, Jens Späth (eds.), 150 Jahre Risorgimento – geeintes Italien?, Trier 2014, pp. 19–35.

# Rulers of the Italian States 1770 to 1870

Republic of Genoa (to 1797)

| Doge | Period of office |
|---|---|
| Giovanni Battista Negrone | 1769–1771 |
| Giovanni Battista Cambiaso | 1771–1773 |
| Ferdinando Spinola | 1773–1773 |
| Pier Francesco Grimaldi | 1773–1775 |
| Brizio Giustiniani | 1775–1777 |
| Giuseppe Lomellini | 1777–1779 |
| Giacomo Maria Brignole Sale | 1779–1781 |
| Marco Antonio Gentile | 1781–1783 |
| Giovanni Battista Airoli | 1783–1785 |
| Gian Carlo Pallavicino | 1785–1787 |
| Raffaele De Ferrari | 1787–1789 |
| Alerame Maria Pallavicini | 1789–1791 |
| Michelangelo Cambiaso | 1791–1793 |
| Giuseppe Maria Doria | 1793–1795 |
| Giacomo Maria Brignole | 1795–1797 |

Kingdom of Italy (from 1861)

| Kings | | Period of reign |
|---|---|---|
| Savoy | Victor Emmanuel II (b. 1820) | 1861–1878 |

## Papal States

| Popes | Period of office |
|---|---|
| Clement VIV | 1769–1774 |
| Pius VI | 1775–1799 |
| Pius VII | 1800–1823 |
| Leo VII | 1823–1829 |
| Pius VIII | 1829–1830 |
| Gregory XVI | 1831–1846 |
| Pius IX | 1846–1878 |

## Duchy of Modena and Reggio (to 1860)

| | Dukes | Period of office |
|---|---|---|
| Este | Francis III (b. 1698) | 1737–1780 |
| | Hercules III (1727–1803) | 1780–1796 |
| | Francis IV (b. 1779) | 1814–1846 |
| | Francis V (1819–1975) | 1846–1860 |

## Kingdoms of Naples and Sicily, from 1816 Kingdom of the Two Sicilies (to 1861)

| Kings | | Period of office |
|---|---|---|
| (Spanish) Bourbon | Ferdinand I (b. 1751) | 1759–1825 (1798–1799 and 1805–1814 limited to Sicily) |
| | Francis I (b. 1777) | 1825–1830 |
| | Ferdinand II (b. 1810) | 1830–1859 |
| | Francis II (1836–1894) | 1859–1861 |

## Duchy of Parma and Piacenza (to 1860)

| Rulers/Dukes and Duchesses | | Period of reign |
|---|---|---|
| Bourbon (-Parma) | Ferdinand I (1741–1802) | 1765–1801 |
| Habsburg-Lothringen | Marie Louise (b. 1791) | 1814–1847 |
| Bourbon (-Parma) | Charles II (1799–1883) | 1847–1849 |
| | Charles III (b. 1823) | 1849–1854 |
| | Louise Marie / Robert I (1848–1907) | 1854–1859 |

## Kingdom of Sardinia (to 1861)

| Kings | | Period of reign |
|---|---|---|
| Savoy | Charles Emmanuel III (b. 1701) | 1730–1773 |
| | Victor Amadeus III (b. 1726) | 1773–1796 |
| | Charles Emmanuel IV (b. 1751–1819) | 1796–1802 (since 1796 limited to Sardinia) |
| | Victor Emmanuel I (1759–1824) | 1802–1821 (to 1814 limited to Sardinia) |
| | Charles Felix (b. 1765) | 1821–1831 |
| Savoy-Carignan | Charles Albert (b. 1798) | 1831–1849 |
| | Victor Emmanuel II (b. 1820) | 1849–1861 (then King of Italy) |

## Grand Duchy of Tuscany (to 1860)

| Dukes | | Period of rule |
|---|---|---|
| Habsburg-Lothringen | (Peter) Leopold I (b. 1747) | 1765–1790 |
| | Ferdinand III (b. 1769) | 1790–1801 and 1814–1824 (1801–1824 Napoleonic) |
| | Leopold II (1797–1870) | 1824–1859 |
| | Ferdinand IV (1835–1908) | 1859/1860 |

## Republic of Venice (to 1797)

| Doges | Period of office |
|---|---|
| Alvise Mocenigo IV | 1763–1778 |
| Paolo Renier | 1779–1789 |
| Luigi Manin | 1789–1797 |

# Selected Bibliography


Chapter 1: The Ancien Régime

Campbell, Angus, Sicily and the Enlightenment. The World of Domenico Caracciolo, Thinker and Reformer, London 2016.

Cantarutti, Giulia, Fra Italia e Germania: studi sul transfert culturale italo-tedesco nell' età dei Lumi, Bologna 2013.

Capra, Carlo, La Lombardia austriaca nell'età delle riforme (1706–1796), Turin 1987.

Cazzaniga, Gian Mario (ed.), La Massoneria. Storia d'Italia, Annali 21, Turin 2006.

Delpiano, Patrizia, Church and Censorship in Eighteenth-Century Italy, New York/London 2018.

Donati, Alberto, Giambattista Vico. Filosofo dell'illuminismo, Ariccia 2016.

Ferri, Sabrina, Ruin's Past. Modernity in Italy, 1744–1836, Oxford 2015.

Ferrone, Vincenzo, The Politics of Enlightenment. Republicanism, Constitutionalism and the Rights of Man in Gaetano Filangieri, London 2012.

Galasso, Giuseppe, Il regno di Napoli. Il Mezzogiorno borbonico e napoleonico (1734–1815), Turin 2007.

Imbruglia, Girolamo, Venturi, Franco, Cantimori, Delio, Illuminismo e storicismo nella storiografia italiana, Naples 2003.

Paolucci, Gianluca (ed.), Illuminatismo tra Germania e Italia nel tardo Settecento, Rome 2019.

Ricuperati, Giuseppe, Lo stato sabaudo nel Settecento. Dal trionfo delle burocrazie alla crisi d'antico regime, Turin 2001.

Tazzara, Corey, Findlen, Paula, Soll, Jacob (eds.), Florence after the Medici. Tuscan Enlightenment, 1737–1790, New York/London 2020.

Trampus, Antonio, Storia del costituzionalismo italiano nell'età dei lumi, Rome 2010.

Traversier, Mélanie, Le journal d'une reine. Marie Caroline de Naples dans l'Italie des lumières, Ceyzérieu 2017.

Venturi, Franco, Italy and the Enlightenment. Studies in a Cosmopolitan Century, London 1972.

Chapter 2: Italy under French Rule 1789–1814

Addante, Luca, Le colonne della democrazia: giacobinismo e società segrete alle radici del Risorgimento, Bari 2024.

Ambrosini, Filippo, L'albero della libertà. Le repubbliche giacobine in Italia, 1796–99, Turin 2013.

Baccini, Elisa, L'impero culturale di Napoleone in Italia: stampa, teatro, scuola secondo il modello francese, Rome 2023.

Broers, Michael (ed.), The Napoleonic Empire and the New European Political Culture, Basingstoke 2012.

Capra, Carlo, L' età rivoluzionaria e napoleonica in Italia 1796–1815, Turin 1978.

Carmigniani, Juan-Carlos, Boué, Gilles, Napoleon in Italy: 1805–1815, Paris 2016.

Connelly, Owen, The Wars of the French Revolution and Napoleon, 1792–1815, Hoboken 2012.

Conte, Paolo, Da esuli a francesi: gli italiani oltralpe in età napoleonica (e oltre), Bologna 2024.

Cuccia, Philipp R., Napoleon in Italy. The Sieges of Mantua, 1796–1799, Norman 2014.

De Francesco, Antonino, Rivoluzione e costituzioni. Saggi sul democratismo politico nell'Italia napoleonica, 1796–1821, Naples 1996.

Ibid., L'Italia di Bonaparte. Politica, statualità e nazione nella penisola tra due rivoluzioni, 1796–1821, Turin 2011.

Donato, Maria Pia et al. (ed.), Atlante storico dell'Italia rivoluzionaria e napoleonica, Rome 2013.

Gregory, Desmond, Napoleon's Italy, Madison 2001.

Levati, Stefano, L' esperienza napoleonica in Italia: un bilancio storiografico, Milan 2023.

Morandini, Tazio, "I giorni di Bruto": lotta democratica e progetto nazionale nel giacobinismo piemontese, 1789–1799, Turin 2023.

Musiani, Elena, L'Europa liberale: un modello per i notabili dello Stato pontificio, Rome 2022.

Pillepich, Alain, Napoléon et les Italiens. République italienne et Royaume d'Italie (1802–1814), Paris 2003.

Ibid., Milan, capitale napoléonienne. 1800–1814, préface de Jean Tulard, Paris 2011.

Poggi, Stefano, Cultures of Identification in Napoleonic Italy, c.1800–1814, London/New York 2024.

Planert, Ute (ed.), Napoleon's Empire. European Politics in Global Perspective, London/New York 2016.

Schneid, Frederick C., Soldiers of Napoleon's Kingdom of Italy. Army, State and Society, 1800–1815, Boulder, Coll. 1995.

Ibid., Napoleon's Italian Campaigns: 1805–1815, Westport, Conn. 2002.

Stramaccioni, Alberto, La rivoluzione francese e le repubbliche d'Italia, 1789–1799. Lo Stato della Chiesa, Perugia e i Giacobini, 1798–1799, Perugia 2011.

Turi, Gabriele, Guerre civili in Italia 1796–1799, Rome 2019.

Villani, Pasquale, Rivoluzione e diplomazia. Agenti francesi in Italia, 1792–1798, Naples 2002.

### Chapter 3: The Congress of Vienna, Restauration and Revolution

Balzani, Roberto, Fiorentino, Carlo M., Risorgimento: costituzione e indipendenza nazionale: 1815–1849/1849–1866, Soveria Mannelli 2022.

Barone, Giuseppe, Città in guerra. Sicilia 1820–1821, Bari/Rome 2022.

Bistarelli, Agostino, Gli esuli del Risorgimento, Bologna 2011.

Brice, Cathérine, Diaz, Delphine (eds.), Mobilités, savoir-faire et innovations, in: Revue d'histoire du XIXe siècle 53, 2016/2.

Bruni, Francesco, Idee d'Italia: da Napoleone al Quarantotto, Bologna 2021.

Caron, Jean-Claude, Luis, Jean-Philippe (eds.), Rien appris, rien oublié? Les restaurations dans l'Europe postnapoléonienne (1814–1830), Rennes 2015.

Caruso, Amerigo, Nationalstaat als Telos? Der konservative Diskurs in Preußen und Sardinien-Piemont 1840–1870, Berlin/Boston 2017.

Daum, Werner, Oscillazioni dello spirito pubblico. Sfera pubblica, mercato librario e comunicazione nella Rivoluzione del 1820–21 nel Regno delle Due Sicilie, Naples 2015.

Ibid.,/Späth, Jens (eds.), Un primo liberalismo transnazionale? Verso il bicentenario delle rivoluzioni mediterranee del 1820–23, in: Rivista Storica Italiana CXXX, fasc. II, 2018.

Delpu, Pierre-Marie, Un autre Risorgimento. La formation du monde libéral dans le Royaume des Deux-Siciles (1815–1856), Rome 2019.

Diaz, Furio, L'incomprensione italiana della Rivoluzione francese. Dagli inizi ai primi del Novecento, Turin 1989.

Isabella, Maurizio, Risorgimento in Exile. Italian Émigrés and the Liberal International in the Post-Napoleonic Era, Oxford/New York 2009.

Ibid., Southern Europe in the Age of Revolutions, Princeton/Oxford 2023.

Jarrett, Mark, The Congress of Vienna and its Legacy: War and Great Power Diplomacy after Napoleon, London 2013.

Laven, David, Venice and Venetia under the Habsburgs: 1815–1835, Oxford 2010.

Lentz, Thiery, Le congrès de Vienne. Une refondation de l'Europe 1814–1815, Paris 2013.

Mascilli Migliorini, Luigi, Metternich. L' artefice dell'Europa nata dal Congresso di Vienna, Rome 2014.

Meriggi, Marco, Gli stati italiani prima dell'Unità. Una storia istituzionale, Bologna 2011.

Michelon, Domenico, Palermo al tempo dei Borbone: storie di rivoluzioni, di patrioti, di generali inetti, di camicie rosse e picciotti, Palermo 2022.

Rovinello, Marco, Drafting Italy: Conscription and the Military from 1814 to 1914, London/New York 2023.

Šedivý, Miroslav, Si vis pacem, para bellum: The Italian Response to International Insecurity 1830–1848, Vienna 2021.

Späth, Jens, Revolution in Europa 1820–23. Verfassung und Verfassungskultur in den Königreichen Spanien, beider Sizilien und Sardinien-Piemont, Cologne 2012.

Vick, Brian E., The Congress of Vienna. Power and Politics after Napoleon, Cambridge/London 2014.

### Chapter 4: The Economy

Bevilaqua, Piero, De Clementi, Andreina, Franzina, Emilio (eds.), Storia dell' emigrazione italiana, Vol. 1: Partenze, Vol. 2: Arrivi, Rome 2001.

Caglioti, Daniela Luigia, Vite parallele. Una minoranza protestante nell'Italia dell'Ottocento, Bologna 2006.

Ibid., (ed.), Special Issue: Elite Migrations in Modern Italy: Patterns of Settlement, Integration and Identity Negotiation, in: Journal of Modern Italian Studies, 13 (2) 2008, S. 141–258.

Cohen, Jon S., Federico, Giovanni, The Growth of the Italian Economy, 1820–1960, 2001.

Conca Messina, Silvia A., Leading the economic Risorgimento: Lombardy in the 19th century, New York/London 2022.

Davis, John A., Gramsci and Italy's Passive Revolution, Hoboken 2014.

De Simone, Ennio, Alle origini del sistema bancario italiano, 1815–1840, Naples 1993.

Felisini, Daniela, "Quel capitalista per ricchezza principalissimo". Alessandro Torlonia principe, banchiere, imprenditore nell'Ottocento romano, Soveria Mannelli 2004.

Hearder, Harry, Cavour, Hoboken 2014.

LoRomer, David G., Merchants and Reform in Livorno, 1814–1868, Berkeley 1987.

Maggi, Stefano, Le ferrovie, Bologna 2003.

Moroni, Andrea, Antica gente e subiti guadagni. Patrimoni aristocratici fiorentini nel'800, Florence 1997.

Petrusewicz, Marta, Latifundium. Moral Economy and Material Life in a European Periphery, Ann Arbor 1996.

Poettinger, Monika, Deutsche Unternehmer im Mailand des neunzehnten Jahrhunderts. Netzwerke, soziales Kapital und Industrialisierung, Milan 2012.

Ibid., Roggi, Piero (eds.), Florence. Capital of the Kingdom of Italy, 1865–71, London et al. 2018.

Romeo, Rosario, Cavour e il suo tempo, 3 Voll., Rome 2012.

Schram, Albert, Railways and the Formation of the Italian State in the Nineteenth Century, Cambridge 1997.

Soliani, Riccardo (ed.), Economic Thought and Institutional Change in France and Italy, 1789–1914. A Comparative Study, Cham 2017.

## Chapter 5: Culture and Society

Banti, Alberto Mario, The Nation of the Risorgimento. Kinship, Sanctity, and Honour in the Origins of Unified Italy, London 2020.

Baumeister, Martin, Ciampani, Andrea (ed.), The First Vatican Council and Modernity, Rome 2020.

Bianchi, Raffaella, A Cultural History of La Scala in the Risorgimento (1814–1848), Turnhout 2022.

Borutta, Manuel, Antikatholizismus. Deutschland und Italien im Zeitalter der Kulturkämpfe, Göttingen 2010.

Bouwers, Eveline G., Public Pantheons in Revolutionary Europe. Comparing Cultures of Remembrance, c. 1790–1840, Basingstoke 2012.

Broers, Michael, The Politics of Religion in Napoleonic Italy. The War against God, 1801–1814, London/New York 2002.

Caglioti, Daniela Luigia, Associazionismo e sociabilità d'élite a Napoli nel XIX secolo, Naples 1996.

Cardia, Claudio, Risorgimento e religione, Turin 2011.

Cardoza, Anthony L., Aristocrats in Bourgeois Italy. The Piedmontese Nobility, 1861–1930, Cambridge 1997.

Casalena, Maria Pia, Tradurre nell'Italia del Risorgimento. Le culture straniere e le idee di nazione, Rome 2021.

Cavicchioli, Silvia, Famiglia, memoria, mito. Il Ferrero della Marmora, Turin 2004.

Ibid., Anita. Storia e mito di Anita Garibaldi, Turin 2017.

Ibid., I cimeli della patria; politica della memoria nel lungo Ottocento, Rome 2022.

Clemens, Gabriele B., Sanctus Amor Patriae. Eine vergleichende Studie zu deutschen und italienischen Geschichtsvereinen im 19. Jahrhundert, Tübingen 2004.

Ibid., Le vendite d'arte della nobiltà romana: una base per il collezionismo europeo, in: Il Risorgimento 70, 2 (2023), pp. 70–94.

Cotticelli, Andrea, L'ultimo gran ballo della Roma pontificia: ritratti e storie familiari della nobiltà dell'Ottocento, Rome 2023.

Della Peruta, Franco, Società e classi popolari nell'Italia dell'800, Milan 2005.

Formigoni, Guido, L'Italia dei cattolici. Dal Risorgimento a oggi, Bologna $^{2}$2010.

Ferraresi, Alessandra, Signori, Elisa (eds.), Le università e l'unità d'Italia (1848–1870), Bologna 2012.

Izzo, Francesco, Laughter between Two Revolutions. Opera Buffa in Italy, 1831–1848, Rochester, N.Y. 2013.

Körner, Axel, Beyond *Nationaloper*. For a Critique of Methodological Nationalism in Reading Nineteenth-Century Italian and German Opera, in: Journal of Modern Italian Studies 25/4, 2020, S. 402–419.

Levra, Umberto, Fare gli italiani. Memoria e celebrazione del Risorgimento, Turin 1992.

Liermann, Christiane, Rosminis politische Philosophie der zivilen Gesellschaft, Paderborn 2004.

Macry, Paolo (ed.), Borghesie urbane dell' Ottocento, in: Quaderni storici 56/2, 1984.

Ibid., Ottocento. Famiglia, élites e patrimoni a Napoli, Bologna 2002.

Malatesta, Maria: Storia di un' élite: la nobiltà italiana dal Risorgimento agli anni Sessanta, Turin 2022.

Marchi, Maria Christina, The Heirs to the Savoia throne and the construction of 'Italianità', 1860–1900, Cham 2022.

Mazzocca, Fernando, Sisi, Carlo (eds.), 1861. I pittori del Risorgimento [Roma, Scuderie del Quirinale 6 ottobre 2010–16 gennaio 2011], Milan 2010.

Meriggi, Marco, Milano borghese. Circoli d'élites nell'Ottocento, Venice 1992.

Patriarca, Silvana (ed.), The Risorgimento Revisited: Nationalism and Culture in Nineteenth-Century Italy, Basingstoke/New York 2012.

Pollard, John Francis, Catholicism in Modern Italy. Religion, Society, and Politics since 1861, London 2014.

Porciani, Ilaria, La festa della nazione. Rappresentazione dello stato e spazi sociali nell'Italia unita, Bologna 1997.

Romani, Gabriella, The Formation of a National Audience in Italy, 1750–1890. Readers and Spectators of Italian Culture, Madison 2017.

Sarracino, Vincenzo, Corbi, Enricomaria, Storia della scuola e delle istituzioni educative (1830–1999). La cultura della formazione, Naples 1999.

Schächter, Elizabeth, The Jews of Italy, 1848–1915. Between Tradition and Transformation, London 2011.

Signorelli, Alfio, Catania borghese nell' età del Risorgimento. A teatro, al circolo, alle urne, Milan 2015.

Skokan, Isabel, Germania und Italia. Nationale Mythen und Heldengestalten in Gemälden des 19. Jahrhunderts, Berlin 2009.

Smart, Mary Ann, Waiting for Verdi: Opera and Political Opinion in Nineteenth Century Italy, 1815–1848, Berkeley 2018.

Sorba, Carlotta, Teatri. L'Italia del melodramma nell' età del Risorgimento, Bologna 2001.

Ibid., Politics and Sentiments in Risorgimento Italy: Melodrama and the Nation, Cham 2021.

Traniello, Francesco, Cattolicesimo conciliatorista. Religione e cultura nella tradizione rosminiana lombardo-piemontese (1825–1870), Milan 1970.

Vella, Francesca, Networking Operatic Italy, Chicago/London 2021.

Villari, Anna, "Poter dire sono italiano". La pittura di storia dalla rivoluzione del 1848 al primo decennio dell'Italia unita, Milan 2007.

Whrigley, Richard, Roman Fever. Influence, Infection, and the Image of Rome, 1700–1870, New Haven 2013.

### Chapter 6 : The Revolutions of 1847–1849

Clark, Christopher, Revolutionary Spring. Fighting for a New World, 1848–1849, London 2023.

Couzin, Thierry, Originalité en politique, le cas du Piémont dans la naissance de l'Italie (1831–1848). Gouverner le Royaume de Sardaigne à l' époque de Charles-Albert, Zurich 2001.

Embree, Michael, Radetzky's Marches. The Campaigns of 1848 and 1849 in Upper Italy, Solihull 2011.

Kroll, Thomas, La rivolta del patriziato. Il liberalismo della nobiltà nella Toscana del Risorgimento, Firenze 2005.

Monsagrati, Giuseppe, Roma senza il Papa. La Repubblica romana del 1849, Rome 2014.

Rapport, Mike, 1848 – Revolution in Europa, Stuttgart 2011.

### Chapter 7: The Path to the Nation State


Armenteros Carolina, Ungari, Andrea (eds.), A Companion to Italian Constitutional History (1804–1938). The House of Savoy and the Making of the Nation-State, Leiden/Boston 2023.

Cafagna, Luciano, Cavour, Bologna 1999.

Caiani, Ambrogio A., Losing a Kingdom, Gaining the World. The Catholic Church in the Age of Revolution and Democracy, London 2023.

Case, Lynn M., Franco-Italian Relations, 1860–1865. The Roman Question and the Convention of September, Philadelphia 2016.

Coppa, Frank J., The Origins of the Italian Wars of Independence, London 1992.

De Fort, Ester, Esuli e migranti nel Regno Sardo: per una storia sociale e politica del Risorgimento, Turin 2022.

Dell'Arti, Giorgio, Cavour. Vita dell'uomo che fece l'Italia, Venice 2011.

Di Fiore, Laura, Gli Invisibili. Polizia politica e agenti segreti nell'Ottocento borbonico, Naples 2018.

Esposito, Gabriele, Armies of the Italian Wars of Unification 1848–1870, 2 Bde., Oxford 2017/2018.

Fiorentino, Carlo M., Il garbuglio diplomatico: l'Italia tra Francia e Prussia nella guerra del 1866, Milan 2021.

Gentile, Pierangelo, L' ombra del re. Vittorio Emanuele II e le politiche di corte, Turin 2011.

Girardi, Giacomo, I beni degli esuli: i sequestri austriaci nel Lombardo-Veneto (1848–1866), Rome 2022.

Hérisson, Arthur, Pour le pape-roi: Les catholiques français face à l'unification italienne (1856–1871), une mobilisation internationale de masse entre politique et religion, Rome 2023.

Hearder, Harry, Cavour, London 1994.

Heyriès, Hubert, Italia 1866. Storia di una guerra perduta e vinta, Bologna 2016.

Isnenghi, Mario, L'Italia in piazza. I luoghi della vita pubblica dal 1848 ai giorni nostri, Bologna 2004.

Jaeger, Pier Giusto, Le mura di Sebastopoli. Gli Italiani in Crimea 1855–56, Milan 1991.

Levra, Umberto (ed.), Cavour, l'Italia e l'Europa, Bologna 2011.

Macry, Paolo, Unità a Mezzogiorno. Come l'Italia ha messo assieme i pezzi, Bologna 2012.

Magliani, Stefania, XX settembre 1870: "Roma tutta appartiene agli Italiani", Milan 2021.

Mazzonis, Filippo, La Monarchia e il Risorgimento, Bologna 2003.

Poettinger, Monika, Roggi, Piero (eds.), Florence. Capital of the Kingdom of Italy, 1865–71, London 2020.

Riall, Lucy, Garibaldi. Invention of a Hero, New Haven 2007.

Romeo, Rosario, Vita di Cavour, Rome 1998.

Severini, Marco (ed.), La terza guerra d'indipendenza. Tra centro e periferia, Fermo 2016.

Stramaccioni, Alberto, L'impero e la nazione. I britannici e il Risorgimento italiano (1848–1870), Rome 2024.

Tafuro, Azzurra, Dare madri all'Italia. Patriote e filantrope nel Risorgimento (1848–1871), Rome 2021.
Talamo, Giuseppe, Cavour, Rome 2010.
Viarengo, Adriano, Cavour, Rome 2010.
Viarengo, Adriano, Vittorio Emanuele II, Rome 2017.

Chapter 8: The Nation State: Consolidation and Resistance

Armino, Pino Ippolito, Brigantaggio politico nelle Due Sicilie. Condizioni socio-economiche del regno di Napoli e storia dei movimenti reazionari contro l'unità italiana, Reggio Calabria 2015.
Biondi, Rocco, Storiografia del brigantaggio postunitario. Dal 1860 ai giorni nostri, Milan 2018.
Cammerano, Fulvio, Storia politica dell'Italia liberale 1861–1901, Rome 1999.
Capaldo, Nunziante, Carmine Crocco Donatelli. Il protagonista controverso della rivoluzione lucana del 1861, Lecce 2008.
Ciconte, Enzo, La grande mattanza. Storia della guerra al brigantaggio, Bari 2018.
Daniele, Vittorio, Malanima, Paolo, Il divario nord-sud in Italia 1861–2011, Soveria Mannelli 2011.
Del Bianco, Nino, Marco Minghetti. La difficile unità italiana da Cavour a Crispi, Milan 2008.
Dickie, John, Blood Brotherhoods: the Rise of the Italian Mafias, London 2011.
Fiore, Antonio, Camorra e polizia nella Napoli borbonica (1840–1860), Naples 2019.
Ghisalberti, Carlo, Silvio Spaventa. Tra Risorgimento e stato unitario, Naples 2003.
Macry, Paolo, Unità a Mezzogiorno. Come l'Italia ha messo assieme i pezzi, Bologna 2012.
Meriggi, Marco, La nazione populista: il Mezzogiorno e i Borboni dal 1848 all'Unità, Bologna 2021.
Moe, Nelson, The View of Vesuvius. Italian Culture and the Southern Question, Berkeley 2002.
Monnier, Marc, Histoire de brigandage dans l'Italie méridionale, Paris 2015.
Paolini, Gabriele (ed.), La prima emergenza dell'Italia unita. Brigantaggio e questione meridionale nel dibattito interno e internazionale nell' età della Destra storica, Florence 2014.
Perrone, Nico, L' agente segreto di Cavour. Giuseppe Massari e mistero del diario mutilato, Bari 2011.
Pinto, Carmine, La guerra per il Mezzogiorno. Italiani, borbonici e briganti, 1860–1870, Bari 2019.
Rogari, Sandro (ed.), Luigi Carlo Farini. Statista liberale, Ravenna 2018.
Romano, Valentino, Dalle Calabrie agli Abruzzi. Il generale José Borges tra i briganti di re Francesco II, Nocera Superiore 2018.
Sarlin, Simon, Le légitimisme en armes. Histoire d'une mobilisation internationale contre l'unité italienne, Rome 2013.

Satto, Christian, "Un leone alla catena corta". Bettino Ricasoli politico nell'Italia unita (1861–1880), Florence 2019.

Sonetti, Silvia, La guerra per l'indipendenza. Francesco II e le Due Sicilie nel 1860, Soveria Mannelli 2020.

Vaccari, Roberto, Enrico Cialdini. Il generale di ferro, Modena 2017.

Vigna, Marco, Brigantaggio italiano. Considerazioni e studi nell'Italia unita, Novara 2020.

Wawro, Geoffrey, Austria' s War with Prussia and Italy in 1866, Cambridge 1996.

# Image Credits

Fig. 1: © KHM-Museumsverband Vienna GG 2346.

Fig. 2: © Workshop of Titian active about 1506; died 1576 Venus and Adonis. © The National Gallery, London.

Fig. 3: © Museo Civico di Reggio Emilia.

Fig. 4: © Rome, Galleria Nazionale d'Arte Moderna e Contemporanea. Su concessione del Ministero per i Beni Culturali e Ambientali e del Turismo.

Fig. 5: © Foto di Mauro Ranzani, 2011. © FAI – Fondo Ambiente Italiano.

Fig. 6: © Pinacoteca di Brera, Milan.

Fig. 7: © Public domain (Nationalmuseum Stockholm Inv.-Nr. NMK 33/1920).

Fig. 8: © Stadtmuseum Simeonstift Trier, Inv.-Nr.: III 2236, Picture: Stadtmuseum Simeonstift Trier.

Fig. 9: © Biella, Palazzo La Marmora, Centro Studi Generazioni e Luoghi – Archivi Alberti La Marmora.

Fig. 10: © bpk Berlin / RMN – Grand Palais.

Fig. 11: © Rome, Galleria Nazionale d'Arte Moderna e Contemporanea. Su concessione del Ministero per i Beni Culturali e Ambientali e del Turismo.

Fig. 12: © Comune di Milano – all rights reserved – Milan, Palazzo Moriggia, Museo del Risorgimento.

Fig. 13: © Galleria d'Arte Moderna di Palazzo Pitti, Florence, per concessione del Ministero per i Beni et le Attività Culturali e per il Turismo.

Fig. 14: © Turin, Gam – Galleria Civica d'Arte Moderna e Contemporanea, Ferruccio Rampazzi 1992, su concessione della Fondazione Torino Musei.

Fig. 15: © Museo Nazionale del Risorgimento Italiano di Torino. Proprietà: Città di Torino – Galleria Civica d'Arte Moderna e Contemporanea.

Fig. 16: © Gallerie degli Uffizi, Florence, per concessione del Ministero per i Beni e le Attività Culturali e per il Turismo.

Fig. 17: © Museo Nazionale del Risorgimento Italiano di Torino.

Fig. 18: © ullstein bild – adoc-photos / Fratelli d'Alessandri.

Fig. 19: https://it.wikipedia.org/wiki/Presa_di_Roma#/media/File:BrecciaPortaPia.jpg (public domain)

Fig. 20: © FLHC 82 / Alamy Stock Foto

# Index

## Persons

## M

## Places